The Power of Metaphor in the Age of Electronic Media

Raymond Gozzi, Jr.

Ithaca College

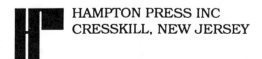

HAMPTON PRESS INC
CRESSKILL, NEW JERSEY

Printed in the United States of America.

Library of Congress Cataloging-in-Publication Data

Gozzi, Raymond.
    The power of metaphor in the age of electronic media / Raymond Gozzi, Jr.
       p. cm. -- (Hampton Press Communication Series)
    Includes bibliographical references and index.
    ISBN 1-57273-122-2. -- ISBN 1-57273-123-0 (pbk.)
    1. Mass media and language. 2. Metaphor. I. Title
    II. Series
  P96.L34G69   1999
  302.23'01'4--dc21   99-18902
                                             CIP

Illustrations and cover design by Paul Dennithorne Johnston

Hampton Press, Inc.
23 Broadway
Cresskill, NJ 07626

To my father, Raymond Gozzi, Sr.
my mother, Irene Murray Gozzi
my sister, Elizabeth Youngberg
my wife, Barbara Logan

Contents

Preface

Underlying these chapters are three themes which have preoccupied me over the decade of the Nineties. First, a respect for the creativeness of humanity, as expressed in its ever-changing language and metaphors.

Second, a conviction that as we move into a society dominated by electric media, our relationship to language is changing. This is difficult to talk or write about, since we must use language to communicate. To use language to discuss language, we are inevitably pushed into metaphor. In Chapter 3, I have proposed that the discourse of our entire society is being pushed toward what Jakobson (1971) calls the metaphoric pole, by the iconic imagery of electronic media.

Third, our metaphors sometimes lead us astray--point us in unproductive and self-defeating directions. This is particularly true when our metaphors define new areas of experience, such as those created by new media or technologies. These metaphors illuminate, but they also cast shadows. For example, cyberspace is not space--in fact it annihilates space (see Lippert, 1996). Yet many writers about cyberspace expect it to be a frontier, to be settled like the Wild West. This metaphor hides from us just how new and strange cyberspace is, and misses cyberspace's potential for complete surveillance of all transactions (see Strate, 1996, and Chapter 21).

Section I of this book contends that electronic media redescribe the world in symbolisms that clash with the already functioning print-based descriptions of the world (Chapters 1 and 2). This clash brings the existing "objectivist" descriptions of the world into question. The clash raises epistemological issues which require metalanguages to be developed, and produces culture wars (Chapters 3 and 4). Examples of such metalanguages are postmodernism and deconstruction, which rely heavily on a new trope, the oxymetaphor, an unstable combination of metaphor and oxymoron (Chapter 4).

This is not the first time that a new communication medium has changed discourse, knowledge, and culture. Chapter 5 provides an overview history of this process from the media ecology perspective, and discusses metaphor in oral, writing, print, and electronic cultures. Chapter 6 describes theories of metaphor. Chapter 7 gives guidelines on how to do a metaphorical analysis.

The rest of the book consists of separate discussions of important metaphors in media (Section II), computer technology (Section III), late 20th Century culture (Section IV), the fields of education and knowledge (Section V), and language (Section VI). These chapters may be read in any order, although Section I's Chapters 1-5 should be read in sequence.

* * *

Many people have assisted me in conceptualizing and putting together this book. I received encouragement and a pragmatic point of view from Hermann Stelzner, now Professor Emeritus at the University of Massachusetts, Amherst. Professor Jane Blankenship, also Professor Emeritus at the University of Massachusetts, Amherst, imparted her love of metaphor.

Jeremy Klein, editor of *ETC., a Review of General Semantics*, gave me suggestions, support, and stimulating conversation. Thanks to *ETC.* for granting permission to reprint many of these chapters. Paul Dennithorne Johnston's excellent illustrations appeared with many of these articles in *ETC.*, I am pleased they can be included here.

Lance Strate, Media Ecology Series Editor of Hampton Press, gave me the benefit of his seemingly boundless knowledge of the communication literature, and provided valuable guidance in turning a collection of articles into a book.

Neil Postman provided morale-building encouragement, and I am very pleased he has agreed to write the Foreword.

Three very intelligent typists have worked on these articles and manuscripts. They include Kim Blankenship of Bradley University, Karen Brown Armstrong of Ithaca College, and Bes Schomacker of Ithaca College.

My debts to my parents, Raymond Gozzi, Sr., and Irene Murray Gozzi, go back farther than I can remember, to the encouragement of an inquiring mind. I also need to express my great love and gratitude to my wife, Barbara Logan, and my sister, Elizabeth Youngberg.

Foreword

Neil Postman
New York University

All language is metaphorical, and often in the subtlest ways. In the simplest sentence, sometimes in the simplest word, we do more than merely express ourselves. We construct reality along certain lines. We make the world according to our own imagery. Consider, for example, a straightforward question such as, "Do you see the point I am trying to make?" Why *see* the point? and why a *point?* Is an idea something you can see? Is it something that converges, or drives a wedge, or indicates a direction? Can an idea fade from view? Can it illuminate a problem? Can someone's ideas jump around from place to place? Can they be marched forward in an orderly fashion? What is an "idea" anyway—a point, a light bulb, a jumping bean, a regiment? Well, ideas are all of these things, and anything else we wish to make them, depending, I suppose, on how we construe the "mind." Is the mind a dark cavern, which is illuminated by ideas? Is it a vessel, which is filled by ideas? Or is it a muscle which may be strengthened? Or a garden to be cultivated? Or a shapeless piece that may be carefully molded?

Obviously, there is no answer to these questions. I raise them to make plausible the idea that language is a design for living. To talk is to imagine a world of make-believe, to hypothesize that everything is like something else. A molecule is like a billiard ball, and a billiard ball is like a planet, and a planet is like a speeding rocket, and a rocket is like a bird, and a bird is like a leaf floating in the wind. Of course, our best poets and scientists are those who have created the most vivid and enduring metaphors: The Lord is my shepherd; life is a stage; the universe is a great clock; the mind is a seething cauldron of emotions covered over with a thin coating of civilization. In poetry and science, such metaphors are usually called to our attention. They are, in fact, forced on our awareness by being placed at the center of what we are to consider, and they may be rigorously examined. But in everyday speech situations we are apt to be unaware of how we are using our metaphors, and therein lies a source of considerable confusion.

To make us aware of how we are using our metaphors (and how they are using us) in everyday speech situations is the task undertaken by Raymond Gozzi. He has been doing this for years with insight and dedication, and offers us in this book, collected for the first time, the essays that his readers have enjoyed and learned from.

It is of special importance that this book be read with care because the role of the metaphor in how we construe the world is rarely taken seriously in school. For the most part metaphor is taught as an ornament to poetic expression; which is to say, something that is used only by poets in order to increase the vividness of their imagery. The whole of Gozzi's work is an attempt to refute that idea, to show us by example after example that metaphor creates the world we believe to exist. If there is any more important project being undertaken by an educator, and undertaken with such style and sophistication, I don't know what it is or by whom. It is, therefore not an exaggeration to say that if every teacher would read this book, the very nature of education would be radically altered. Indeed, if every citizen read this book, the nature of political discourse, of necessity, would be altered. Can anyone give a higher recommendation to a book than this?

section one

The Power of Metaphor

one

The Intimate Relations Between Metaphor and Media

The second half of the 20th century in the United States can justifiably be called the *age of electronic media*. During these years, more and more people have perceived reality through the lenses of the electronic media—in particular cinema, television, and computers. By 1965, 93% of U.S. households had television; 98% did by the 1990s (DeFleur & Ball-Rokeach, 1989).

Also, in the second half of the 20th century, *metaphor* emerged as a central topic in discourse. Metaphors were discovered everywhere, by students of the humanities and the sciences, by engineers describing new technologies, by reporters covering complex events. The processes of metaphor received serious attention from linguists, psychologists, anthropologists, students of communication, and others. After centuries of being relegated to minor supporting roles, metaphors became celebrities in discourse.

My thesis is that these two developments are related. The coming of electronic media has moved discourse toward metaphor.

It has done this in three main ways: producing metaphors for media, internalizing media as metaphors, and moving meaning-making and discourse toward the metaphoric pole.

First, by presenting new objects to be named and new actions to be conceptualized, electronic media (and new technologies generally) have required metaphors to describe them and their effects. I call this *producing metaphors for media*. These metaphors have power because they name the new objects, and structure how we perceive and encounter them.

Second, electronic media have presented new models of thoughtlike processes, new ways to *process information*, which have been internalized as deep, unstated metaphors. The computer, in particular, has become a deep metaphor for the brain, the mind, and thought. And television has become a deep metaphor for processes of social discourse. I call this *internalizing media as metaphors*. These metaphors have power because, unseen and unacknowledged, they serve as cognitive models to shape our self-images as individuals and as a society.

The third way electronic media have influenced discourse toward metaphor is a result of the forms of their symbolisms. Television, cinema, radio, and the telephone all produce symbols that are concrete, specific, and iconic. These contrast with print symbolism, which is abstract, general, and only has a conventionalized relationship to its referent.

When the concrete and iconic symbols of electronic media enter the discourse of the culture, they favor meaning-making processes related to metaphor, according to the linguist Jakobson (1971). These include the emphasizing of similarities, focusing on specifics rather than generalities, and use of argument from analogy. I call this *pushing discourse toward the metaphoric pole*. Here it is the metaphoric *process* that has power, metaphor as opposed to metaphors because it structures discourse itself and becomes more prevalent than other discursive alternatives.

I discuss the movement of discourse toward Jakobson's metaphoric pole in more detail in chapter 3. In this chapter, I discuss the first two ways media and metaphor are related— through the production of metaphors for media, and through the internalization of media as metaphors.

METAPHORS FOR MEDIA

First, particular metaphors have power because they name and describe new media. The metaphor tells us what a new medium is, and the structure of the metaphor can guide discourse about future potentials and effects. *We encounter media, and technology generally, through a screen of metaphors.* This metaphorical structuring of thought and perception can begin quite early in the process of development of the technology, and can influence the decisions made by scientists and engineers, as well as users and regulators of the new technology.

Such metaphors as *the computer has a memory*, or *the computer caught a virus*, play an important role in most people's understanding of computers. (In fact, the term computer is itself a metaphor. Before the 1930s a computer was a *person* who computes.) These metaphors let us understand the unfamiliar in terms of the familiar. But metaphors hide some aspects of the new technology and its effects. They may keep us from appreciating just how strange and new some new technologies really are. They may blind us to certain potentials for which we should be preparing.

Still, metaphor becomes necessary when a new technology appears. The new object creates blank, unnamed regions on our linguistic and conceptual *maps* of experience. There is a new thing to be named, and new actions to be comprehended. Through metaphorical extensions of terms, and through giving the new objects and actions the names of something else, metaphor starts to exert its subtle but pervasive power. A quick, seemingly harmless example is afforded by the little device known as a TV *remote control.*

The Remote Control

We are given a small, rectangular piece of plastic with "buttons" on it. We are told it is a "remote control." We point it at the television, move our thumb, press a "button," and the channel changes. What are we doing? What do we call this action?

In a situation like this, people come up with all sorts of phrases. There is no dictionary definition to guide us. Because we are dealing with a new technology, there is not much precedent on which to go. This new technology has created a new region of experience, which does not have a verbal map to follow. And so, people get creative. They let their imaginations go. They improvise. They extend meanings. They produce *metaphors.*

Probably the most popular metaphor for what we do with the remote control is that we go *channel surfing*. Television viewers, formerly just placid *couch potatoes*, are now *surfers*. More than that, when a commercial comes on that we do not want to watch, we can *zap* it. We have the power of a science fiction hero or heroine, able to *control* our televisions with our *remotes*.

When you stop and think about it, we do not get all that much control—we can just *select* between preprogrammed items. And it isn't all that *remote*—we have to be in the same room. So even the name *remote control* is metaphorical, implying that we have more *control* than we do.

But these are not the only metaphors that have been created to describe this new interaction between human beings and a new technology. A different set of metaphors has appeared in discourse. Viewers are described as *grazing* when they *click* the *remote*. By contrast to the physically fit and tanned *surfer* image, a *grazer* conjures up images of peaceful cows or other farmyard animals. And instead of *zapping* like Buck Rogers, *clicking* implies that you are not doing much at all, or at most, are using your computer *mouse* (another metaphor describing a new technology).

But the metaphor-creating process has not stopped here. As I was writing this chapter, I came across a social science research article studying *grazing*. When people were observed actually using their *remote control devices* (RCDs), six more terms had to be invented to describe their actions accurately (Eastman & Newton, 1995).

1. *Punching* in a specific channel number.
2. *Jumping* to a new channel by using the "previous channel" button.
3. *Arrowing* by pressing down on the up or down arrows continuously.
4. *Scanning* for using the arrow button slowly to see each channel.
5. *Inserting* for putting more than one channel simultaneously on screen.
6. *Muting* the sound with the mute button or volume controls. (Actually, adjusting the volume could be a whole new category, perhaps called *volume upping* or *downing*.)

Will any of these new terms catch on? Will millions of people start telling each other to *punch* in the other channel? Will parents tell their children to stop *arrowing?* I doubt it, but no one can say for sure. This uncertainty is a fascinating aspect of studying the metaphors that grow up around new technologies. The choice of metaphors, their development and elaboration, are all unpredictable. And fun to watch.

The metaphors also tell us something about ourselves, about how we like to view ourselves. If we think of ourselves as *channel surfers* perhaps we are compensating heavily for sitting in front of the television actually doing nothing. If the industry calls us *grazers,* perhaps they do not have too high an opinion of us. The metaphors people use give us insights into their conceptual and fantasy worlds. More than that, the metaphors shape how we perceive our "real" world, and what we are doing in it. We may think we are describing our actions, or the future of a new technology, when all we are doing is following out the implications of our metaphors.

And do these metaphors hide something truly new in the language of the familiar? The *remote control* allows people to easily *zap* commercials, yet television exists to show commercials to audiences. This little device alters the viewing relationship which is the economic foundation of current American television. Advertisers must now find new ways to get their messages across to an increasingly restless population of viewers. Dramatic scriptwriters must pace their dramas faster, so the audience won't be tempted to switch channels after a few dull seconds.

The ripple effects from the *remote control* are only beginning to be felt. Perhaps we should not get too comfortable with these *grazing* and *zapping* metaphors, because we still need to think about the developing implications of this little piece of plastic.

MEDIA AS METAPHORS

So far I have discussed the sometimes messy process where metaphors are created to describe new media, new technologies, actions, and effects. At the same time, however, another metaphorical process occurs, where the media or technologies themselves become metaphors.

The human mind is always looking for ways to understand itself, and the knowledge that shapes it. This quest inevitably leads into metaphor. People are also constantly seeking ways to conceptualize themselves as social beings, and the societies in which they live. Again, metaphor becomes necessary.

Historically, certain technologies have become important metaphors for the mind, knowledge, and social process. Bolter (1984) called these "defining technologies". Clearly, the electronic computer has become such a defining technology for the mind in 20th-century culture, as Bolter claimed. But alphabetic writing, print, and television have also been internalized as deep, unacknowledged metaphors.

McLuhan (1964) was the first to highlight this process, referring to media as both metaphors and translators, and turning Robert Browning's poetic line, "a man's reach should exceed his grasp, or what's a heaven for?" into one of his famous puns: "a man's reach should exceed his grasp, or what's a metaphor." He went on to write:

> All media are active metaphors in their power to translate experience into new forms. The spoken word was the first technology by which man was able to let go of his environment in order to grasp it in a new way. Words are a kind of information retrieval that can range over the total environment and experience at high speed. Words are complex systems of metaphors and symbols that translate experience into our uttered or outered senses. They are a technology of explicitness. By means of translation of immediate sense experience into vocal symbols the entire world can be evoked and retrieved at any instant. (p. 57)

All communication media can provide a model, a structure, for how thought and discourse function. Ong (1977) noted that media have structuring power within the mind:

> each of the so-called "media" . . . makes possible thought processes inconceivable before. The "media" are more significantly within the mind than outside it . . . writing and print and the computer enable the mind to constitute within itself . . . new ways of thinking, previously inconceivable questions, and new ways of searching for responses. (1977, p. 46)

Ong made the point that Western culture from ancient Greece onward internalized patterns of thought from the techniques of alphabetic writing, and generalized them into a metaphor for knowledge and the mind. Writing reconstitutes the spoken, evanescent word in a permanent, visual space. It therefore encourages us to think of knowledge as something fixed, organized in linear fashion, and representable visually on a plane or in space. It presents us with lists, indexes, tables, graphs, and charts as visual metaphors for knowledge (Ong, 1982). The mind is thus often seen as a blank page, or tabula rasa.

It may be worth recalling that knowledge is created by the brain after integrating all the senses, and probably does not take the form of representations from one sense. For some people, knowledge may not take the form of any external sense representation. Representing knowledge visually is a metaphorical act because it maps mental knowledge processes and products onto the structure of vision.

Furthermore, writing "separates the knower from the known" (Ong, 1982, p. 44). It "fosters abstractions which disengage knowledge from the arena where human beings struggle" (p. 43). Again, it may be worth recalling that knowledge is generated from within lived experience, and its priorities and emphases are related to that experience. The radical decontextualization of knowledge implied by writing and later print helps give rise to the view of the world called *objectivism*, which is discussed more fully in chapter 3.

Ong's point is that media can be internalized and function as metaphors for the mind and for knowledge. Internalized media metaphors can also structure a culture's discourse. Postman (1985) wrote:

> although culture is a creation of speech, it is recreated anew by every medium of communication. . . . Each medium, like language itself, makes possible a unique mode of discourse by providing a new orientation for thought, for expression, for sensibility. . . . The forms of our media . . . are rather like metaphors, working by unobtrusive but powerful implication to enforce their special definitions of reality. Whether we are experiencing the world through the lens of speech or the printed word or the television camera, our media-metaphors classify the world for us, sequence it, frame it, enlarge it, reduce it, color it, argue a case for what the world is like. (1985, p. 10)

Postman gave a clear example of media effects on discourse by his historical comparison of political debates. In the print-dominated 19th century, the Lincoln-Douglas debates were "clearly modeled on the style of the written word" (p. 48). The debaters spoke for hours, used long and complex sentences, read long quotations from previous speeches, and referred to numerous statements made by their opponents. By contrast, a late 20th-century presidential "debate" amounts to little more than the display of competing sound bites. The underlying model for this discourse is, Postman claimed, the television commercial.

Media forms and formats can be internalized, then, and function as unacknowledged deep metaphors which structure the conduct of thought and discourse.

In the currently fashionable terminology of cognitive psychology, we could say that these deep media metaphors form cognitive models which organize thought and action.

Ong, Postman, and other thinkers in the *media ecology* tradition, are not preaching technological determinism. The *interaction* between humans and media technology is their subject. As Ong (1977) said, his thought is relationist, not reductionist. Postman (1979) adopted the *ecology* metaphor to describe the complex interplay of humans, technologies, and environments. I look more closely at the processes of change in the next chapter.

two

New Media Redescribing the World

METAPHOR'S RISE TO STARDOM

In the second half of the 20th century, metaphors have been called on to star in all sorts of arguments and explanations. They have been found underlying many significant discourses, including the supposedly "objective" domains of science. They have been claimed to be central elements of thought itself.

This 20th-century fame is in stark contrast to 2,000 years of relegation to supporting roles. Since the Roman Empire, metaphor has been considered a mere ornamental use of language, a pretty turn of phrase rippling along on the surface of discourse. Granted, metaphor was always promoted by poets, mystics, and religious thinkers. But the *serious* business of language, it was held, had to do with matters of accuracy, reference, and objectivity. Here metaphor had no place because it named one thing in terms of another. How could two separate things be the same? Clearly, in this view metaphor was a kind of *mistake*. Metaphor might be an amusing bit part player in the subplots of discourse, but the central roles went to nouns, verbs, and that style of discourse known as *literal language*.

Then came the 20th century. Critic Wayne Booth, speaking at a conference on metaphor in 1978, said:

> There were no conferences on metaphor, ever, in any culture, until our own century was already middle-aged. . . . Explicit discussions of something called metaphor have multiplied astronomically in the past fifty years. . . . Along with the immense increase in bibliography about something previously *called* metaphor has gone an immense explosion of meanings for the word. . . . No matter how we define it, metaphor seems to be taking over not only the world of humanists but the world of the social and natural sciences as well. (Booth, 1978, pp. 47-48)

What brought about the historically sudden change of fortune for metaphor? What factors played a role in elevating it from a bit part player to one of the superstars of discourse?

My thesis holds that a main factor is a change in the predominant media of communication within Western society during these years.

At the beginning of the 20th century, writing and print were the dominant media of communication. Writing had been central to Western culture since ancient Greece, and print had amplified and extended this dominance since the 1500s. In 1900, people in the United States got their distant news from newspapers. They learned about the world around them from books. Magazines were a bold new medium, housing the investigative journalism of the muckrakers.

By the end of the 20th century, the dominance of writing and print had been at least partly eclipsed by electronic media. Cinema, radio, and television changed the ways people got their news, and learned about the world around them. The number of newspapers was declining, the hours spent watching television were increasing. Print and electronic media were in competition for people's time and attention. Although no clear winner had emerged from this struggle at the time of this writing, major cultural adjustments were under way.

A lot else has happened as well. Discourse has become more complex, unwieldy, contentious. Epistemological issues have come to the foreground, meanings have become relativized, old certainties have dissolved into new indeterminacies. I contend that these developments, too, are related to the growing ascendancy of electronic media, as they encroach on a territory once described primarily by print media.

But to support my thesis, I need to get a little more specific. What happens when humans interact with their communication technologies? In the short run, they send and receive messages. But in the longer run, a communication medium exerts other influences, more subtly, all through a culture. This longer range influence is harder to categorize, more difficult to study. The "effects" may take centuries to become apparent, and then be so mixed in with other "causes," so "overdetermined," that the exact influence of the medium may not be "isolable."

However, for my purposes here, I focus on one process. As people interact with and through communication media, over time they produce a redescription of the world. This redescription process is central to the changes in discourse, and I turn to it next.

DESCRIPTIONS OF THE WORLD

There is a description of the world implicit in all language and social interaction. (I use the term "the world" to refer to the life world of everyday experience, as used by sociologist Alfred Schutz, 1964, and others.) This description is rarely brought to conscious attention, it forms the "background knowledge" against which the events of everyday life unfold. Yet this background knowledge has a structure, described by Schutz in terms of "zones of relevance." Each zone has its own appropriate forms of knowledge, from the personal knowledge of zones close to home, to the typified knowledge of zones we only know through media. (See essays in Schutz, 1964.) The description of the world is always emergent and incomplete, constantly being updated with new "gossip" and "information."

This concept of a description of the world has appeared in many disciplines, under many names. The linguist, M. A. K. Halliday (1987), wrote of a description of the world that is encoded in words, "lexical items," as well as in the deeper grammar, syntax, and relational patterns of a language.

The cultural description of the world is called by Boulding (1956) "the Image." Boulding traced out how the image plays a central role in the life of the culture. It sets out what people collectively believe to be true. It guides behavior. It assists people in deciding what is possible and what is impossible.

Perkinson (1995) noted that new media "recode" the culture, and allow it to be criticized. Perkinson said that through this criticism, culture is improved, and progress results. I share Perkinson's conviction that the redescription process is an important result of a new medium. However, I think Perkinson overlooked the dislocations and disorientation caused by new media. He also used an oversimplified model of rational criticism producing cultural progress. Sometimes, new media redescriptions lead to irrational and destructive criticisms. Furthermore, I expect culture rarely improves from criticism alone. Culture improves through cooperation, coordination, and creativity.

To summarize my argument so far, every new medium contains the potential to *redescribe* the world of everyday life. This redescription occurs over a period of time, as people interact with the new medium. The redescription involves generating new symbolic forms, genres, and conventions that are learned and diffuse through the culture.

The redescription of the world foregrounds some aspects of the world and minimizes others. It implies that some people, places, events, and problems in the redescribed world are more important than others. It allows people to imagine and model possible actions that might be taken in the redescribed world, and that may not have seemed possible in the older descriptions. Over time, there will be more things to discuss, and more ways to discuss them as the redefinition of the world enters more into the discourse of everyday life.

The redescription of the world allowed by a new medium must enter into a culture that already has functioning descriptions of the world. The new medium's redescription of the world will disturb the cultural balance of descriptions of the world, whatever that may be, by adding new perspectives on the same events. Therefore, these old and new descriptions of the world will become subjects of discussion and debate in a new, relativistic metalanguage.

Metalanguages From Redescriptions of the World

I use the term "metalanguage" in Halliday's sense (1987) of a new subset of language that is concerned largely with epistemological issues of language, knowledge, and meaning. Metalinguistic operations are part of normal functioning, when we turn our attention to the specifics of what was said, or how it was said. The metalanguage opens "new semantic spaces" (Halliday, 1987, p. 146). It provides new and complementary ways of describing the same set of phenomena.

Every language is constantly renewing itself, changing in resonance with changes in its environment. But this is not an incidental fact about language; it is a condition of its existence as a system. . . . Such a system is good for thinking with and good for doing with, these being the two complementary facets of all human semiosis. When either of these facets comes under pressure, the system responds by creating special varieties of itself to meet the new demands. So in a period of rapid growth of science and technology, new metalanguages appear. These new forms of language are both created by and also create the new forms of knowledge. (Halliday, 1987, pp. 138, 140)

The metalanguages are produced by people as they recognize and attempt to settle issues raised by the existence of a new redescription of the world. The metalanguages will tend to bring all descriptions of the world into consciousness, put them into discourse, and question them. This generates an extremely relativistic outlook that many people in the culture will find unsettling.

In a discourse produced by metalanguages, epistemology becomes an overriding intellectual concern, even if not explicitly recognized as such. *For in a metalanguage, all former "facts" in descriptions of the world become mere "assumptions" in the metalanguages.*

As descriptions of the world get called into question, cultural harmony becomes more difficult to maintain. A sense of drift, disorientation, alienation becomes generalized. Communication seems increasingly problematic.

Some people will stubbornly resist the new relativism, and lapse into a "fundamentalist" attitude of resistance to change in the descriptions of the world. Others will become cynical about all descriptions. Others will eagerly try many varieties of description, moving from one to another without becoming committed to any. (See Lifton's, 1993, description of "protean" and "fundamentalist" personality types for further illustrations of these phenomena.)

Metalanguages Disturbing Culture

I am claiming that a new medium's redescription of the world comes into contrast (and sometimes conflict) with existing cultural descriptions. As a result, people must consciously examine these formerly "background" descriptions. This process generates "metalanguages," or "languages about language."

Thus, in the second half of the 20th century, the United States has seen several phenomena that are, according to this view, related.

First is the growing pervasiveness of a new class of communication media, the electronic media of television, cinema, telephones, radio, and computers.

Second is the renewed and deepened interest in metaphor, in many fields of study, as well as in ordinary discourse.

Third is a huge expansion in the lexicon of the language, an almost unprecedented addition of new words (see Gozzi, 1990).

Fourth is a proliferation of specialized languages, some technical, but many relating to processes of signification, communication, and language. Prominent among these are the highly relativistic metalanguages of postmodernism, structuralism, poststructuralism, and deconstruction.

Fifth is a series of political and economic redefinitions of the world that have shaken the processes of ordinary political and social life. These include redefinitions made by ethnic civil rights activists, the peace movement, feminists, abortion opponents and proponents, environmentalists, and religious fundamentalists. Not to be left out is the relativistic "market economics" of the radical right.

REDESCRIPTION AS AN ECOLOGICAL PROCESS

I contend that all of these phenomena are related, not in a linear cause-and-effect manner, but in complex ecological interactions. To discuss such matters, we are pushed into metaphor. The metaphors I choose to work with come from the *media ecology* tradition of Postman (1979), Meyrowitz (1985), and others. I discuss the media ecology metaphor at greater length in chapter 5, for now suffice it to say that the metaphor stresses the interrelatedness of cultural phenomena. Because culture is constituted in communication, when the means of communication change, everything in the culture will change also—not necessarily all at once, or together, but they will be affected.

Postman (1976) stressed the importance of the information environment to human interaction. Meyrowitz (1985) defined a social situation as an information situation, requiring an agreed on definition of the situation. I am attempting to expand on their theories by using the concept of a redescription process. (For a different description of the redescription process, see Perkinson, 1995.)

This redescription of the world begins in the information environment, as a new medium is increasingly used and its descriptions of the world contrast with existing cultural descriptions. Then the "definition of the situation" becomes less clear, more debatable. This leads to the production of metalanguages.

These metalanguages produce an increased complexity of discourse, which leads to a corresponding density and opacity to social and cultural processes. Times of redescription of the world make everyone uncomfortable, and tend to produce *culture wars*.

How do the strains of the redescription process get eased? How do the social divisions and cultural antagonisms heal? If history is our guide, time is the healer—not the prescriptions of one or another party in the *culture wars*. As the new medium becomes more familiar and absorbed into the institutions of the culture, its redescription of the world becomes "naturalized," and is incorporated into the educational and social life of the culture.

But this naturalization has not occurred yet, and may take many decades. In the late 1990s, we are still in a painful transition stage. In the next chapter, I discuss in more detail the existing world descriptions based on print media, and how electronic media redescriptions have destabilized them.

three

Jrom Print to Electronic Descriptions of the World

A particular description of the world has been supported by writing and print media for the past 2,000 years in Europe and North America. This description of the world has been called by many names: a *scientific* worldview, a *Cartesian* philosophy of the strict separation of subject and object, a *materialistic* philosophy of the primacy of material objects, a *skeptical* approach to all data, an *empirical* method of producing knowledge, and so on. For the sake of brevity, I will use Lakoff and Johnson's (1980) term objectivism to describe this view of the world.

OBJECTIVISM

Objectivism says that there is a "real" world out there, made up of objects with properties. Humans are separate from this world, and can know this world only through their senses. Because humans are fallible, they need the methods of science, empirical testing, to give a correct, definitive account of reality. But there ultimately is only one, correct, account of reality, and science will eventually achieve it.

We understand the objects of the "real" world through categories and concepts, which, if they are correct, correspond in a one-to-one fashion with the properties the objects have in themselves. Our words should also correspond in a one-to-one fashion with the "real" world. Words should therefore have fixed meanings, for the job of language is to refer to the pre-existing, "real" world. "Objective" language properly fits reality, with no bias or human "subjectivity" distorting its representations. The reasonable use of language joins concepts logically into propositions that mirror the structure of reality. To use language in this objective fashion is to be rational. (See Lakoff & Johnson, 1980; also Johnson, 1987.)

Objectivism is a "set of shared commonplaces in our culture" (Johnson, 1987, p. x). It provides a common sense description of the world, which has served for several hundred years. In fact, no one in the culture has been able to get completely away from it, even those who criticize it most eloquently.

But there are problems with objectivism. In the 20th century, objectivism showed signs of exhaustion as a useful philosophical approach (see Langer, 1951). For example, it may be true that a physical object exists and has properties apart from what people think, but when we come to more complex "objects" like people, families, groups, customs, belief systems, institutions, societies, these are not "objects" in the same sense. What people think—and say—about these social objects helps make them what they are at any given moment. In these cases, language does not merely refer to outside objects, it helps constitute what those objects become (see MacPhail, 1994).

Even in the realm of the physical sciences, objectivism was in trouble around the beginning of the 20th century, as physicists started exploring the strange, discontinuous world of subatomic particles and the relativistic, non-Euclidean properties of space and time near the speed of light. Physicist Werner Heisenberg even propounded an Uncertainty Principle, which held that the presence of the experimenter altered the results of the experiment.

OBJECTIVISM, WRITING, AND PRINT

Objectivism was born in the era of alphabetic writing, and came to fruition in European culture during the same centuries that the printing press became the dominant medium of communication. Although I would be reluctant to say that writing and print were the only causes, or even the main cause, of objectivism; clearly the two were (and are) related. The case for such a relationship has been made by Ong (1982), Eisenstein (1979), McLuhan (1962), and others. We can see some of the reasons print supports objectivism by looking at the *form* of the print medium.

In general, the media ecology approach assumes that the form of a medium encourages a number of things. First, a particular medium's form is internalized as a metaphor, and encourages certain cognitive habits on the part of its users (see discussion in chapter 1). Second, a medium tends to favor certain types and patterns of symbolization, and exclude others.

I believe there is always a human element as well as a technological one, in the equation. So I speak of communication technologies as *encouraging* or *facilitating* certain patterns of thought and behavior, but I try not to imply that these are inevitably determined by the technology.

The *forms* of writing and print encourage, for example, the *expression of symbols in linear, sequential order.* (Order wrong of words unlogical sign is.) In the terms of philosopher Suzanne K. Langer (1951), writing and print are *discursive symbolisms*, in which issues of sequence, order, permissible contiguities are foregrounded. Discursive symbolisms have a fixed vocabulary, that can be defined in a dictionary, and that can be translated into other discursive symbolisms. Discursive symbolisms also have a syntax, rules for combining vocabulary into larger propositions. Discursive symbols are good for conveying general concepts.

These discursive symbolic forms became internalized as metaphors for the proper conduct of thought and discourse. On these metaphors are built Western conceptions of logic, reason, and orderly proofs, all of which must proceed linearly from premises to conclusions without missing a step.

The forms of writing and print also encourage *abstraction* in symbolism and thought. Alphabetic letters bear only a conventional relation to that which they symbolize—sounds. These letters and their conventional relationships must be laboriously learned over many years. Furthermore, the abstractions of the alphabet are arrived at through a process of separation, analysis, and division. This process of abstraction through analysis and division was internalized as a metaphor. It reappears in many artifacts of Western thought and culture, including the experimental method of science, industrialism, the assembly line, "Taylorism," and so on (see Logan, 1986).

The abstract symbolism of writing and print makes it possible to think of the world of symbols as completely separate from the world it is being used to symbolize. Writing separates the knower from the known, as Ong (1982) put it. This separation is one of the assumptions of objectivism.

If the world of symbols is completely separate and different from the world it symbolizes, then a set of questions becomes appropriate to ask. How *objectively* do these separate and arbitrary symbols reflect the pre-existing nonsymbolic world? What factors might distort the accuracy of the symbolic representations? In this view, *objective* symbolism is most highly valued because it corresponds most closely with the presumed *objective, real world out there* beyond the reach of our symbols.

We can see the connections between writing and the analytical, objective frame of mind emerging in ancient Greece. In the Platonic dialogue *Phaedrus*, Socrates explained the proper way to write a speech:

> The conditions to be fulfilled are these. First, you must know the truth about the subject that you speak or write about; that is to say, you must be able to isolate it in definition, and having so defined it you must next understand how to divide it into kinds, until you reach the limit of division. . . .

Note that the "truth" is obtained from "isolating" the subject from its context, and then "dividing" it as far as possible.

These assumptions remain 2,000 years later, providing the format for a valid, proper argument in the print medium. These principles are taught in introductory composition classes. First, students must define their topic and state their assumptions. Then they should proceed by analyzing the situation, taking it apart into its component parts. They must proceed sequentially, step-by-step, with logical relationships between steps, not missing any. Then, and only then, a conclusion may be reached and considered "supported,"

Note that arguments in writing and print are usually abstract. Arguments in print rarely rely on explicit visual images, instead they depend on logical relationships.

Note also what the print medium requires of its users. As Postman (1985) called on his readers to do, simply consider "what is demanded of you *as you read this book*" (p. 25). You must remain still, concentrate on abstractions, pay no attention to the shapes of the letters on the page but instead go to the meanings of the words they form, judge the quality of an argument while delaying your own verdict. In other words, a specific set of skills is required by the medium, skills that it takes years of effort to achieve.

These skills required by print are exactly the same skills required by scientific, empirical investigation, as it developed in European culture during those centuries. (Other cultures, we now know, have developed different approaches to science.) In particular, the use of analysis, logic, sequential steps, and extreme skepticism are essential elements of Western science. And a crucial step of the scientific method is *publication* of procedures and results, so a larger scientific community can conduct discourse.

As alphabetic writing, and later print, entered into the ongoing discourse of culture, they highlighted these skills of abstraction, analysis, discursive symbolism, linear logic, and objectivity. This formed the superstructure for the thought and activity of the "Golden Age of Greece" in the 5th century BCE, and for the 16th- and 17th-century European Renaissance and the 18th-century Enlightenment. These centuries produced Western science, the Protestant Reformation, an age of democratic revolution in Western Europe and North America, and the Industrial Revolution, which has not yet exhausted itself. Certainly, these massive historical movements were not solely *caused* by writing and print media, but they were made possible by the internalized metaphors of writing and print. And they took their particular historical forms in part because of the *biases* of writing and print.

We can see these biases more clearly in the later 20th century because a different set of communication media, with different biases, has attained prominence. (See Table 3.1 later in this chapter.)

THE FORMS OF ELECTRONIC MEDIA

Perhaps the clearest difference between the forms of print and electronic media is in the levels of abstraction of their symbolism. Print is highly abstract, arbitrary marks on a page that have only a conventionalized relationship to their referents. Electronic media symbolism is much more *concrete.*

Cinema and television use pictures, the radio and telephone produce a copy of the human voice. To perceive and understand these media, no special training is required, no complex memorization of associations and meanings is needed. As Messaris (1994) demonstrated, people only need to use their ordinary perceptual skills when encountering television and cinema. The same is true with the radio and telephone—if you can understand spoken language, you can understand the messages.

Concentrating on cinema and television for a moment, I would like to discuss their use of pictures. In the terminology of Peirce, (1932) these symbolisms are *iconic*, bearing a structural resemblance to that which they symbolize; for Langer (1951), pictures are *presentational symbols*, as opposed to the discursive symbols of print. Presentational symbols give all their pieces at once, rather than serially, one after the other, as in discursive symbolism. Presentational symbols do not have basic units, such as phonemes or morphemes. Therefore, presentational symbolism does not have a fixed vocabulary of terms, and there is no dictionary possible. Because there is no dictionary of meanings, presentational symbols must derive meaning from their relationships to particular contexts. Because all the information is presented at once, there are no rules of syntax (see Langer, 1951).

It is certainly true that cinema and television, because they use moving pictures and string them out in a sequence, have elements of discursive symbolism. However, the visual pictures do not provide a fixed vocabulary in the discursive sense. Therefore, I place them closer to presentational symbolism than to discursive symbolism.

Let us now examine the form of a "valid," "proper," argument made on television—a commercial, for example. Commercials do have sequential structures, as the words and images proceed through time. But they rarely start at the beginning, making assumptions explicit. Rather, television throws you into the action somewhere after it has started. Television then carries you along through changes that may not be at all logical. The conclusion, if there is one, will not have been demonstrated so much as arrived at (see discussion in Postman, 1985).

Note that the iconic symbolism of television aims for our emotions. Gone is the cold abstraction of print. Instead we get affectively tinged visual images, in quick succession. The visuals come at us all at once, with many facets presented simultaneously. Gone are the rigors of logical analysis. Instead we get the "fact" of one image succeeding another, and we usually must "fill in the gaps" on our own. We are engaged emotionally, nonverbally.

Think about what skills are required to view television. Because the medium mimics ordinary sights and sounds, we do not need any special training to tune in and see what is going on. (I strongly believe we do need special training to view television in the proper way, but that is a different question.) We do not even need to stay still, we can move about and watch or listen. We do not need to struggle with abstractions, television puts it all there before our eyes. The qualities called into play are primarily those of emotion and empathy, instead of the removal and reflection called for by print. (See chapter 9 for an extended discussion of the differences between television and texts.)

Another contrast in the forms of print and electronic media comes from the fact that print is silent and still, whereas electronic media are noisy and full of motion. They mimic the actual perceptual situation, presenting concrete details, one after the other. As a result, electronic media do not give their users the time to reflect and review that print does. There is always another image coming; electronic media hate dead air.

The concrete, iconic symbolism of electronic media make it possible to think of the world of symbols as very much like the world it symbolizes. This leads to a view of electronic media as powerful agents within the real world. In the 20th century, a whole area of research grew up around studying electronic media as they present "role models" for "social learning," and produce "effects" that have been the subject of controversy.

ELECTRONIC MEDIA VERSUS OBJECTIVISM

My point in the last sections is that, because they have different forms, electronic media describe the world differently than do print media. Even if the content seems to be the same "subject," electronic media descriptions will be different from print.

The different forms of print and electronic media favor different ways of linking symbols together into descriptions of the world. The world described by writing and print tends to be held together by rules of logic and processes of reason. Even in a novel, a writer is constrained to give reasons for events occurring, coincidence is looked on as an unacceptable plot device.

In electronic media, the world is usually described by narrative, or in terms of drama. Drama emphasizes conflict instead of reason. Electronic narrative can often be just one thing after another, with no clear relationships. In movies or TV, coincidences occur more acceptably than in print.

The different forms of print and electronic media also favor different processes of making meaning. The discursive symbols of writing and print derive their meaning from fixed definitions, frozen into dictionaries, severed from particular contexts. The direction of meaning-making is toward the abstract, the disembodied, the universal.

By contrast, the presentational symbols of electronic media derive meaning from ties to their particular contexts. The direction of meaning-making is toward the concrete, embodied, particular. This is why it is so difficult to illustrate an abstract or general concept on television—the imagery is always moving toward the particular.

Not surprisingly, as electronic media permeated U.S. culture in the 20th century, with their concrete, iconic, dramatic symbolisms, the new descriptions of the world came into conflict with the older print-based descriptions. Challenges arose to the objectivist worldview.

The new electronic descriptions particularly challenged the hallowed objectivist separation of knower from known, of observer from observed, of subject from object. The "world" was no longer seen as pre-existing, "out there," separate from human activity. Instead, it came to be seen as constantly being formed through human symbolic interactions. One result of this intertwining of observer and observed is that there can be no totally "objective" reporting about the "world"—in media, science, or anywhere else—because our symbolisms are implicated in the construction of that world.

In this cultural situation, metalanguages have become necessary. These metalanguages have been called many names, such as *postmodernism, social constructivism, structuralism,* or *deconstruction.* We are in a transitional stage, which may last a long time, away from the comforting dichotomies of objectivism, and toward a messier, interactional model that has not yet received a satisfactory name. Lakoff and Johnson (1980) proposed the term "experientialist synthesis" for that mixture of reason and imagination that underlies all thought.

The formal differences between print and electronic media may be summed up as done in Table 3.1.

Understanding these formal properties of media will help us appreciate just how different the symbols of the new electronic media are, as they have entered into the discourse of the culture. I turn to this issue next.

Table 3.1. Formal Differences Between Media.

Print Media Formal Properties and Biases	Electronic Media Formal Properties and Biases
Still, unmoving	Moving, active
Silent	Noisy
Abstract symbols, with only conventional relations to objects	Concrete symbols, with iconic relations to objects
Discursive symbolism, emphasizing linear sequential relations	Presentational symbolism, emphasizing similarity, with no discrete vocabulary or syntax
Connections of logic, reason	Connections of narrative, drama
Meanings of symbols from convention, dictionary	Meanings of symbols from relations to particular context

THE METAPHORIC AND METONYMIC POLES OF DISCOURSE

In this section, I claim that, because of the forms of electronic media, the discourse of the culture has been pushed toward metaphor, using linguist Jakobson's typology (1971).

Jakobson distinguished between two poles of discourse, based on his studies of how the brain processes language. Jakobson studied child language and patients with linguistic disorders, or aphasia. The two poles correspond to the tropes of metaphor and metonymy.

Jakobson claimed that normal language use blends two functions. The first function he called the "significative" function, which involves relationships of *similarity*, combines language into *units of higher complexity*, emphasizes issues of *context*, and produces *metalinguistic operations*. When this significative function is emphasized, discourse is at the "metaphoric pole." Many metaphors and similes are produced, metonymy is absent, poetry is produced, and romanticism is the aesthetic mood.

The second function he called the "distinctive" function This function involves issues of *selection* and *substitution*, and involves relations of *contiguity*, or nearness, which govern the formation of sentences. When this distinctive function is emphasized, discourse is at the "metonymic pole": Metonymy and synechdoche appear often, metaphor is absent, prose is emphasized, and realism is the aesthetic approach.

All discourse combines and falls between these poles of metaphor and metonymy. But print, and especially prose, are identified with the metonymic pole (see Jakobson, 1971).

Because print is so abstract and must discursively give symbols one after the other, it must rely on the processes Jakobson called "relations of contiguity." It must foreground the rules of syntax and order. Therefore, it will emphasize synechdoche (using the part to represent the whole) and metonymy (using an associated quality to represent the whole). And metaphor will be downplayed or absent.

To give an historical illustration, when writing and print entered into culture, they also disturbed the existing descriptions of the world, and they also produced metalanguages. But *the metalanguages generated by writing and print went toward the metonymic pole.* One of the results of alphabetic writing in ancient Greece, for example, was the discipline of history, which sought relatively objective accounts—in prose—of events to replace the mythological—and poetic—approaches of the earlier oral culture (see Goody, 1977). And when print became established in Europe, the "scientific worldview" was fostered, which redescribed the world in terms of numbers, perhaps the ultimate metonymy (see Eisenstein, 1979). Meantime, metaphor was seen as simply a surface ornament or linguistic mistake.

By contrast with print, electronic media rely primarily on presentational symbolism. This type of symbolism rests on relations of similarity, and depends for meaning on contextual information. In terms of our argument here, *electronic media emphasize the processes at the metaphoric pole of discourse* (see Langer, 1951; Meyrowitz, 1985).

I highlight here two key points of similarity between Jakobson's metaphorical pole of discourse and the meaning-making processes of presentational symbolism. First, metaphor and presentational symbols must both be comprehended as wholes. Breaking down into atomistic elements will not help us understand them, in fact, it will hinder our understanding.

Second, metaphor and presentational symbols can only be understood in relation to their particular context. When the context changes, the symbol changes its meaning(s). In principle there cannot be an abstract dictionary of meanings which give unvarying definitions for metaphors or presentational symbols.

This would indicate that as electronic media enter into the discourse of the 20th century, they are pushing the discourse toward the metaphoric pole. And so the metalanguages generated by the process of redescribing the world tend to favor metaphor. They tend to rely on relationships of similarity and pay more attention to contexture, as occurs at the metaphoric pole. They tend to favor linguistic combinations of increasing complexity, as the significative function of language is stressed.

The contrasts between poles are summed up in Table 3.2.

Those readers familiar with the research on right-brain and left-brain functions may have noticed similarities between this research and Jakobson's polarities (see discussion in Logan, 1986). The left-brain functions govern linear sequencing of information, similar to Jakobson's metonymic pole. The right-brain functions govern recognition of patterns all at once, similar to Jakobson's metaphoric pole. I note the similarities here without necessarily endorsing brain specialization research—it provides some insights, but may segment the brain's workings too artificially.

ROCK POETRY AND "LIKE"

So what evidence can I cite that discourse is moving away from the metonymic pole (favored by print) and toward the metaphoric pole (favored by electronic media)? I point to two important intergenerational changes in language that co-occurred with the rise of television. One began in *the Sixties*, which of course spread through *the Seventies*. This was the phenomenon of *rock poetry*. The other occurred in *the Eighties* and *the Nineties*. It was the verbal tic "like", saying "like" like, all the time. (For a further discussion of these "decade" metaphors, see chapters 34 and 35.)

Rock Poetry

As the first television generation got access to an electronic medium—radio—it produced a new kind of music generically called *rock-'n-roll*. But this *Sixties* rock music was very different from its predecessors of *the Fifties*. Apart from being louder, its lyrics were much more personal, expressive, and complex. Rock music became poetry, expressing emotions and feelings that were beyond the scope of earlier rock music, and also beyond the scope of written poetry. The poetry and music of performers like Bob Dylan, Simon and Garfunkel, Jackson Browne, the Beatles,

Table 3.2. Jakobson's Poles of Discourse.

Metonymic Pole	Metaphoric Pole
Relations of contiguity	Relations of similarity
Severing from context	Relations to context
Selection and substitution of terms	Combination into units of higher complexity
Produces prose	Produces poetry
A "realist" aesthetics	A "romantic" aesthetics
Much use of synechdoche and metonymy	Much use of metaphor and simile
Emphasis on parts	Emphasis on wholes
Little use of metaphor	Little use of metonymy
Emphasized by print media	Emphasized by electronic media

and the Grateful Dead redefined the genre. It became a status symbol for performers to write their own songs, and fill a long-playing record with them, rather than just singing other people's songs. Poetry suddenly became "relevant."

When McLuhan and Ong considered this outburst of poetry, they were reminded of the central role of poetry in cultures that relied primarily on oral communication. McLuhan (1964) thought rock music fostered a *new tribalism*, and Ong (1971) wrote about the *literate orality* of lyrics in Simon and Garfunkel songs. These phrases, with their metaphoric pairing of opposite terms, were early *oxymetaphors*, which I discuss further in chapter 4.

Like . . . Another Example

Another intergenerational shift in language occurred as later television generations came along in *the Eighties* and *the Nineties*. This is the notorious use of the term "like". Many older people who listened to the talk of young people during these years found the "like" tic extremely annoying. But there are two important aspects of it that I mention here. (I try to put "like" more in the context of its generation in chapter 34.)

I have listened closely to when "like" appears in conversations. It is used to set a scene, to signal a change in focus. As Plat (1995) said, *"like" signals a new camera angle.* The storyteller using "like" is a TV director calling a new shot. *The television show has become a deep metaphor for the conduct of discourse.*

Take this random conversation I recently overheard between two teens in a mall, as closely as I can recall. One girl was speaking, with only occasional murmurs of assent from the other. "My mother, like, wanted to take me shopping for clothes, you know? So I'm like, okay. But she like goes to these fancy stores. I'm like, 'not that, Mom.' These clothes she wants me to get are like too expensive, you know? . . ." Here the conversation jumps from scene to scene, mimicking a television camera. In different scenes, different tones of voice and expression are used, similar to the progression of a TV show.

Another point about "like" is that it turns everything into a simile. A simile is a comparison using like or as, and is often regarded as the weaker version of a metaphor. Like the metaphor, it focuses on similarities. And, when used in a similar fashion to directing a TV camera shot, "like" pushes discourse toward presentational symbolism as well.

So, as television and other electronic media became more prevalent and powerful through the second half of the 20th century, the discourse of the generations that grew up with it changed. And as my examples of rock poetry and "like" indicate, the discourse moved toward more poetic, visual, metaphoric usages. As the analysis of "like" indicates, television has been internalized as a metaphor or cognitive model for the production of discourse by many in the TV generations.

SUMMARY

Why has metaphor become such a star of discourse in the 20th century, after centuries of being considered a bit part player? My analysis (or synthesis) suggests that the coming of electronic media have played an important role in the process. Electronic media have provided us with redescriptions of the world that have come into contrast, and conflict, with existing cultural descriptions of the world. This contrast has led to the generation of metalanguages to discuss the new issues raised.

The *forms* of electronic media have played a key role. These media privilege presentational symbolism, which relies on similarity or iconicity. Thus, their redescriptions of the world push discourse toward the metaphoric pole. The culture had previously been dominated by print media, whose descriptions of the world favored the metonymic pole.

If this reasoning is accepted, the outlines of the situation that has produced the complex and contentious discourse of the 20th century become clearer. As discourse shifts from the metonymic pole to the metaphoric pole, as symbolism becomes less discursive and more presentational, pervasive cultural disorientation results. The objectivist description of the world, supported by discourse at the metonymic pole, starts to crumble. Logic gives way to reasoning by analogy. Metaphors are discovered everywhere. Contradictions abound. And a new trope, a new type of metaphor has emerged to articulate them. I discuss oxymetaphors and some of their more prominent promoters in the next chapter.

four

Metalanguages of Paradox: McLuhan and Derrida

Historically, as Langer (1951) wrote, paradoxes "always mark the limit of what a generative idea, an intellectual vision, will do" (p. 21). The paradoxes of the 20th century signify the exhaustion of the generative idea that drove Western' philosophy and culture for several centuries. Langer identified this generative idea as the Cartesian separation of subject and object, inside and outside. This is one of the bases of what I call "objectivism."

The coming of electronic media has, I contended, generated new descriptions of the world which have come into contrast and conflict with existing cultural descriptions of the world. Print-based objectivism is, as a result, no longer the only respectable language game in town. But what to replace it with? What can accommodate the images of the world spewing out of electronic media, with their quickly changing imagery, their narrative frames, their simplified concrete symbolism?

As of this writing, the definitive replacement of objectivism has not arrived. The old description of the world is discredited, but no new description has been agreed on. We are in a transitional stage, with transitional names like *postmodernism* or *poststructuralism*. Metalanguages are being generated, with some sense of excitement and apprehension in academic discourse. But in this early stage, the metalanguages are still bound up with objectivism, and its print-based biases. Many of the metalanguages are concerned to demonstrate and remedy the shortcomings of objectivism. To do this, they often rely on paradox.

As language produces metalanguages within itself and beyond itself, it stretches and deforms the definitions of its own parts. I claim that the metalanguages of the second half of the 20th century have generated and been generated by a new trope—the *oxymetaphor*. In this chapter, I provide illustrations of oxymetaphors from two influential thinkers: media theorist Marshall McLuhan, who proclaimed that

the medium is the message

and Jacques Derrida, a literary critic and philosopher and prophet of deconstruction, who claimed, among other things, that

every reading is a misreading.

The oxymetaphor has become the superstar of academic discourse, bedeviling objectivists, beguiling postmodernists, and begetting controversy inside academe and out. Like any superstar, the oxymetaphor must appeal to a wide range of people, so it must appear to say something different to different audiences. It must also leave room to maneuver when pinned down in debate. The oxymetaphor has performed admirably well on both counts. Let us take a closer look at this trope.

THE OXYMETAPHOR

The oxymetaphor is a combination of metaphor and oxymoron. These two tropes are not as different as they might seem. An oxymoron is a quick paradox (Blumenfeld, 1989). But Aristotle noted that metaphor is like a puzzle or riddle. To give more formal definitions, a metaphor asserts a structural similarity between two domains normally thought to be separate. An oxymoron yokes together two domains normally thought to be opposite.

The oxymetaphor is a shifting trope, with two poles and (at least) two levels. The two poles are metaphor and oxymoron, and any given oxymetaphor may fall closer to one or the other of these poles. The two levels are what the words say—the object level—and how the phrase is used in discourse—the "meta" level. In many cases, the oxymetaphor is an oxymoron used as a metaphor.

The propositional process is, after all, the heart of discursive symbolism. It relies on rules, order, logic, and reasonably fixed definitions of terms. It produces propositions that are supposed to be logical, reasonable descriptions of the world. Oxymetaphors are like little explosives placed into propositions. When they are used in discourse, their self-opposing tendencies can explode propositions. At the very least, they create high tension by their yoking together of opposites. They help generate metalanguages. They provide energy to move discussion in new directions. Some of these directions are unproductive and destructive, whereas others are fertile and powerful.

Oxymetaphors create a discursive situation where suddenly attention is focused on the processes of language and definitions of terms. Discourse immediately becomes more dense and opaque. All definitions become stressed, every sign starts to look polysemic. It becomes harder to talk about anything, for first you must talk about talking about it.

Oxymetaphors provide powerful weapons for surprise attacks in academic debate, but these weapons are always in danger of exploding their user's positions as well as those of the opponent. But oxymetaphors also provide exhilaration and entertainment—forbidden thrills of self-contradiction, playing outside the rules. Stodgy academics can feel like they are *transgressing boundaries,* and *subverting meanings.*

In the following discussion, I do not attempt to give a thorough or systematic critique of the "systems" of thought of McLuhan or Derrida. I simply list and discuss some of the more prominent oxymetaphors propounded by these thinkers. Because my thesis is that new media redescriptions of the world have propelled the creation of metalanguages, I am also on the lookout for traces of media influence. In the case of McLuhan, media influence was everywhere, because this former English professor turned himself into a celebrity commentator on the media. In the case of Derrida, we can also make a case that television structures many of his oxymetaphors.

MCLUHAN

In the 1960s, McLuhan, a Canadian professor of literature, somehow became a "media guru," with international recognition for his cryptic and suggestive observations about media. McLuhan's career came to be symbolized by his famous pronouncement that

> *"the medium is the message"* (McLuhan, 1964, p. 23).

This oxymetaphor is, in part, an oxymoron. In our normal understanding, the message passes through the medium and is gone, while the medium remains. The oxymetaphor is also used as a metaphor for a new approach to studying media.

This oxymetaphor did what good paradoxes do—it enraged some people, while it challenged others to think about familiar processes in new ways. Clearly, in the short run, the medium is not the message, the message is the message. But over the longer term, the nature of the medium can shape messages, can affect how the medium redescribes the world, and can become a message in itself.

McLuhan explained this process using another oxymetaphor, based on the metaphor that a medium creates a new environment:

> *"TV is environmental and imperceptible,*
> *like all environments"* (McLuhan, 1964, p. ix).

It is surely oxymoronic to claim that TV is imperceptible, when the machine is blaring in the living room many hours a day. But this oxymetaphor again challenges us to think of a medium as more than just a *pipeline carrying messages,* as more traditional views have it. (I discuss the *conduit* metaphor for communication at more length in chapter 18.)

As television expanded around the world, McLuhan came up with another oxymetaphor to envision the result—we would all live in a

> *"global village"* (McLuhan & Fiore, 1969).

I discuss this fascinating oxymetaphor in chapter 11. Here I just point out that a village is very small and intimate, whereas any global institution is inevitably quite large and impersonal. And yet this oxymoron can be effectively used as a metaphor to describe a potential development of electronic media. Although I have my doubts that the *global village* is possible, this oxymetaphor has stimulated the imaginations of many people to think farther ahead than they would have otherwise.

In his last book (McLuhan & McLuhan, 1988) completed by his son, McLuhan summed up many of his thoughts on different media, using many oxymetaphors in the process. The telephone, for example, makes obsolete the old barriers between physical spaces:

"there is here and here is there" (p. 153).

The reaction to the "invasion from Mars" radio drama of 1938, when many people panicked:

"World reverses into talking picture:
audience as actors
participating in their own audience participation" (p. 172).

The computer creates:

"projections of present as future, of future as present:
retrieval of now as alltime" (p. 188).

And the xerox machine:

"With reader as publisher,
the reading public disappears" (p. 145).

I do not attempt to explicate these McLuhanisms, beyond saying that they combine oxymoron and metaphor in creative and original ways. They create and are created by a metalanguage concerning the new electronic media and their effects. The logical certainties of the print-based descriptions of the world come into question in the metalanguage.

McLuhan's Colleagues

McLuhan was one of a number of theorists who studied the nature of the medium itself as a central topic (see discussion in Meyrowitz, 1985, on "medium theory"). Ong (1971), one of McLuhan's colleagues, came up with an oxymetaphor of his own when describing popular culture in the 1960s:

"literate orality" (p. 284).

"Orality" usually refers to the communication and culture of groups that do not have writing. Being "literate" implies certain cognitive styles, communication patterns, and cultural qualities that are very different from those of oral cultures. But these opposites are being combined in the emergent culture of electronic media. Ong noted some of the differences with another oxymetaphor:

"For primitive man, happenings occurred. Today,
we program happenings . . . we plan unplanned events,
and we label them happenings" (p. 285).

Postman is another thinker in the medium theory tradition. He produced some notable oxymetaphors to convey his critical attitude toward electronic media. The title of his 1985 book is:

Amusing Ourselves to Death.

Usually, we do not do something so serious as die when we are merely amusing ourselves. But Postman used this oxymoronic phrase as a metaphor for the death of public discourse in the television era. Another oxymetaphor describes television's definition of news:

". . . news as pure entertainment" (p. 100).

This oxymetaphor is increasingly subscribed to in newsrooms around the country.

In a later book, *Technopoly* (1993), Postman critiqued electronic technology with another oxymetaphor. He noted (chapter 4) that:

we have more information, but understand less about the world.

The world is a less coherent place, according to Postman, because of the great amounts of information brought by electronic media. This oxymoronic situation is used as a metaphor for the overall plight of our culture.

The media ecology tradition has the potential to generate more oxymetaphors. Because electronic media combine the (apparent) intimacy of oral communication with the distance of print communication, they can put senders and receivers in paradoxical situations. Gozzi and Haynes (1992) note that receivers of electronic media messages can experience

"a distant presence," (p. 218)

and respond with

"uninvolved involvement" (p. 221).

McLuhan, Ong, and Postman used oxymetaphors effectively to generate a metalanguage dealing with the complex subject of the electronic media and their effects. These oxymetaphors convey something of the sense of disorientation that always accompanies technological change. At the same time, they promise to begin the process of reconceptualizing that is made necessary by the presence of new media redescriptions of the world. I discuss this approach to the study of media more in chapter 5.

Next, I turn to another metalanguage—deconstruction— that also uses oxymetaphors and that shows media influences.

DERRIDA AND THE DECONSTRUCTIONISTS

In the 1980s, "deconstruction" swept across the academic landscape like an unruly storm from France. This critical metalanguage was promoted by its own "star," Derrida, an Algerian-born philosopher. Deconstruction called the canons of literary criticism into question, and proceeded to expand its claims to cover all signs and sign systems. Like an intellectual horror movie, both scary and exciting, deconstruction reveled in the exhilaration of using language to cancel itself out. In our terms, it relied heavily on oxymetaphors.

One of the main axioms of deconstruction was that

meaning is indeterminate.

(See discussion in Culler, 1982.) This is partly oxymoronic, because meanings, by definition, are supposed to determine something. However,

every reading is a misreading, and
all interpretation is misinterpretation.

(see Ellis, 1989). No final reading is possible, no meanings are "univocal," because of the

infinite play of signification

(see discussion and quotes in Ellis, 1989). This, too, is oxymoronic because signification works by limiting the possibilities of meaning and interpretation.

In the deconstructive attitude, the author of a text loses his or her place of authority, for

the author is dead, only readers create meanings,

and therefore authors intentions are irrelevant, and a text may mean whatever any reader seriously believes it to mean (see Lehman, 1991; quotes in Ellis, 1989).

Deconstruction arrives at these oxymetaphors because of Derrida's criticism of what he called the "metaphysics of presence," or "logocentrism," which has dominated Western thought since Plato. In this book, these ideas are called "objectivism"—which insists on the desirability of a one-to-one correlation between external reality and the signs we use to represent reality in language. Deconstruction critiques objectivism by foregrounding the complexities and uncertainties of language, text, and reader.

Deconstruction, then, fits into our model of a relativizing metalanguage brought about by the clash of descriptions of the world produced by electronic media. The discourse of deconstruction definitely moves toward the metaphoric pole. Derrida himself, besides producing many suggestive oxymetaphors, claimed that metaphors are central to philosophy and thought (see Culler, 1982).

Deconstruction and TV

But can we find evidence of the influence of electronic media on deconstruction? I believe we can, and in this section I amplify a remark by Poster (1990), who said that deconstruction may be "defined as TV viewing applied to books" (p. 65). In the terms of this book, we can say that television is used as an unstated deep metaphor to generate some of deconstruction's positions.

Many of the discoveries of deconstructionists about "texts" bear a striking resemblance to the everyday facts of television. The *infinite play of signification* is a pretty good description of any segment of the "flow" of daily television, particularly if one is *channel surfing*, where random and contradictory signs succeed one another in bewildering profusion.

The *indeterminacy of meaning*, and the *endless displacement of meanings*, is actually sought for by writers of mass media dramas. These shows must appeal to large audiences, with differing political opinions, personal tastes, and so on. The mass market dramas cannot get too didactic, and must allow alternative interpretations to be drawn, to keep from alienating sectors of its audience. Being obvious or "preachy" is a major sin for mass media writers.

Mass media "texts" are therefore often designed to be "polysemic," intentionally keeping open alternative interpretations. It is good for business to have people talking and arguing about the show around the water cooler the next day. Television and cinema are industries devoted to the *indeterminacy of meaning.*

Deconstructionists have said we can never get at the "real" thing, only signs (see C. Norris, 1991.) This is certainly true of watching television to get our information. We only see signs on television.

Deconstructionists also subsume the world to "text," all is an

"open text"

(see C. Norris, 1991). This sounds a lot like a TV news show. We know the general format, but never know what specifics will be on the show on a particular night. Although a printed text is fixed, the electronic texts of television are flowing and changeable.

Derrida also claimed that writing is primary to speech,

"there is no linguistic sign before writing"

(see Ellis, 1989, pp. 18-23). Again, this is true of television where almost everything is scripted, even those "spontaneous" conversations on talk shows.

Many commentators noted that deconstruction is a rhetoric of "transgression," "violent opposition," and "disruption" (C. Norris, 1991, p. 32). Here, the similarity to everyday television drama is apparent. Such terms could be used in any day's program descriptions in the newspaper.

What are we to make of these homologies between deconstructionist pronouncements about printed language texts, and the character of everyday television? I believe that a deep metaphor is at work. The forms and formats of television have been internalized. These structure the observations, claims, and assertions of deconstruction. The everyday experience of television viewing gives plausibility to these claims. This is one explanation for the power and fascination exerted by the deconstructionist metalanguage, and its cousins in the *poststructuralist* or *postmodern* pantheon of discourse. (For a detailed discussion of these latter approaches and their relation to electronic media, see Poster, 1990.)

Deconstruction in the Media Spotlight

Deconstruction has spilled over from academia into the glare of the mass media more than any other metalanguage. It has not gotten very good press. de Man, one of its celebrity academic proponents, was discovered to have written anti-Semitic cultural criticism for the Nazis during World War II (see Lehman, 1991). A major philosophical forebear of Derrida, Heidegger, a German philosopher, also has been found out to be a more active Nazi than previously suspected (see McMillen, 1993).

In the articles and counterarticles generated by the de Man controversy, the deconstructionist technique of reversing polar opposites was used for rhetorical effect, but failed to be convincing. As critic Lehman (1991) wrote:

> There was, first of all, Derrida's statement that a condemnation of de Man would "reproduce the exterminating gesture." A critic of de Man was, in other words, no better than an exterminating Nazi. . . . Most bizarre of all was Richard Rand's argument that de Man and his partisans were the real Jews in the case. (p. 243)

A critical method that cannot tell the Nazis from the Jews surely leaves much to be desired.

However, as far as I know, no one in the debate pointed out the usefulness of a collaborator's skills in the muddied environment of academic discourse. In both collaborating with the Nazis, and writing for the U.S. academy, a certain ruthlessness and slipperiness can come in handy. Also useful is the ability to redefine terms after you have used them, giving you the ability to generate *indeterminate meanings*.

Then there were some public incidents where Derrida implicitly claimed that the tenets of deconstruction were not really to be applied to him. One such incident involved Derrida's objection to the publication of a translated interview with him, in a book entitled *The Heidegger Controversy* (see L. Lewis, 1993; McMillen, 1993). Derrida complained that there were "heavy, heavy" mistakes in the translation (McMillen, 1993). However, deconstruction had long claimed that *meanings are indeterminate*. Further, *meanings were created by readers, and the author's intentions were irrelevant*. As L. Lewis (1993) wrote:

> Here is the Grand Poo-Bah of Deconstruction, the author of the Death of the Author, a card-carrying anti-intentionalist and born-again indeterminist whining about having been mistranslated, misunderstood, and (gasp!) misrepresented . . . was I sleeping in class when Derrida exempted his own words from the general run of linguistic utterances? (p. B3)

For all its failings, however, deconstruction does participate in the metalinguistic project of replacing (or reframing) objectivism, which is a necessary cultural response to the new descriptions of the world from electronic media.

I once heard Derrida (1996) speak. In his presentation he provided a number of paradoxical statements:

> *(Algeria, his homeland) "from which I emerged*
> *without emerging from it"*

and, his efforts in France to be

> *"more, and less, French than the French."*

When discussing language, he remarked that

> *"in a sense nothing is translatable,*
> *in a sense everything is translatable."*

And one of his oxymetaphors was, I thought, quite beautiful. He was describing "A dream, to make something happen or arrive to the language, where

> *language loses itself by finding itself,*
> *turns from itself to itself."*

In a moment of candor, he did admit, "In short . . . I exaggerate, I always exaggerate."

SUMMARY

In this chapter, I provided a quick tour through some of the paradoxical terrain produced by metalanguages in the second half of the 20th century. As discourse moves away from the metonymic pole, with its objectivist description of the world, and toward the metaphoric pole, with its interactionist descriptions of the world, everything suddenly seems up for grabs. The old certainties become just another set of assumptions. (For another description of this process, written from within the *map-territory* metaphor, see chapter 15.)

In the next chapter, I provide some historical context to this discussion, and trace out changes in metaphor's fortune as they relate to changes in media.

five

A Media Ecology History of Metaphor

THE MEDIA ECOLOGY METAPHOR

The history of metaphor can be understood using the media ecology approach to communication history. But first it is useful to discuss the term *media ecology*, which is itself a metaphor. The metaphor emphasizes the role of media as environment. Postman (1979) explained the metaphor by pointing out that when a culture's main medium of communication changes, everything else in the culture changes as well. Communication is one of the central activities of any culture. Therefore, when the means of communication changes, we can expect the rest of the culture to be affected. Maybe all the changes do not come at once, or all together, but eventually the culture is transformed.

This metaphor asserts that *a culture is an ecology*, where all parts are related in some way. When one aspect of an ecological system is disturbed, repercussions are felt through the entire system. Media *compete* with each other in this ecological system. Each medium tends to seek out its own *niche*. Sometimes media *pollute* the culture with too much irrelevant information.

When media change, the old cultural forms will feel strains, new cultural forms will arise, and social conflict will result. Traditionalists will fight to keep the old ways, whereas innovators will struggle for recognition and legitimacy.

Such a struggle is seen in the late 20th-century U.S. culture, where institutions of the print-based culture—schools, libraries, governmental elections, among others—are being impacted and changed by electric media. Television and computers are speeding up social processes and changing the ways we communicate. Young people are reading fewer books, and watching more television. Postman (1993) described this as a war of media. But this is not the first such war of media, as is seen from the media ecology approach to history.

THE FOUR STAGES OF COMMUNICATION HISTORY

In the media ecology tradition, the history of human communication is divided into four eras: oral, writing, printing press, and electric communication.

Stage 1: Oral Communication

The era of oral communication was when humanity lived in tribes and villages with no written language. The role of oral language in memorizing and transmitting culture has been studied by Ong (1982) in *Orality and Literacy*.

State 2: The Era of Writing

Next comes the era of *writing*. The first writing was pictographic, and each character stood for an entire word. This writing system was called *cuneiform*, it appeared around 3500 BCE, in Mesopotamia, and its use was limited to a special caste of scribes. It was not until 1500 BCE that the alphabet was invented, probably by the Semites in the Mediterranean basin. Each symbol of the alphabet stood for a sound.

The Greeks added vowels to the alphabet, turning it into a system that could be used by many people. We get a good description of the changes brought about by writing from discussions of the subject held by Socrates, Plato, and other early Greek philosophers. Havelock's (1963) *Preface to Plato* describes the vast culture changes brought about as writing technology disrupted the values and traditions resting on the older oral methods of education and cultural transmission. We can see relativistic metalanguages emerging in the thought of the Sophists and the new schools of rhetoric.

State 3: The Printing Press

The third main period in human communication history was brought about by the printing press, invented in Europe in the 15th century. The first book Gutenberg printed was the Bible, and within 100 years, the Catholic Church's monopoly of knowledge about the Bible was broken. One of the results of this was the rise of Protestantism in all its varieties. Another result of the printing press was the rise of a scientific community, committed to open publication of experiments, methods, and results (see Eisenstein, 1979).

Other histories of the print era can be found in Innis' *Empire and Communications* (1950), and *The Bias of Communication* (1951). Innis stressed the importance of monopolizing a medium of communication for political power. McLuhan's *The Gutenberg Galaxy* (1962) connects print with the rise of individualism, the dominance of the visual mode of perception, and the creation of "the public" and the nation-state. Sometimes the writing and print stages of communication history are blended together in media ecology thought, but they probably should be kept separate.

Stage 4: Electric Communication

The fourth stage of human communication history comes with electric communication. This begins with the electric telegraph first used in the United States in the 1840s. By the end of the 20th century, electric communication media have spanned the globe and reached into space. The changes in culture, education, and consciousness produced by electric communication media are the subject of many media ecology studies, which often look back to the changes caused by earlier communication media as a guiding analogy.

Understanding Media (McLuhan, 1964) is the groundbreaking media ecology work dealing with electronic media. McLuhan made the case that electronic media undermine the individualistic, visual and analytical biases of print, replacing them with collective, "tactile," and holistic biases. Some of the metaphors from this insightful but uneven book are critiqued in chapters 10 and 11.

Postman, in *Teaching as a Conserving Activity* (1979), traced out the consequences for education of these differences between print and electronic media. Postman argued that electronic media present a "hidden curriculum" of intrinsically gratifying, present-centered images. This hidden curriculum, Postman claimed, opposes print-based analytical, rational, and logical styles of thought.

Postman's *Amusing Ourselves to Death* (1985) continues these themes, as it claims television has turned the public discourse of news, religion, and education into entertainment. Postman's *Technopoly* (1993) argues that the information overload from television and computers has damaged U.S. culture's sense of coherence. It also deplores the technological mindset's inability to provide moral guidance to society.

Meyrowitz's *No Sense of Place* (1985) develops a theory of the social changes produced by television, which stresses the destabilizing of former social boundaries by increased information. This helped lead, Meyrowitz said, to movements for equality for Blacks, women, and bringing political figures down to the levels of everyday people. Both Meyrowitz and Postman (1982) made the case that electronic media have increasingly dissolved the distinction between children and adults. The metaphor of the *disappearance of childhood* is discussed in chapter 13.

The media ecology approach to history is sweeping, yet intuitively understandable. The older means of communication have not disappeared—we still engage in oral communication for most of our important life's work. We write, we read printed materials, we watch television. So each of us has some experiential basis for understanding the basic categories of the media ecology approach to history.

However, some thinkers find the media ecology approach too broad and sweeping. They claim that it oversimplifies complicated relationships, and gives too much power to communication media. Although these objections must be considered, they partly lie in a misreading of media ecology thinkers, who, except for McLuhan in his expansive moments, were careful to avoid technological determinism, qualify their generalizations, and place media in their historical context.

LITERATE ORALITY

One of the main metaphors the media ecology tradition uses to comprehend the transition to electric media is that, in many ways, *electric media are returning us to a kind of orality.* Ong (1982) called this a "secondary orality", because, of course, writing and print still exist (although they are increasingly mediated through electronic media). I prefer Ong's (1971) phrase *literate orality,* to describe the complex and contradictory blend of contemporary media and culture.

Many habits of thought from oral cultures seem to be returning in the world of electric media. Ong (1971) pointed to the use of poetry, rhythm, and formulaic repetition in popular music, which are similar to the repetitive formulas of oral education. Postman (1985) noted, with dismay, the abandonment in public discourse of literate habits of logical and sequenced arguments, and their replacement with images and slogans. He traced this to the presentational forms of television symbolism. McLuhan (1964) looked at rock concerts and called radio a *tribal drum.*

The idea of a new orality brought on by electric media is an oxymetaphor formed by conceptual blending. We cannot simply map the properties of oral societies onto our own—modern (or postmodern?) society is too big and complex to be compared with the small, relatively insulated tribal groups of oral culture. But we can conceptually blend oral and print characteristics into a new structure: part metaphor and part oxymoron. I believe the main promise of the media ecology tradition for explaining electric media's effects on culture and consciousness lies here.

METAPHOR IN ORAL SOCIETIES

For many thousands of years, humans lived in small tribal groups with no written language. In such groups, spoken language played a central role in collective memory. There were no libraries with books filled with writing to preserve the insights and knowledge of the past. Whatever got remembered had to be memorized by someone, repeated to others at appropriate times, and passed on to future generations.

As a result, education in oral societies tended to involve much repetition, memorization, reciting aloud. Many devices were used to aid memory—rhymes, poetry in rhythm, mythological stories. Clearly, in such a system, metaphors, proverbs, stories, and myths played a central role. Furthermore, as pointed out by Lippert (1996), oral cultures have relatively few abstract terms in their vocabularies, and metaphor allows them to use concrete imagery to think about abstract topics. Thus, metaphor is one of the main supports of oral societies' predominantly analogical thinking processes, as described by Levi-Strauss (1966).

But there is more to the situation. For in oral societies, language was thought to hold an intimate relationship with the real world. If you knew the name of a thing, you had power over that thing—animate or inanimate, human or spirit. The "object" and the "sign" were connected in a real but little understood manner. Such connections formed the basis of *magic*, where you were thought to be able to influence something at a distance by chanting its name, burning its image, or some other symbolic method.

Many oral societies were organized around groups that had certain spirits or animals as their "totems." Thus, a portion of a tribe might describe themselves as the "buffaloes," for example, or as the "crows." To modern anthropologists studying such groups, these terms are metaphors in our sense—giving the name of one thing to something else. But to the participants, the totemic terms were metaphors in the oral society's sense—an expression of a real bond between the group and the animal, or the spirit of the animals, or other spirits. People in the totemic clans would describe themselves as buffaloes, and seek to emulate the desirable qualities of their totemic animals. In rituals and ceremonies, members of the totemic clans would don the appropriate masks and costumes, and be thought to transform themselves into the totemic spirits. (For an anthropologist's discussion of the use of metaphor in ritual to "predicate an identity" on participants, see Fernandez, 1977.)

In oral cultures, then, metaphors are taken very seriously. They are more than suggestive comparisons, they express real connections. Metaphors are at the basis of religious and magical ceremonies that are intended to communicate with the spirit world and produce results in this world. Only the most learned and powerful figures may explicate and understand the meanings of the metaphors in the tribal myths, legends, and tales. In oral societies, you don't mess with metaphors.

WRITING CULTURE AND METAPHOR

By the time we get to Aristotle, in the 4th century BCE, many changes have taken place in the world. Large civilizations have emerged in the Middle East, India, China. World trade is going on. Huge cities dot the landscape.

In this larger, cosmopolitan world the old magical attitudes toward language have started to fade. Greek philosophers are debating whether names have a necessary connection with their objects (*physis*), or whether they are just arbitrary collective agreements (*nomos*).

Literal language has come into being. The fixity of writing makes it a privileged form of speech for legal and accounting tasks. "Get it in writing" is still a phrase we use today when we want to be sure of the terms of a contract or agreement.

As writing spread through the culture, it redescribed the world in terms of fixed marks on a surface. It encouraged skills of analysis and abstraction. It provided a metaphor or cognitive model for envisioning the world of thought as radically separate from the world of things. In literate discourse, completely abstract objects could be discussed, free of all connections to particular places and times (Havelock, 1963). Furthermore, writing allowed different versions of tradition to be compared, and encouraged skepticism about the old oral traditions. This skeptical attitude produced the disciplines of philosophy and history (Goody, 1977).

In Jakobson's (1971) terms, oral society was heavily at the metaphoric pole of discourse. As writing entered more into the discourse of Greek culture, it moved that discourse more toward the metonymic pole. The older oral metaphor-based reasoning principles of similarity and analogy were discredited by the newer, writing-based principles of logic and analysis (see Havelock, 1963). The old concrete analogical symbolism of orality was superceded by the new abstract logical symbolism of writing. The nature of the word changed, from evanescent sound to fixed visual form (see Ong, 1982).

Havelock (1963) wrote that the new literate discourse broke the "spell of the concrete" and replaced it with the "discipline of the abstract" (p. 295). In this transitional stage, new metalanguages emerged, pointing out paradoxes in language and thought, and raising uncomfortable epistemological questions. The teachers propounding these new metalanguages were controversial figures in Greek culture. The Sophists and rhetoricians were accused of corrupting tradition and promoting immorality in an ancient Greek *culture war* (see Havelock, 1963).

As writing took over more tasks in the culture, it began to impose new forms of education. The old orality-based ways of learning involved students practicing speaking and memorization through repetition of formulas. The new literate-based learning required reading—a solitary and mostly silent activity. In the oral-based education, you learned when it was appropriate to speak, and when it was appropriate to keep quiet; you also learned how to address specific audiences. The writing-based education, however, trained people to produce written documents, which addressed everyone in the same manner. And although writing appeared to be intelligent, as Plato pointed out in *the Phaedrus*, writing could not answer questions put to it.

Writing required precision and accuracy. Metaphor was clearly a form of inaccuracy—giving something the name of something else. And so, metaphor lost the status that oral societies had bestowed on it. Its function of providing access to abstract thought was made obsolete by abstract alphabetic writing. As discourse moved toward the metonymic pole, metaphor was repressed. Writers from Aristotle on tended to treat metaphor as a *stylistic device,* an embellishment, but nothing essential to language or thought itself.

The Roman educator Quintilian, for example, called the metaphor "the supreme ornament of style," and "the most beautiful of tropes." He presented his own version of how the "transference" worked. Metaphor could transfer from the (a) inanimate realm to the animate, (b) animate to the inanimate, (c) inanimate to the inanimate, and (d) animate to the animate. Already we see the proliferation of definitions for metaphor, which have continued until the present (see Hawkes, 1972).

PRINT CULTURE AND METAPHOR

The notion of metaphor as a surface embellishment of language has persisted in the "educated" classes up until our own times. *Real* language was held to be "literal" language, fixed and accurate like writing. In this scheme, metaphor is a difficulty, an inaccuracy—occasionally useful for illustrating a point, but having nothing to do with the important business of writing or thinking.

Print amplified writing's redescription of the world as fixed, objective, and abstract. It anchored discourse at the metonymic pole, encouraging the use of synechdoche and metonymy and repressing the use of metaphor. One of the main achievements of print culture was, in fact, the scientific method. Science rested on the ultimate metonymy—number. The world through science was seen most accurately as numbers, measurements, precise and abstract. Science also insisted upon mathematical accuracy in language, clear communication between scientists so experiments could be repeated. No room for metaphor here—or so it seemed, until philosophers started noticing the metaphors embedded in scientific theories themselves—such as the atom as a miniature solar system (see Black, 1962, *Models and Metaphors*).

But if print fostered notions of "literal" language, eventually it supported the publication of opposing views about language and metaphor. The tradition of "magical" language had never fully disappeared—but it tended to be relegated to "unreliable" sources, such as mystical thinkers, illiterates, women healers, and others. But in the 19th century, a group of poets, called the "romantic poets," published their views, which placed metaphor at the heart of language.

The English poets (Shelley, Keats, and Coleridge) all saw language as "vitally metaphorical" (see discussion in Hawkes, 1972). Far from being an appendage to language, metaphor was basic to its job of conceptualizing and communicating.

Thus, was begun the split between the "classical" and the "romantic" views of metaphor. The classical view, according to Hawkes, sees metaphor as "detachable" from language, and useful mainly as an ornamental device. This classical view also sees language as separate from the reality it tries to describe. Clearly, the classical view is supported by and reinforces objectivism.

By contrast, the romantic view sees metaphor as central to language, and finds even abstract and "scientific" thinking resting on "root" metaphors. The romantic view sees language as an integral part of the reality it describes, and therefore language plays a role in shaping that reality. (See also Shibles, 1971, for an annotated list of thinkers on metaphor, with valuable quotations.)

METAPHOR IN THE ELECTRONIC ERA

Electronic media redescribe the world in moving, noisy images. Their symbolism is concrete and iconic. They have jarred discourse away from the metonymic pole supported by print. Their formats have provided new deep metaphors for envisioning knowledge and reasoning. They have moved culture back toward the metaphoric pole of oral societies, producing a *literate orality*. In response to this shift, metalanguages have emerged, highlighting metaphor and paradox. A new trope, the *oxymetaphor*, has been produced, joining together metaphor and oxymoron (see chapter 4).

In this environment, metaphor became increasingly visible to thinkers in many different areas. By the second half of the 20th century, the romantic view of metaphor had received more verification than Keats or Shelley could ever have dreamed. And it came from a group of people calling themselves "scientists"—"cognitive scientists".

This new "scientific" elaboration of the romantic view of metaphor was announced in the book *Metaphors we Live By*, by Lakoff and Johnson (1980), and summarized by Lakoff (1993). Lakoff and collaborators analyzed ordinary phrases to discover pervasive conceptual metaphors that shape thought and language. They found a widespread system of "conceptual metaphors," rooted in bodily experience (see further discussion of this work in chapter 6).

The views of Lakoff and his collaborators fall directly in the "romantic" view of metaphor. However, the classical view of metaphor has not gone away, although it has been transformed. The classical view of metaphor lives on in the branch of cognitive science which takes a "computational" approach to metaphor (see Martin, 1996).

This branch of cognitive science is seeking to program computers to "understand" and translate natural languages. The ultimate goal is shown in various corporate videos of the technological future (see AT&T, 1993). The idea is to have a person in the United States, say, speak into his or her phone in English, and have a person in Japan, for example, hear the conversation in Japanese. The computers in the phone system will allow people to talk to each other without having to learn a new language.

This is an appealing vision, a reversal of the Biblical Tower of Babel story. However, the effort to program computers to understand and translate natural language has not produced the hoped-for results. I discuss this issue more in the third section of this volume, but in brief, I do not think that natural language, as spoken by humans, will ever be fully apprehendable in computer form because the computer needs to have its operations symbolized and specified. Natural language, however, makes metaphorical jumps and turns that cannot be specified in advance.

I imagine some interesting results will come out of the computational approach to language and metaphor. However, I think that it rests ultimately on a fallacy—thinking is not computing, and the brain is not a computer. I contend in Part III that these are oxymetaphors, which paradoxically unite opposites.

And so we have, in the electronic era, the continuation of the classical versus romantic split. Lakoff and colleagues say metaphor is central to all language, and having a body is central to all metaphor. The computational approach says you can put all language into a computer program—language, in other words, can be reduced to disembodied symbols and rules.

But in the electronic era, the division becomes more extreme. The classical view has fulfilled a potential in Enlightenment-scientific thought. It describes human language in terms of machine programming. What used to be thought of as essentially human—language—is conceived as mechanical. Against this view stand the Lakoff romantics insisting on the primacy of embodied experience.

six

Theories of Metaphor

A metaphor is a transference, naming one thing in terms of another, according to Aristotle's ancient definition. It sounds so simple—and *is* simple enough for people to use metaphors every day. Yet there seems to be no end to theorizing about metaphor. Since ancient Greece, thousands of treatises have been written on theories of metaphor (Noth, 1995).

In the 20th century, the term "metaphor" has expanded its scope, and it has often been used as a shorthand term to describe any similarity or analogy. As discourse has become increasingly fragmented, metaphor is also used as an all-purpose connector term. These uses do relate to the etymological sense of metaphor as *a bridge*, involving a *carrying over*. This is from the Greek roots "meta" (beyond, above) and "pherein" (carrying, or bearing; see Merriam-Webster, 1983).

Yet sometimes the *bridge* leads into the unknown. Metaphor is often applied to new situations, to expand the reach of language and thought. Thus, metaphor has creative power, and is one of the main resources that language uses to conceptualize and communicate about a changing reality (Langer, 1951). This property was recognized long ago by Aristotle in his *Rhetoric:*

we all naturally find it agreeable to get hold of new ideas easily: words express ideas, and therefore those words are the most agreeable that enable us to get hold of new ideas. Now strange words simply puzzle us; ordinary words convey only what we know already; it is from metaphor that we can best get hold of something fresh.

Unfortunately, this classic insight has been overlooked by many thinkers today. You can read a long list of current books on language, semiotics, linguistics, communication, and social science without ever encountering the notion that language is open and creative. Perhaps this is because our age loves machines, and gravitates toward closed-system mechanistic theories that try to put everything in neat boxes.

Metaphor refuses to be contained in neat boxes. In fact, part of *what a metaphor does is break the conceptual boxes that routine language uses*. Metaphor is messy and unpredictable. It does not conform to neat rules and does not follow rational paths. It is a major expression of that part of language which falls outside the boundaries of scientific inquiry, called "the remainder" by Lecercle (1990). Let us take a look at some of the ways metaphor breaks through boundaries.

MAPPING

Lakoff and Johnson (1980) said that "The essence of metaphor is understanding and experiencing one thing in terms of another" (p. 5). They described the metaphorical transfer process as *mapping*. When we use metaphor, we *map* features from a *source domain* onto a *target domain* (see Figure 6.1). This terminology is simple, intuitive, and useful. (But note that we must use metaphors to describe metaphors—*mapping* is a suggestive metaphor, as is *target*. Are we conceiving of metaphor as some kind of military operation?)

For example, the metaphor *life is a drama* is a common but very productive trope. It maps the properties of the source domain—drama—onto the target domain—life. When used in discourse, this metaphor can be the basis for thinking about life and living, and can generate new insights or points of view. We can apply what we know about drama to what we do not know about life. In fact, this metaphor is one of the enduring metaphors in the fields of philosophy, sociology, anthropology,

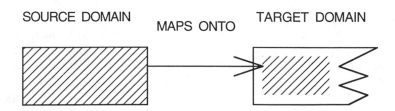

Figure 6.1. Metaphorical mapping of structure

communication, and literary criticism. As I point out in chapter 12, this metaphor probably has a bright future in the everyday language of the *television generations.*

SYSTEMATICITY

Yet another way metaphor can extend meanings is through the "systematicity" of metaphors, to use Lakoff and Johnson's (1980) terminology. Metaphors are often coherent and systematic, especially if they rest on analogy. This means that metaphors can map entire structures of relations from one domain to another.

The property of systematicity is foregrounded in my working definition of metaphor:

A metaphor asserts a structural similarity between two domains normally thought of as separate.

When metaphors are used as bridges into the unknown, they gain power from showing us structural similarities, and suggesting paths to follow to discover new insights into the unknown domain.

This property of following out implications of structure is a major source of the power of metaphor to generate creative thought and insight into unknown domains.

CONCEPTUAL BLENDING

The "conceptual blending" (see Figure 6.2) approach of Turner and Fauconnier (1995) is an outgrowth of the Lakoff and Johnson work on metaphor, but adds to the understanding of the conceptual processes at work. Lakoff and Johnson referred to metaphor as *mapping* structure from a *source domain onto a target domain.* Turner and Fauconnier noted that in some metaphorical expressions, something else seems to be taking place. They call this conceptual blending.

In a conceptual blend, two or more domains may be involved. The metaphor does not necessarily *map* from one domain to the other. Rather, the domains may be *blended* into a separate conceptual *space,* which takes on aspects of both domains and has emergent structure of its own.

For example, the metaphor *cyberspace* is a conceptual blend. It blends the notion of a computer network with the notion of physical space, producing something that is a combination of both but having distinct new properties of its own. In fact, I contend in chapter 21 that *cyberspace* can also be considered an *oxymetaphor,* the conceptual blending together of opposite terms. (For more on *oxymetaphors,* see chapter 4.)

Another thinker has elaborated ways that metaphor can extend or create meanings. Wheelwright (1962) coined the terms *epiphor* (extension of meaning through comparison), and *diaphor* (creation of new meaning by juxtaposition or synthesis). Epiphor seems to be similar to Lakoff and Johnson's mapping. Diaphor seems to be similar to conceptual blending.

LEVELS OF METAPHOR

Most theories of metaphor acknowledge that metaphor works on more than just one level of thought or language. There is disagreement, however, on just how to define these levels. I propose a taxonomy of metaphors using this metaphor of *levels: deep metaphor, surface metaphor,* and *meta-metaphor.*

Most metaphorical theories from the past 2,000 years dealt with *surface metaphors,* the actual words used and replaced by metaphors. From the objectivist description of the world favored by the dominant writing and print media, metaphor was simply an ornamental use of words, a matter of surface appearances that might help make a point more effectively. As the objectivist view of

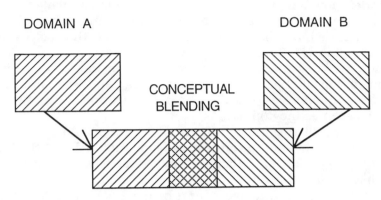

Figure 6.2. Conceptual blending

the world came into question in the 20th century, metalanguages emerged to deal with the epistemological issues raised by electronic media's competing descriptions of the world (see chapters 2 and 3). Then as the smooth surfaces of language fractured, metaphor was discovered everywhere, both in the deep foundations of thought and discourse, and in metalinguistic processes that expanded definitions and concepts. Most of the theoretical attention has gone to the deep metaphors, and I begin there.

Deep Metaphor

A *deep metaphor* structures discourse, even though it may not ever be explicitly stated in that discourse. It serves as a blueprint, or a ground plan, guiding the discourse. It can be detected by the relations between the many surface metaphors that appear in the actual discourse. I sometimes call this process a master metaphor aligning mini-metaphors. Many thinkers have highlighted this structuring aspect of deep metaphor.

In a classic book, philosopher Pepper (1942) identified *four root metaphors* that he claimed underlie the major philosophical systems in Western thought. One is *mechanism,* which relies on images of levers, electric fields, technology in general. Another is *organicism,* which focuses on integrating processes that form an organic whole, transcending the sum of their parts. A third *root metaphor* Pepper called *contextualism,* which studies every event as a strand in a historical context. The fourth is *formism,* which relies on an intuition of similar forms in dissimilar phenomena.

MacCormac (1985) also claimed that all philosophical theories have an underlying, or *basic* metaphor, which provides an insight that undergirds an entire approach. This is also true, he contended, for theories of metaphor, which themselves need a *basic* metaphor. This can lead metaphor theorists into circular logics, as they use metaphor to explicate metaphor This is a problem for an objectivist view of language and logic, but I expect as discourse moves toward the metaphorical pole, this circularity will be seen as inevitable.

One of the most influential formulations of this *depth* relationship in metaphor comes from Richards (1936) in *The Philosophy of Rhetoric*. Richards introduced two technical terms to distinguish the different ideas that metaphor gives us. The *vehicle* is the actual word or phrase used, the *tenor* is the underlying idea, subject, or situation. These two *interact* in the metaphor—thus Richards' theory is called the *interaction theory* of metaphor. (Today the term "tenor" is often replaced by "topic," which accurately describes the function of this underlying idea.)

Sometimes, deep metaphors are called *models*, and there has been much discussion over whether or not models are metaphors (see Black, 1962, for the affirmative position). Certainly, models and metaphors share the property of providing structure, although models are usually thought of as visual diagrams or abstract structures of relations, whereas metaphors are usually considered to be words or ideas.

One concept that joins these domains is Peirce's (1932) notion of *iconicity*, or resemblance. Iconicity has proved difficult to define precisely (see Noth, 1995). I expect as discourse moves more toward the metaphoric pole, defining iconicity will seem less of a problem, because the metaphoric pole emphasizes the discovery of similarity as one of the main functions of discourse. In the future I also expect metaphor will be generally considered to be both iconic and a model.

The Usefulness of Excavating Deep Metaphors. Deep metaphor can be found working in serious political speeches and policies. When we examine the metaphors used by a speaker or advocate for a particular position, we can discover much about their underlying assumptions, which often are not made explicit. When we discover these underlying assumptions, we can examine them, critique them, and suggest other ways of looking at the situation. Often this takes the form of suggesting other deep metaphors.

For example, Schon (1979) examined the discourse of city planners and social policymakers, and found that urban housing was often described in terms of *blight* metaphors. This problem-setting metaphor then implied a solution—urban *renewal,* which involved the complete destruction and redesign of an urban area to eliminate the *diseased* section. Yet a competing metaphor emerged from different observers—the slum as a *natural community.* This "problem-setting metaphor" defined the situation differently and pointed to different solutions, namely trying to support the rooted communities where they were. The different metaphors made it difficult for the conflicting parties to engage in fruitful discussions about social policy.

Many other areas of discourse exhibit the pervasiveness of deep metaphor, and illustrate the problems for dialogue between those with different metaphorical understandings.

Ivie (1987) found metaphors underlying much of the thought of opponents of the Cold War. The rhetoric of idealists like Henry Wallace, William Fulbright, and Helen Caldicott resorted to a system of metaphors to describe the nuclear stalemate using *madness, sickness, pathology,* and *force.* Ivie contended that these metaphors failed to effectively counter the *crusade* metaphor of Cold War supporters. He called for a new set of metaphors that "legitimizes collaboration between antagonists," and suggested some kind of *symbiosis* metaphor be identified and elaborated.

Metaphors also can be found at work in news stories. Mumby and Spitzack (1983) found metaphors in the language of TV news stories. For example, a metaphor implying that *politics is war* was found underlying expressions like *prime target, defeated, fought* the press, *running for cover.* At the same time, politics was metaphorized as a game, as in a description of a *lobbying team, with first- and second-rate players.* Also politics was conceived as a drama, with people *playing a lesser role,* or *doing a balancing act.*

Likewise, Blankenship (1976) found pervasive metaphors of a campaign as a *horserace* when studying news coverage of the campaign for the Democratic nomination of 1972. The *race* had its *front-runners,* who were *out ahead of the pack,* its *dark horses,* and *also-rans.* Mixed in to the news reports were also metaphors of politics as *war,* and politics as *drama.*

Mumby and Spitzack suggested that an alternative deep metaphor of *politics as a work of art* would allow us to judge politics in ways that the current metaphors do not. We could speak of an *ugly policy,* or a *genius for shaping ideas.*

Not only politics, but intellectual disciplines during particular historical periods can have underlying deep-metaphorical assumptions. The thought and creativity of the period is then shaped by its metaphors. Stelzner (1965) discovered many mechanical metaphors in speech communication theories of the 19th century. He found a shift to biological metaphors taking place in the 20th century. Clearly, when the underlying metaphors of a field shift, thought and language suddenly have many new paths to follow.

Technology as Deep Metaphor. Several thinkers noted that technologies can form deep metaphors that influence a culture in many areas. Bolter (1984) called these "defining technologies". As discussed in chapters 1 through 3, media ecology thinkers have traced how communication technologies can be internalized and serve as metaphors for the conceptualizing of many processes of thought and discourse. Mumford (1963) discussed the clock as a defining technology for the early industrial-scientific culture of Europe. Edge (1974) found the steam engine to be a deep metaphor in the thought of 19th-century thinkers like Marx and Freud, with their concerns about *pressure* and *release.* Bolter (1984) viewed the computer as today's defining technology.

But clearly *the machine,* in a somewhat abstract sense, is the deep metaphor most implicated in the thinking of science, and objectivist culture generally. Turbayne (1962/1970) found an underlying "hidden" metaphor that the *universe is a machine* at work in influential early scientific thinkers like Descartes and Newton. On this deep metaphor has been erected a whole scaffolding of "scientific truth." He claimed that many scientists have become "victims" or "prisoners" of the mechanistic metaphor, mistaking the entailments of one deep metaphor for the only acceptable way to "do" science.

> The victim of metaphor accepts *one* way of sorting or bundling or allocating the facts as the *only* way to sort, bundle, or allocate them . . . he confuses a special *view* of the world with the world. (p. 27, italics added)

Turbayne tries to show the arbitrariness of this deep metaphor by substituting another: *nature speaks a universal language.* This would lead, he claimed, to a different, but no less scientific, practice of "science."

Edge (1974) found mechanical metaphors as the basis of much thinking about society, and had concerns about their authoritarian implications for social control. If *society is a machine,* then it seems reasonable to appoint trained engineers to run it, and not leave it to the whim of fickle electorates. Edge suggested that another series of deep metaphors, that *society is a work of art*, could lead to a more participatory and creative set of assumptions.

Conceptual Metaphor. Perhaps the most influential work on deep metaphor is coming from cognitive scientists associated with Lakoff and Johnson's (1980) approach articulated in *Metaphors We Live By.*

Lakoff (1993) and collaborators claimed that "ordinary, everyday English is largely metaphorical" (p. 204). He and others discovered "a huge system of everyday, conventional conceptual metaphors," which they claim has "destroyed" the traditional distinction between "literal" and "figurative" language (p. 204).

Lakoff (1993) claimed that "the locus of metaphor is not in language at all, but in the way we conceptualize one mental domain in terms of another" (p. 203). An example of these "conceptual metaphors" at work in English is A STATE IS A PERSON (Lakoff and collaborators capitalize conceptual metaphors in print). This leads to descriptions of states as *friendly, hostile, healthy, generous, heroic,* and so on. These expressions may provide a misleading sense of purpose and unity to the complex maneuverings of foreign policy and diplomacy, which are, after all, the resultants of many conflicting groups and interests.

Where do these conceptual metaphors come from? Lakoff and Johnson insist that they come from the actual embodied experience of everyday life (see Johnson, 1987; Lakoff & Johnson, 1980). The system of conceptual metaphors cannot be separated from our bodies. These metaphors rest upon internal images of the body and its action—"image-schemas" in the group's terminology.

Many of these image-schemas are described by Johnson in his book, *The Body in the Mind* (1987). For example, from our bodies we have a sense of the differences between up and down. More than this, we associate different feelings and states with up and down. So *up* tends to be associated with feelings of liveliness and happiness, while *down* is associated with feelings of tiredness or sadness.

Johnson found an underlying metaphor of *physical appearance is a physical force* in many common expressions. Thus, someone can be said to have *striking* looks, we can be *knocked off our feet* by a beautiful person, movie stars are described as *bombshells,* we can be *blown away,* and so on.

These conceptual metaphors play a role in our thinking as well as in our descriptions. Johnson (1987) discussed how the *physical appearance is a physical force* metaphor leads to a chain of argument that claims that women are responsible for producing sexual desire in men. This metaphorical argument goes like this: (a) A woman is responsible for her physical appearance. (b) Physical appearance is a physical force exerted on other people. (c) Therefore a woman is responsible for the force she exerts on men. This chain of argument could be used to "explain" instances of rape, and excuse men from controlling their own desires.

The larger point of the Lakoff and Johnson work is that our metaphors are ultimately grounded in our experience of our bodies. Bodily experience influences even our most "literal" attempts to be objective.

I find the work of Lakoff, Johnson, Turner and colleagues to be the most exciting work currently occurring in metaphor. I sympathize with their efforts and share most of their assumptions and conclusions. I would question, however, their sharp separation between thought and language, when they claim that metaphor is a "figure of thought," not of language. I find it difficult to separate thought and language so completely— rather they are intertwined, each making the other possible. This separation seems even more inappropriate because Lakoff and company are busy eliminating the distinctions between thought and the body, the old "mind-body" dualism underlying objectivism. If this dualism is laid to rest, as it should be, then why import another, just as arbitrary?

Surface Metaphor

Surface metaphors are explicitly stated in discourse. They imply some analogy or structural similarity between two domains of reference. They may be connected to other surface metaphors—in which case a deep metaphor is probably operating. Surface metaphors, however, can also be one-hit wonders, shining brightly for a moment and then vanishing.

Most of the action in metaphor theory is in deep metaphor, as the previous sections indicate. Surface metaphors, however, used to be in the theoretical spotlight. In fact, many of the theories of metaphor from the past 2,000 years have come from within the objectivist view of the world, located at the metonymic pole of discourse (see chapter 3). This perspective downplays the importance of metaphor and its associated discursive operations. Metaphor seemed to be simply a matter of replacing words in the *substitution theory*, or a matter of suggesting analogies in the *comparison theory* (see Noth, 1995).

From the objectivist perspective, metaphor is a kind of *mistake*, because the job of language is to refer accurately to a pre-existing outside world. Proper language is *literal*, according to objectivism. Those figures of speech that did not conform to this prescription were called *tropes*, or turnings because they turned away from the proper referential function of language.

Literal language *literally* means written language, therefore fixed and permanent. So the objectivist view of language rested in part on the deep metaphor provided by technologies of writing and print. It prescribed the qualities of written and printed language for all proper language. So, as Lakoff (1993) pointed out, the notion of literal language *is itself a metaphor*.

Oral language is always fluid and changing (see Ong, 1982, for a discussion of the differences between sound-based oral language and permanent, silent written language). As electronic media move the culture away from the dominance of writing and print, the literal figurative dichotomy is coming more into question

Instead of using this dichotomy, I propose a different approach to understanding surface metaphor and its role in language. We might think of language as occurring along a *spectrum* from "completely defined and understood terms" on the one side, to "incoherent, not understood terms" on the other side. I represent this spectrum in Table 6.1. Of course, there are not the clear boundaries between the phases of language that the table layout implies.

No language is completely codified, there is always variation in meanings because contexts of language-use keep changing. But let us take the codified pole as one necessary tendency—all language needs agreed on definitions, or it is useless for communication.

Everyday language, in this view, is located somewhere between the poles of codification and incoherence. It is *pulled in both directions at once*. It needs to rely on shared definitions and understandings (pulled toward the codification pole), but it also needs to be flexible and creative (pulled toward metaphorical language and incoherence pole).

This spectrum of surface language matches well with Postman's (1976) "continuum of semantic flexibility," which competent communicators must be able to use. However, he noted:

> Semantic flexibility has its limits. At one end of the continuum lies role-fixation, and stupid talk is its most characteristic symptom [i.e., talk which does not know what environment it is

Table 6.1. Surface Language From Codification to Incoherence.

Codified and defined language	Objective reporting	"Everyday language	Metaphorical and creative language	Incoherence

> in]. At the other end lies schizophrenia, and crazy talk is its hallmark every time [i.e., talk that sustains an unreal environment]. But in between lies a wide range of opportunities for self-development and for its expression through talk that is effective, productive, and above all, sane. (p. 118)

Role fixation and its resulting stupid talk would lie beyond the codification pole, whereas schizophrenia and its crazy talk would lie beyond the metaphorical pole.

Something interesting happens to language when a country is occupied by a hostile foreign power (or when a tyrannical government takes over). All of a sudden, everyday language is pushed toward the metaphorical language pole. No longer is it desirable to "say what you mean." You might get in trouble for objective reporting. So people speak metaphorically, allowing a wide range of interpretation to what they say, so they cannot have their words used against them by informers or "thought police."

The efforts of schools and English classes are usually to move the discourse of students toward the codification pole.

I would locate Jakobson's *metonymic pole of discourse* toward the codification pole, and his *metaphoric pole of discourse* toward the metaphorical and creative side of the spectrum. These conceptualizations are not identical, however, they are dealing with slightly different aspects of the complex totality that is human language. Jakobson's poles deal with *deeper* aspects of discourse than this surface language continuum.

This spectrum of codification-incohenence is offered as an alternative to the older "literal-figurative" distinctions of language. As was pointed out earlier, the concept of "literal language" hides the fact that much of our supposedly "literal" language rests on metaphorical foundations.

Meta-Level Functions of Metaphor

The third sense of metaphor focuses on its creative aspects, and foregrounds its function in expanding our linguistic and cognitive maps (note the map metaphor). I call this the *meta-level* of metaphor, the prefix "meta" meaning "above" or "beyond."

Sometimes metaphors can expand our frames of reference by linking specific phenomena with larger, "archetypal" concepts. Osborn (1967) pointed out how the rhetorical use of archetypal metaphors of light and darkness (and associated metaphors of the sun, heat and cold, and the change of the seasons) can function to increase the motivational power of persuasive appeals.

Sometimes a metaphor can seem to multiply the associations and meanings of a specific term. This insight is used by Jaynes (1976), who used the metaphor of multiplication to explicate the process of metaphor itself. In arithmetic, a multiplier works on a multiplicand, to generate a new result. In metaphor, a *metaphier* works on a *metaphrand*, to produce a new result. The lesser known thing to be described is the *metaphrand*, the better known relation used to elucidate it is the *metaphier*.

Sometimes the term *metaphor* is used in a very large sense to describe a cultural totality. Chesebro and Bertelsen (1996) claimed that media can provide the "dominant cultural metaphor" of a period. The dominant cultural metaphor fostered by electronic media is still in formation, they claim. They discussed one suggestion, from Gozzi and Haynes (1992), that the dominant metaphor will be "empathy at a distance," which will foster paradoxical attitudes of noninvolved involvement and compassionate detachment. They concluded, "At this moment, we are cautious, and we have yet to be convinced that 'ironic empathy' will be the dominant metaphor of the electronic media age" (p. 57).

The general property of "metaphor" as creative instrument is most fully explored in a long-neglected book, *Symbol and Metaphor*, by Foss (1949). Foss contrasted symbols and metaphor along the lines of Table 6.1. "Symbol" seeks to codify language, to freeze it within forms. "Metaphor" seeks to expand language, make it more fluid. But Foss' discussion, heavily rooted in the ancient Greeks, is more subtle than this description implies.

Foss focused on existence as a process. This process is never fully describable by fixed "symbols," which chop up the fluid process and substitute static parts, which are then treated as if they are wholes. Any symbolic classification will always be contingent and incomplete.

Foss contended that the processes of existence are best captured by the *processes* of language. He pointed to *metaphor as a process*, the process of expanding language and concepts. The metaphorical process is therefore messy and unpredictable, very unappealing to those who want to rely on the regularities of symbolic reductions. Foss anticipated many of the independent findings of the Lakoff and Johnson cognitive scientists, and grounds them in a philosophical base.

> . . . it is not so much in the single word, but in the process of speech itself, stretching over and beyond single words, in which the metaphorical move toward extension of knowledge is to be found. Only in the process of speech can the metaphorical task be fully achieved, that is, to oppose the tendency of the word toward smooth and expedient fixation in familiar fences, and to draw it into the disturbing current of a problematic drive. . . .

> In blasting the symbols and shattering their customary meaning the dynamic process of the searching, striving, penetrating mind takes the lead. . . . It is what Aristotle aims at when he calls the metaphor energy. (pp. 59-60)

Like all metaphors, the metaphor of *levels* has its strong and weak points. I hope this discussion of the three main levels provides a tolerably useful *map* of theoretical approaches to metaphor.

TWO ADDITIONAL PERSPECTIVES

As I have been studying and writing about metaphor from a mainly practical orientation, I have come across two approaches that are not covered by the previous metaphorical levels of theory. These are *embodied metaphors* and the idea of *the senses as metaphors.*

Embodied Metaphors

Occasionally, I have come across something that seems to be a physical embodiment of some larger concept. The physical thing is actually a metaphor for an idea. Take, for example, the fast food restaurant, as discussed in chapter 31. The actual franchise is a metaphor for the larger idea of *the perfect repeatable system,* beloved of gamblers everywhere. It involves a mapping of the idea of the *perfect system* onto the production of hamburgers, or sandwiches, or whatever. We have become so used to this particular embodied metaphor that the very syllable "Mc" can transform any word into a representative case of McDonald's *perfect system.* (I discuss "McMetaphors" in chapter 32.)

Perhaps I am flirting with neo-Platonism here, seeing material objects as partaking of some eternal form. All I can say is this concept has proved useful on occasion, when dealing with what used to be called the *real world.* (See also chapter 36, where I discuss the supermarket as an embodied metaphor for the abstract market system; and chapter 40, where putting together a jigsaw puzzle is treated as an embodied metaphor of the knowledge acquisition process.)

The Senses as Metaphors

The philosopher Nietzsche (1873/1992), among others, noticed that phenomena like "sounds" do not exist in nature, they result from the constructions of our senses. So he described the sensation of "sound" as itself a metaphor.

> A nerve stimulus, first transformed into a percept! First metaphor! The percept again copied into a sound! Second metaphor! . . . When we talk about trees, colors, snow, and flowers, we believe we know something about the things themselves, and yet we only possess metaphors of the things, and these metaphors do not in the least correspond to the original essentials. (p. 62)

Our whole sense-environment, in this sense, is metaphorical. In the *real world* there are no colors, no high sounds, no heat. These are all "metaphors" created by our senses, although I am not sure how Nietzsche knew that these sense-metaphors "do not in the least correspond to the original essentials."

It is a healthy exercise to question our sense-data and our world-constructions. If this approach to metaphor can help, it should be included in any survey of metaphorical usages. (I discuss these issues more in chapter 17 on virtual reality and chapter 39 on psychological projection.)

Next, I turn to a more practical matter—how to perform a metaphorical analysis.

seven

How To Do
a Metaphorical Analysis

The following outline of a method is meant to be a guideline, not a bible. It includes the important steps in the process, but some steps may be disregarded and others may be substituted.

STEP 1: IDENTIFY THE METAPHORS

It all starts with recognizing metaphors when you encounter them. You will encounter *surface metaphors* first. They can easily slip by as you read or listen, but *usually a metaphor catches your attention a bit more than do the surrounding words*. Notice when your attention is caught by some new, different, thought-provoking, infuriating, or funny *turn of phrase*. This can become intuitive with practice, and is a useful skill to have.

Once you have identified a metaphor, look around to see if other, related metaphors also appear. Metaphors often come in clusters because there often is a *deep metaphor* at work. A deep metaphor structures a part of discourse—I call the process *master metaphors aligning mini-metaphors*. See if many of the *surface* metaphors imply some common theme or model.

This clustering of metaphor results from the property of *systematicity* (Lakoff & Johnson, 1980). Systematicity results from the fact that metaphorical mappings involve structure, not just hit-or-miss associations. This property is very useful when searching for metaphors. Some metaphors might slip by you until you start to notice others that are similar. Then you look back and realize there has been a structure of metaphor operating all along.

Recognizing systemicity can be useful if, for example, someone makes an argument based on a series of metaphors. The argument may seem convincing, but you may sense something is wrong. If you can excavate the deep metaphors, you might be able to show how the metaphors do not apply, or only partly apply, and you have given a powerful counterargument. Or, you might find that the metaphors are mixed, that they do not work together coherently. This, too, is important information in evaluating metaphor-based arguments.

An example of a deep metaphor would be *the body is a machine*. Some biology text, for example, may state this openly, but it may not. The metaphor hunter will have to figure this metaphor out by noting the turns of phrase the textbook uses in supposedly matter-of-fact descriptions. Is the arm described as a *lever*? Is the digestive system a *chemical factory*? Is the brain described as a *computer*, *thermostat*, or *guidance system*? When you list all such expressions, you can then discover the underlying deep metaphors that structure much of the surface discourse.

You will come across metaphors everywhere: in everyday conversation, newspapers, magazines, talk shows, TV news, as well as poetry, novels, philosophy. Metaphors are particularly common when new technologies are introduced, or explained. It may be a scientist or engineer speaking, but the language can be just as metaphorical as that of a poet.

See if you can find the metaphors in the following sentences:

1. Time flies.
2. The representative from the rural district was concerned that the Information Superhighway wouldn't have any on-ramps in his district.
3. Metaphor is a key that unlocks many different areas of study.

These metaphors are as follows:

1. *Flies*—time does not really fly, we don't actually know what it does.
2. There is a master metaphor here—the *Information Superhighway*, which is not a highway but a network of electrical lines. There is also a mini-metaphor, aligned with the master metaphor—*on-ramp*. This is an example of how metaphor can be systematic. We would not talk about a *trap door* to the Information Superhighway—the metaphor would be a *mixed* metaphor, not structurally consistent.
3. *Key*—metaphor is a word, phrase, or idea, not a key. *Unlocks*—areas of study are not locked containers, although sometimes they may seem that way.

STEP 2: EXPLORE THE IMPLICATIONS OF THE METAPHORS

Any metaphor or system of metaphors will highlight some things, and ignore others. Some aspects of the phenomenon being described will be pushed forward, into bold relief by the metaphors. But other aspects will be pushed back, into the shadows, to be ignored and forgotten. Part of the job of a metaphorical analysis is to bring these neglected aspects into the light, where they can be given equal consideration. What is downplayed or ignored by the choice of metaphors? What is highlighted, and does it deserve to be?

(Quick question—What is the deep metaphor structuring the previous paragraph? Did you notice all the references to *light*, and *shadow*? Perhaps *metaphor is a spotlight*?)

A metaphorical system will often lead to certain implied conclusions. For example, the *Information Superhighway* metaphor implies that the electrical-wire network of the proposed *superhighway* will be like the concrete roads of the interstate Highway system. It is "common knowledge" that the interstate Highway system produced great economic benefits for the country and many jobs for many people. Therefore, discussions of the Information Superhighway often imply that this system will also provide economic benefits and many jobs. This implied conclusion, however, may not be accurate. Shuttling messages across wires is a very different process from sending physical goods along real roads. A metaphorical analysis should discuss these differences clearly, without being led by the force field of the metaphor into a predetermined conclusion. (For a more thorough discussion of this metaphor, see chapter 23.)

STEP 3: SUGGEST ALTERNATE METAPHORS

Nothing shows up the biases of a particular metaphorical system better than another metaphorical system. Each system will imply a different structure, and you can more easily find the gaps, the contradictions, the alternate implications and predictions.

So, instead of the *Information Superhighway*, how about calling the proposed electronic network the *video jukebox?* Not so exciting, but able to illustrate different potentialities of the system. No longer are we traveling down a highway, we are sitting at home paying to watch TV. Somehow a *video jukebox* does not seem to be a huge stimulus for the economy as a whole, and we would not expect so many jobs to be generated by a *jukebox* as by a *superhighway.*

Each of these metaphors has its own system of implications, what Lakoff and Johnson called entailments. By suggesting alternate metaphors, the systems of entailments can be compared, and more implications of the situation can be considered.

STEP 4: WHO USES THESE METAPHORS?

Often, metaphor is used as a persuasive device. Someone has an interest in these metaphors, someone wants to imply certain conclusions and ignore other conclusions. It is worth some effort for the metaphorical critic to notice the sources of the metaphors she or he is studying. For example, the *Information Superhighway* metaphor appeared often in the rhetoric of backers of the proposed electronic network, and was mocked in the rhetoric of its opponents.

In public controversies, sometimes different groups will latch onto their own deep metaphors, and the battle of economic or political interests becomes a battle of metaphors. One example of this is discussed in Lakoff's (1996) *Moral Politics.* Lakoff found different underlying models of the family at work as deep metaphors in political discourse.

Lakoff said the deep, or conceptual, metaphor is *the nation is a family.* "Conservative" discourse takes the "strict father" model of the family, and assumes stern discipline is necessary to educate and train family members. Thus, there should not be welfare programs or other government support, because this will not train *family members* to be independent and self-sufficient. "Liberal" discourse takes the "nurturant parent" model of the family. In this model, *family members* grow through love, empathy, and caring. Thus, there should be welfare programs and government support because this will ultimately help *family members,* or citizens.

By *excavating* the deep metaphor *the nation is a family,* Lakoff showed a systematicity to political discourse which was previously not made explicit. Of course, the nation is not a family, and if both sides recognize this, they may be able to communicate more effectively about their differences.

CONCLUSION

Once you have taken these four steps, you will have arrived at a clearer understanding of the subject you are studying. You will understand the language used to communicate about the subject, and you will gain insight into the conceptual worlds of the people involved. You will be able to criticize particular arguments and assumptions because you can see their underlying metaphorical structure. You will also be able to locate the discussion in a larger conceptual framework by supplying alternative metaphors. You will be able to offer different approaches to the issues by using your alternate metaphors. Not a bad payoff from simply looking for those funny little turns of phrase we call *metaphors.*

section two

Media and Metaphors

eight

Deep Metaphors for Television

The medium of television invites metaphors. Television is multifaceted, energetic, fascinating, and unlike anything else we experience. As with any new technology, metaphors need to be developed that can guide thought and discourse. Even scholarly research depends on deep, often unstated metaphors to structure investigation and debate.

These deep metaphors for television in academic discourse have been excavated by Meyrowitz (1993). Meyrowitz found that researchers have used three deep, or basic (MacCormac, 1985) metaphors: *the medium is a conduit, the medium is a language, and the medium is an environment.*

In this chapter, I discuss these metaphors, and attempt to show how they may be combined into the more inclusive metaphor of *the medium is redescribing the world.* Looking more closely at television's redescription, I claim that it embodies the metaphor of *life is a drama.* I predict that the drama metaphor has a promising future, in the form *life is a television show.* We are still in the first century of the television medium, and I believe that the full impact of this metaphor is only beginning to be felt.

TELEVISION AS A CONDUIT

Metaphors for television have political consequences. Debates over "media effects" have raged through much of the 20th century. Media industries have had to defend themselves against charges of political propagandizing, corrupting the youth, increasing violence, promoting immorality, and so on. In these debates, media industries increasingly sought refuge in a metaphor: The medium is just a *conduit*, a *pipeline*. The medium just delivers harmless *information*. What people do with that information is up to them—don't blame the messenger. (See discussion in Davis & Baran, 1981).

The *television is a conduit* metaphor implies that communication occurs only through channels, or conduits. At one end of the pipeline, a sender puts a message into the conduit. The medium conduit then encodes the message, shuttles it along to the other end, and then decodes it for the receiver, who takes it out of the pipeline. The famous Shannon-Weaver (1949) linear model of communication embodies this metaphor. The metaphor of communication through a pipeline is often applied, incorrectly, to all communication (see critique in chapter 18).

The conduit metaphor for communication is deeply embedded in our language—it is a description of the world encoded in lexical items. We speak of *getting our ideas across, giving* someone else an idea, *picking up* someone else's thought, and so on (see examples in Reddy, 1979).

And what is carried through the conduit pipelines? In the original formulation of the metaphor, "ideas" were carried. In the 20th-century elaboration of the metaphor, *information* is the "content" of the conduit. Much of the technological drama of the 20th century has been about building bigger conduits, to carry more information, faster and farther.

The conduit metaphor does not apply well to interpersonal communication (see critique in Ong, 1982, and in chapter 18, this volume). But it provides a plausible model for mediated communication, and has been useful in defending media industries from charges of undue influence.

Political Uses of the Conduit Metaphor

Under the conduit metaphor, television is *just a channel for messages*. It just delivers these small pictures with accompanying sounds. How could it be "powerful"? You can change the channel, you can always turn the TV off.

Television just delivers *information*. Don't blame the messenger for what people do (or don't do) with the messages.

This metaphor formed an underpinning for the limited effects models of television effects from the 1950s onward. As critics of the industry pointed to the many incidents of violence that were shown on television, especially in children's television, the conduit metaphor gave structure to the response. *It's just a pipeline for images*. How could insubstantial images hurt anyone? Perhaps a few disturbed children reacted negatively or aggressively to such images, the argument ran, but you cannot blame the medium for that (see Davis & Baran, 1981; DeFleur & Ball-Rokeach, 1989).

I do not retrace the tortured history of this debate here. Suffice it to say that media industries managed to stave off significant government regulation of their policies or content for the second half of the 20th Century, except for some attempts to regulate children's television and the exclusion of cigarette ads. As the debate proceeded, other observers attempted to replace the conduit metaphorical framework with other metaphors. I turn to these other metaphors next.

IS THE MEDIUM A METAPHOR?

Because media attract metaphors so irresistibly, it has occurred to some observers that perhaps media themselves are metaphors. This position is taken by Postman (1985) in *Amusing Ourselves to Death*, where he does a turn on McLuhan with "the medium is the metaphor" (p. 3), suggesting that a medium, like a metaphor, enforces a certain view of the world. It selects some aspects of the world to convey, and hides other aspects.

McLuhan (1964) himself arrived at this position in *Understanding Media*, and maintained it in his last work (McLuhan & McLuhan, 1988), where he held that all "artefacts" are "a kind of word, a metaphor that translates experience from one from to another" (p. 3).

I think that communication technologies do resemble metaphors in certain respects. A *metaphor*, by ancient definition, is a "bridge," performing a "carrying over" from one domain into another. Certainly, communication technologies do this. This "carrying over" function of media qualifies them as *metaphors* in one of the major uses of this term (see discussion in chapter 6).

Furthermore, it is possible to analyze television's messages in the same manner that metaphors are analyzed, as Larson (1982) demonstrated. Larson noted that the production techniques of a television message *interact* with its pictorial and audio content. This interaction of technique and content is similar, he claimed, to what occurs in a metaphor, using the philosophy of Richards (1936). Richards said a metaphor consists of the interaction between a topic and a vehicle that conveys that topic. Larson identified the production techniques with the vehicle, and the imagery with the topic.

However, it is also possible, as Muir (personal communication, 1994) pointed out, to see media as synechdoche. A synechdoche presents a part of something and implies it stands for the whole. Television presents a part of a situation, and implies that it is bringing us the whole story. Going beyond this, I suspect that *any* of the tropes of language could be applied to media with good results. Television can also be thought of as metonymic—referring to things by characteristics associated with them (usually, how they look, or whatever part of them can be photographed). And the wise viewer will regard all he or she sees on television as a simile—*like* the original but not the real thing. So, although I contended in chapter 3 that television favors metaphor and produces discourse at the metaphorical pole, I agree that other linguistic tropes are also operating.

This leads us to the larger view of the medium as a *language*. A medium seems to be speaking to us, in its own language, and we attempt to decipher the language to *get the message*. This, too, is a deep and powerful metaphor.

TELEVISION AS A LANGUAGE

Meyrowitz (1993) discussed the *medium-as-language* metaphor as it plays a role in academic studies of the media. Some scholars examine the *grammar* and *syntax* of a medium—studying how the medium favors certain ways of putting together messages. Cinema and television, for example, have a whole *vocabulary* of shots—medium shot, close-up, extreme close-up, and so on. How these shots are put together (*grammar and syntax*) influences the telling of the story.

For example, if the director wants us to feel empathy with one character—perhaps a young boy—we will see many close-ups of the boy. We will see shots from the boy's point of view—usually "low angle" shots where we will be looking up at adults. The selection of shots will subtly influence our perceptions of the overt content of the story, leading us to empathize with the boy, and understand his world.

Note, however, that these are metaphorical uses of the terms *grammar* and *syntax*. For the *language* of television does not have a fixed vocabulary, with relatively fixed definitions of terms, as a language must. Instead, its visual imagery relies on changing contexts for its meanings. Even though it contains fragments of spoken language, in itself it does not have the fixed vocabulary a true language requires. Therefore, there are no television *words* to combine, hence no dictionaries of meanings, and no rules of *syntax* and *grammar* (see discussion of presentational symbols in Langer, 1951).

So the academic uses of the *medium is a language* metaphor have not necessarily lead in productive directions. But there is more to a language than grammar and syntax. There must also be *speakers* and *listeners*, who live within a *speech community* of some sort. This aspect of the *language* metaphor promises to lead to more interesting observations.

Communities from Language

If the medium is at least a partial *language*, who *speaks* this *language*? In the case of television, it is easy to assume that we are being spoken to by the characters we see on the screen. However, the situation is more complicated than this. In reality, the *speakers* are usually large corporate institutions. These institutions hire writers, lawyers, programming executives, public relations people, videographers, video editors, and others who are all involved in what can be *spoken*.

What is the *speech community* in which this partial language is spoken? This would be that group of people who watch, listen, and talk about what they saw on TV. But is this vast, mass audience really a *community*? Sometimes network executives speak of the "good old days" of the 1950s and 1960s, when there were only the three networks to watch, and everyone had common experiences from television. But even then, the audience was divided, separated from each other, and not really a community.

Television divides its *speech community* rather sharply between those who *speak* and those who *listen*. This division is downplayed in many ways by U.S. television. The audience is constantly told how important its opinions are. The mechanism of the "ratings" plays a large role in this story, supposedly granting to the silent audience the power over whether programs will stay on the air. Requests for telephone calls (usually toll calls) and e-mail make it appear that the *speakers* really want to hear from the *viewers*. When you consider the huge size of the television audience, such *feedback* mechanisms are narrow, indeed.

Still, we find real *speech communities* forming around television content. Fan clubs, such as the famous Trekkie clubs of *Star Trek* fans, spring up to give reality to the potential for community contained in all communication media. Sometimes the fans get rowdy, as when sports fans trash a city after watching a championship game on TV. Often, the fans just gossip, as their favorite soap opera characters have some pseudo-event occur to them, such as the "birth" of a child, or a "wedding."

We can look at *television as a language* as creating a kind of *virtual grapevine*. People take it to be a web of gossip and information coming to them from a larger group. People participate in the *virtual grapevine* by carrying on gossip themselves, with real people, giving reality to sometimes totally fictional characters and situations. This is the basis for community in the real world.

The fan-club phenomenon is a perhaps trivial case of a very powerful potential of communication media—the potential to bring people together into groups, to coordinate their activities, to provide topics of discourse, and a common *language* to interpret their world.

B. Anderson (1983) studied the role of newspapers in Europe in the 18th and 19th centuries in creating new nation-states. He claims the emergence of a national-language press helped create *imagined communities* which became the basis for nation-states. Local, divided societies were able to be bound together into larger collectivities because they shared the same *language* to interpret their world—not only the actual language of speech, but a media-based *language* of understanding.

One can only wonder what social/political groupings will be brought about through the current communication system, with its global reach of satellites, cables, and fiber optics. Toynbee (1972) speculated that this communication system might be a precursor for a new "universal state," beyond the level of the nation-state. Perhaps this is already occurring with the rise of the multinational corporations, who have their own high-speed communications networks.

The medium as language metaphor should lead us to study how media can create community. It leads us to ask who can speak, who must listen. It highlights for us the potential of communication media to form and coordinate large groups of people. To me, it highlights just how limited the community-building of television has been. Perhaps in some future, there will be more *speakers* in the television *speech community*, and some real communities can be formed. This hope has been held out by various interactive cable systems, and now by the internet and/or the *Information Superhighway* (discussed in chapters 22 and 23). As of this writing, it has not happened.

One final question is posed by the *medium-as-language* metaphor. What is the *language* saying?

Here I contend that in the long run, communication media are *telling us about our world*. Media are redescribing a world we already live in, and telling us how others live, or might live in their world. *The redescribed world is the content of the language of television.* This leads us to the metaphor of the *medium is an environment*.

TELEVISION AS ENVIRONMENT

Another metaphoric perspective identified by Meyrowitz (1993) is that television is an *environment*. Meyrowitz said the medium can be considered an environment in two senses. First, TV is an environment for its own messages—favoring certain kinds of content and excluding others. Second, television can also be considered an element within the larger environment, altering social roles, interacting with cultural codes and customs.

The media ecology approach implicitly uses both aspects of this metaphorical structure. All media are seen as selecting certain content, and becoming elements in a cultural environment. Media then interact in ecological fashion with the rest of the culture and with each other.

In this chapter, I *combine* the *medium-as-environment* metaphorical structure with the *medium-as-language* metaphorical structure, by saying that a *medium redescribes the world*. This redescription occurs within the *language* of the medium, is brought to us through the *conduits* of the medium, and becomes a structuring element in the *environment* of the culture.

In chapter 3 I noted that television redescribed the world in terms of moving visual images with sound—a very different *form* of description than provided by print. Here, I point out some of the *contents* of the redescribed world.

It is clear that the redescribed world of television is *violent,* much more violent, in fact, than the real world (see Gerbner, Gross, Signorielli, Morgan, & Jackson-Beeck, 1979). The world as described by television is also more active, exciting, and jumpy than the world of our direct perception. It is full of people who are thinner and better looking than most people. It contains many products that promise to make us happy and fulfilled. And almost everyone in television's redescribed world has quick verbal skills.

We may summarize this by saying that *the basic nature of life in the redescribed world of television is drama in all its forms.* Drama relies on *conflict.* It aims to heighten emotions. It presents us with people in sharply defined situations, and produces clear outcomes. It deals with heroes, heroines, villains. This is the world as redescribed by television. We are dealing here with a powerful metaphorical structuring of the world, not necessarily with the world as we experience it.

In *real life,* few people are heroes, heroines, or villains. Few situations are clear-cut conflict situations. Often, situations are resolved in ambiguous ways, with no clear-cut winners or losers. Most of life is everyday routine, quite undramatic. Few of us are exceptionally thin, athletic, beautiful, handsome, well-built, or photogenic.

Yet the dramatic redescription of the world is taking hold on the imaginations of *Generation X* and a lot of other people besides (see discussion in chapter 12). I predict that the ancient metaphor of *life is a drama* will have a healthy future in the environment containing television, because television redescribes life in the world as drama.

Life Is a Television Show

The venerable *life is a drama* metaphor has been held hostage in academic discourse by different thinkers. Burke's followers propound one vocabulary, and Goffman's followers another. But the metaphor will burst the bounds of these terminological prisons as the routinized drama of television becomes one of the culture's main descriptions of the world.

I predict that *life is a television show* is going to be a powerful deep metaphorical structure in the future. We already see it in the discourse of the *television generations* who incessantly use the term "like". Each time "like" is used, it signals another camera angle on the story being told (Plat, 1995, see also chapters 3 and 34, this volume). The television show has become an internalized metaphor for how discourse should be conducted.

We are already trying to be the *stars* in our own *shows*. Sometimes we are willing to be just *supporting cast members*. In the *scenes* of our social life, are we *just acting* or are we being *real?* (And how will we know the difference?) How do we come up with the right *lines?* Who will be the *sponsor* of our show? (Either mom and dad or our employer.) These issues are highlighted by a dramatic redescription of the world (see chapter 12).

We can see the enactment of the *life is a television show* in many everyday actions. For many people, for example, it is important to buy *name brand* merchandise, and display the labels. Some clothing manufacturers even put the labels on the outside of the clothing. This makes us into walking advertisements, and illustrates our participation in the television culture.

We enact the *life is a television show* metaphor whenever we calculate the visual effects our appearance will have on another. What clothes to wear, what makeup, hair styles, and so on? We also enact the metaphor when we try out our lines, which we hope will *play well* in a certain situation. We enact the metaphor when we take media figures for our *role models,* either to look, sound, or act like them.

This metaphor has shortcomings when applied to *real life.* We need to remember that not many TV shows get good *ratings.* We need to be reminded that *real people* may not be as quick or witty as those *role models* on TV. We should not be disappointed that the outcomes in real life are more fuzzy and bittersweet than the clear-cut outcomes of TV drama. And we should not expect to solve our problems by purchasing products.

But I predict that the *life is a television show* metaphor will gain in power, as an unexamined deep metaphorical structure, as television pervades more of our everyday routines. This makes it all the more important to understand the deep metaphors of the *medium as conduit, medium as language,* and the *medium as environment,* as they combine to *redescribe the world as drama.*

SUMMARY

In this chapter I examined three deep metaphors for television that have appeared in the discourse of the 20th century. The industry claims that television is a *conduit*, just a pipeline carrying information. Critics see television as a *language*, and as *an environment* that have greater influence on culture than implied by the *conduit* metaphor.

I proposed combining all these deep metaphors into the larger metaphor that *media redescribe the world*. The nature of life in this redescribed world is, for electronic media, *drama*. Increasingly, the world will be described in dramatic frames, and we will interpret our own lives in dramatic ways. The deep metaphor *television redescribes the world as drama* may turn out to be the ultimate winner in the metaphorical efforts to describe television.

nine

Why Television Is Not a Text

A metaphor has crept into common use in academic discourse about television. The metaphor states that a television program is a "text." A companion metaphor describes watching and interpreting the program as "reading." I argue here that these metaphors are not only inappropriate, they are dangerous. They leave us conceptually unable to grasp the roots of a cultural crisis—the decline of literacy.

"Text" has proved to be a popular metaphor in the lexicon of social scientists, deconstructionists, and postmodernists. Geertz (1983) listed "text," "game," and "drama" as three of the central "analogies" underlying the "symbolic turn" of social theorizing. Postmodernist thought occasionally describes all of experience as a "text" (Rosenau, 1992).

Other useful metaphors have been generated from the "text"-"reader" marriage. *Intertextuality, subtext,* and *urtext* have successfully crossed disciplinary boundaries. In television studies, the metaphor of "text" has produced some useful results. It has led to more informed debates over how television messages generate meanings, and has provided new terms for analysis, as pointed out by J. Lewis (1991). Suggestive cues have been taken from reader response theory to guide theorizing about the ways a "text" can constitute its "readers" (Allen, 1987).

This said, I begin my criticism of the text metaphor as it is used in studies of television.

First, I seek to demonstrate how much of a stretch the metaphor really involves, by comparing the actions of reading a written text and watching a television program. These are quite different activities—we conflate them at great risk to our vocabularies and our theories.

Second, I show how the "text" and "reading" metaphors are often not acknowledged as metaphors in television studies. I indicate how this leads to describing very different kinds of signs as if they were the same.

Third, I claim that the "text" metaphor has become overly complex and that it has gathered under its expanding domain several quite different types of activity, which should be conceptually separate.

Why does this matter? Because describing television viewing as "reading" a "text" makes invisible one of the cultural crises of our times: the decline of literacy. Young people have largely stopped reading real texts, and are watching television instead. As a result, much of the cultural tradition encoded in print is being lost. Cognitive habits associated with literacy are in decline. I see this situation as symptomatic of a decline in literacy. It is a cultural crisis of astonishing but not clearly known dimensions. We will not adequately grasp this situation theoretically, much less prescribe cures for it, if we reassure ourselves through our vocabulary that watching television is really just "reading" a "text."

For these reasons, I suggest that if one applies the "text" and "reading" metaphors to television viewing, one should enclose the terms in quotation marks, as I have done throughout this chapter. Of course, I believe it would be preferable not to use these metaphors at all, for reasons I now elaborate.

DIFFERENCES BETWEEN READING A TEXT AND WATCHING TELEVISION

The "text" metaphor (and its associates) are inappropriate because they mask great differences between two very discrete activities.

We notice, for example, that a printed text is silent. The reader, for the first many years of reading, reconstructs an authorial voice in his or her mind (Ong, 1982). This reconstruction is absent in television watching because the medium is not silent. The television is downright noisy—it shouts at us something like a person would.

Another difference: The printed text stands still. In order to get from one word to the next, the reader must exert effort. Television moves on its own, whether we want to move on in the story or not.

When we have reached a sufficiently automated stage of reading, after years of practice, we can form pictures in our minds of what the text is telling us, and can elaborate our own insights and judgments. This capacity I call *imagination*, or *the mind's eye*, although I have seen very little about it in the communication literature and would prefer a more exact term. This effort of imagination is pre-empted by television, which provides pictures, characters, action, sounds, and music for us.

As we know, it takes years to learn how to read. The stages of this process have been described by Chall (cited in Corteen & Williams, 1986) as follows:

> Stage 0—Pre-reading (birth through kindergarten): Children acquire visual, auditory, perceptual skills.
> Stage 1—Initial reading (Grades 1-2): Children learn letters and how to match them with spoken words.
> Stage 2—Confirmation, fluency, obtaining information with less conscious effort (Grades 2-3): Children practice decoding with familiar books, do not yet read for information.
> Stage 3—Reading for learning new material (Grades 4-8): Children begin to read for knowledge and information. Meaning is extracted with minimal memory of actual words.

By contrast, watching television does not take years of learning (although perhaps it should, to create more critical viewing). Television viewing begins during the preschool years and children quickly recognize characters, songs, jingles, and advertising products. Children's awareness of what is happening on television certainly develops over time, but television presents itself with a clarity even a very young child can follow.

Because television is so available to young children, whereas reading requires an effort, watching television may be a displacement activity that reduces time spent practicing reading. Corteen and Williams (1986) claimed that while children are in

Stage 2 of the reading process, which requires arduous practice, television presents itself as a more "fun" activity. This is where television may interfere with development of reading skills. In their study of three Canadian communities, Corteen and Williams concluded that "the weight of our evidence indicates there is a significant negative relationship between reading achievement and amount of television watched, even after IQ is controlled" (p. 67). They tempered this conclusion by noting "the absence of reading practice is, in our view, more important that television per se" (p. 71). Here we find one of the roots of the decline in literacy I discuss in a later section.

Reading a text requires concentration. It is difficult to do much else while you are reading. Television, however, is often "watched" to the accompaniment of other activities (D. Anderson, 1983). Salomon (1984) proposed the concept of amount of invested mental effort (AIME) to differentiate between reading texts and watching television. In his studies of Israeli schoolchildren, Salomon found that "Television is 'easy' and print is 'tough,'" according to their self-reports. Salomon used the metaphor that TV viewing, because it is so easy, *short circuits* the processes of obtaining literacy.

There is also evidence that reading and television viewing have different properties for adults. Kuby and Czikszentmihalyi (1990) gave hundreds of people beepers, and had them fill out forms describing their activities, moods, and so on. whenever the beepers went off during a 2-week period. This experience sampling method produced data about people's activity levels, and so forth, during both reading and watching television, among many other activities.

Summarizing their results, Kuby and Czikszentmihalyi noted that "reading is significantly more demanding cognitively: it is more active and involves more alertness, more concentration, more challenges, and more skills than TV viewing. Furthermore, these differences were significant regardless of whether persons viewed or read alone or with the family" (p. 135).

In both reading and television viewing, subjects reported feeling relaxed, with low affect. However, reading involved much more skill than television viewing, much higher concentration levels, and perhaps this was why people wished they could be doing something else more often when reading than when watching television.

My point in this section is simply that watching television is a very different activity than reading a printed text. It requires different learning, mental effort, skills, and cognitive habits. If we wish to understand either activity in any depth, we would do better to conceptually separate them, rather than terminologically merge them. However, this is done all too often in television studies, as the next section discusses.

UNACKNOWLEDGED METAPHORS HAVE CONSEQUENCES

Our terminology, of course, subtly influences our discourse. Terminology does not determine discourse, but it tends to open up certain pathways, and close down others. This happens all the more when the terms are metaphors that have not been carefully examined.

The "text" metaphor was imported into television criticism from semiotics, often via film criticism. And much of my criticism of the "text" metaphor applies to film as well. Even though the experiences of watching television at home and watching a film in a theater are different, neither of them is sufficiently like reading a printed text to warrant acceptance of the metaphor.

The "text" metaphor is usually presented not explicitly as a metaphor, but as a technical critical vocabulary producing a heightened awareness of television. Usually it undergirds a dense thicket of eclectic terminology.

I could choose many examples, but I offer just one: a generally well-done and insightful textbook on television criticism by Butler (1994), called *Television*. In the glossary, "Text" is defined as ". . . In television criticism . . . a segment of the televisual flow, such as an individual program, a commercial, a newscast, even an entire evening's viewing" (p. 355).

"Reading" is defined as: "The viewer's active interpretation of a text, whether written (e.g., a book) or visual (e.g., a television program or film)" (p. 350).

There is no mention of metaphor here. These are the terms of the critical vocabulary.

In an earlier section of the book, Butler wrote: "it is helpful to think of a star as a 'text,' as a collection of signifiers that hold meaning for the viewer" (p. 55). Here at least "text" is put into quotation marks. But is a star best conceived of as a collection of "texts"? The section is about Roseanne and her star status, which is described as her "intertextuality" because she has been treated by many "texts."

But when we think of Roseanne, what comes to mind? A visual image of a particular person—the face, the body, styles of movement—and auditory images of the voice, this is the stuff of star image. We do not think of a collection of "texts," we think of a representation of a person. The "text" metaphor has made the visual and auditory aspects of this star phenomenon disappear.

The "text" metaphor merges two fundamentally different types of symbolism, as described by Langer (1951). The "text" is a *discursive symbol*, presented in series, using abstractions. The image is a *presentational symbol*, there all at once, in concrete specificity.

These different forms of symbolism carry with them different ways of knowing. The epistemology of printed text is not the same as the epistemology of visual images, or television programs (Ong, 1977). As Messaris (1993) warned:

> As far as our understanding of the nature of visual communication is concerned, this conflation of language and images seems to me to be the exact opposite of what a productive approach should look like. As I see it, what makes images unique as a mode of communication is precisely the fact that they are *not* merely another form of arbitrary signification. Learning to understand images does not require the lengthy period of initiation characteristic of language learning . . . (p. 290)

Graber (1988) interviewed groups of people about issues in the news to study their methods of *information processing*. She found that information from the television was processed differently from print:

> Closeups of human beings were rich information sources for our subjects, because most people have learned to draw inferences from physical appearance and movements....Our subjects considered the information disclosed by pictures invaluable for forming opinions about people, including political leaders. It was deemed particularly crucial at election time. . . . (p. 168)

As I pointed out elsewhere (Gozzi & Haynes, 1992), the epistemology implied by print relies on logical abstractions, rule-following, and requires that argumentation be articulated in words. By contrast, the epistemology of television relies on strong immediate impressions; emotional associations; and receives its warrants from empathetic feelings, either positive or negative. I name the epistemology of electric media *empathy at a distance*. Television combines the visual, auditory, and kinesthetic cues of face-to-face contact with the abstractions and distance of literate communication. This produces a paradoxical experience of uninvolved involvement. Empathy at a distance can be seen in Graber's (1988) observation that "closeups stirred emotions and produced feelings of positive or negative identification with the people shown on the screen. People often expressed a desire to help suffering fellow humans on television" (1988, p. 168).

My point in this section is that unacknowledged metaphors have consequences. The "text" and "reading" metaphors will lead the discourse of their users away from an understanding of the fundamentally different modes of symbolism and their accompanying epistemologies that operate in reading and watching television.

THE OVEREXPANSION OF THE "TEXT" METAPHOR

In this section, I indicate how the "text" metaphor has expanded in the discourse of television studies to cover phenomena that are very different in nature, not simply confusing types of symbolism but types of experience.

For my textual examples, I use a printed text by Fiske (1987), *Television Culture*. In many ways this is an excellent book, and I would not want to undermine its thoughtful discussions of realism versus discursive approaches to understanding narrative and character. However, I believe its application of the "text" and "reading" metaphors to television leads in unproductive directions.

There is some slippage in the definitions of "text" through the book, and the index lists 11 different subheadings of "text"; including "closed," "open," "ghost," "radical," and "writerly." But I begin with the seemingly straightforward definitions of *primary, secondary, and tertiary* "texts": "At one level there is no problem. The primary television text is that pattern of signifiers on the screen and in the airwaves at any one time" (p. 84).

As I have indicated, I believe there is a problem here. Calling the "pattern of signifiers on the screen" a "text" fails to distinguish between two different forms of symbolism. Or, if we wish to use the language of semiotics, as Fiske himself often preferred, we take a cue from Peirce's (1932) terminology. A written text is composed of *symbols,* defined by Peirce as having only a conventionalized link to their referents. A television "text" can include symbols, but also includes *icons* that are isomorphic in form to their referent. Live television, in addition, is *indexical,* in that it is directly linked to what it signifies. (Peirce himself discussed still photographs as being a mixture of iconic and indexical signs.) A television program, then, is composed of a mixture of signs, whereas a written text is composed only of one kind of sign.

In a further elaboration of his notion of primary "text," which somewhat confuses the definition, Fiske added: "But no text is simply a pattern of signifiers; a text is a bearer of meanings . . . there is considerable space for the negotiation of meaning . . ." (p. 84). At an earlier point Fiske wrote that "a program becomes a text at the moment of reading . . ." (p. 14).

This leads to a definition of the "reader" as "the producer of texts, the maker of meanings and of pleasures" (p. 17).

This kind of word play is reminiscent of deconstruction—the reader is the producer of texts, and the author (or authors) disappear. I do not find this perspective particularly illuminating. The "reader" is at most a co-producer of meanings and is constrained by what the author(s) have created, and would have nothing to produce if an author hadn't already produced something.

So Fiske's primary "text" is sometimes the "pattern of signifiers on the screen," and sometimes a complex interaction between this and a "reader" who produces a "text."

Then there are secondary "texts" produced by publicity industries. These include:

> writing about television in a wide variety of forms—journalistic criticism, gossip about the stars, specialist magazines for fans (particularly of soap opera), "novelizations" of television scripts . . . advertisements, posters, and television promos. These may be secondary texts, but they can be read back into the primary text, the transmitted image. (p. 85)

Fiske continued:

> There is also a third level of text—the readings that people make of television, the talk and gossip they produce: these too are part of this web of intertextual relations that must be taken into account when we wish to study television as a circulator of meanings in the culture. (p. 85)

Note the vastly different activities that are gathered together into the domain of the "text" metaphor. These include the pattern of impulses on a television screen, the acts of watching and interpreting television, talking with people about television, producing and reading "gossip," seeing and reading publicity materials, making up our minds about television. All of these are describable as producing "texts."

I am not disputing that these processes occur, or that they are important to study. I think it is important to study the life of signs in society, the circulation of meanings stirred up by television. I do not think we can effectively study them by melding them all together into some version of the "text" metaphor.

THREE SUGGESTIONS FOR REPLACING THE "TEXT" METAPHOR

In this section I offer three suggestions for replacing the "text" metaphor, of differing levels of complexity.

The first option available to those who use the "text" and "reader" metaphors is to continue to use them, but to take the trouble to enclose them in quotation marks, as I have done throughout this chapter. This will make the metaphors visible, indicate some distance from the metaphors, invite further thought about them. When speaking, a short apologia can alert listeners to the need to receive the metaphors skeptically. This is the least drastic of the options I am suggesting.

A second, slightly more drastic suggestion, involves using a *plain English* or *ordinary language* approach. Thus, a television "text" is, in fact, a program, advertisement, evening's viewing, or whatever. Just call it what it is normally described as. Watching television, that complex activity, can be described as the natives do, as "watching"; or, at other times, as "vegging out"; or other terms that ethnographic research can supply (D. Anderson, 1983). A "reading" is an *interpretation*.

I realize that the ordinary language approach will need to have its terminology sharpened in theoretical discourse. That should be a useful endeavor, particularly if native informants are engaged in the process.

A third approach, and the most drastic, is to substitute another theory and its terminology entirely for the "text" metaphor. Many of Fiske's "texts" seem to be psychological constructs. For this aspect of the process, two theoretical substitutes come to mind. One is the *frame theory*, which has been used intermittently in mass communication research for some time (see Davis & Baran, 1981). Here the act of "reading" television becomes "framing", and "giving a preferred reading" would become "applying frames according to the cues in the messages". In many ways, a *frame* metaphor is appropriate for a pictorial medium like television—the TV image always has a frame.

Space here does not allow for an adequate discussion of the frame theory and its ups and downs in studies of the media. That is not the purpose of this chapter, nor the purpose of raising the issue. I merely wish to point to frame theory as an alternative approach to the issues covered by the "text" metaphor that might provide a clearer vocabulary.

A second theory that might substitute for the "text" metaphor is schema theory, from the cognitive sciences. "Schemas" are cognitive structures used for processing new information and retrieving stored information. They consist of organized knowledge about situations and individuals that has been abstracted from experience (see Graber, 1988).

Schema theory has covered much of the same ground as communication and media theory—seeking to understand how people interpret their world, give meaning to experiences, and join together in communities of shared symbolism (Arbib, 1985). Although schema theory has not, to my knowledge, been closely applied to the act of watching television, a translation from the "text" metaphor to schema theory might look like this: "Reading" television would become "selecting and activating schemas", which could occur at different levels of involvement.

To give a "preferred reading" of a television "text" would translate to "accepting the cues in the program, and activating harmonious schemas." To give an "oppositional reading" would be to "resist the cues in the program, and activate dissonant schemas." (I am here importing metaphors of harmony and dissonance, which accord well with the emphasis on sound of secondary orality.)

One more translation: To "read tertiary texts back into primary texts" would be to "link stored information in schemas with currently activated perceptual schemas."

What do we gain by using schema theory? Each reader will have to decide for him or herself. I think schema theory might allow us to be clearer about the psychological processes involved in television viewing than the "text" metaphor allows. Schema may be individual and/or social, so the social processes of circulating meanings may be apprehendable within the theory as well (Arbib, 1985).

On the negative side, there is a certain loss of elegance and eloquence with schema theory. I also confess that I am a little uneasy about the origins of schema theory in artificial intelligence and physiological psychology—there is a tendency toward reductionism and mechanical models of humanity in these disciplines that I find disturbing. Cognitive scientist and philosopher Arbib (1985) assured us that schema theory need not be reductionistic, there is room for a "person". I certainly hope so.

Clearly, this is a larger issue than I can, or wish to, address in this essay. My purpose is to make a positive suggestion in an otherwise negative discussion; to suggest that schema theory might be an alternative to using an overly complex and confusing "text" metaphor.

THE DECLINE OF LITERACY

Why does all this matter? What difference does it make if we substitute *activating schema* for "reading," or some other term, aren't we really just saying the same thing in different ways? I suggest that the use of the "text" metaphor, with its "reading" sidekick, does make a difference—a dangerous difference. For watching television is not "reading" a "text," in fact, watching television is often preferred to reading real texts. These are competing activities. And real reading, of real texts, seems to be in decline, while watching television seems to be on the increase.

In the late 20th century (and on into the early 21st) we are living in an age of declining literacy. There is an ecological struggle or *war* going on between the media, to use Postman's (1985) imagery. Young children—the future—are reading less and watching television more. Various print-based institutions in our culture have noticed the trends. Newspapers and magazines see their readership getting older and older, not being replenished from the ranks of the young. Teachers at all levels have noticed their students' inability to spell, their unfamiliarity with a wide range of books and authors. A whole literate tradition is being carelessly dropped by the wayside, left behind in the hurry and noise of daily life.

It is a tenet of "medium theory" (Meyrowitz, 1985) that different media favor different cognitive skills and habits. Here it is helpful to look at longer historical periods. In general, medium theorists come down on the side of print as favoring reflective, abstract thought; a conception of an autonomous self; and a scientific, "objective" approach to the world (Ong, 1982). These tendencies were subversive in 5th-century Athens, where they undermined the communal, mythic, and ritualistic oral traditions of the day (Havelock, 1963). In turn, these print-based habits of mind are being undermined by electric media, particularly by widespread television viewing, which displaces practicing reading, in the second half of the 20th century.

Some alarmists have predicted the end of reading, the disappearance of the book altogether. I do not think this will happen—the book is too much of a good value—cheap, portable, and crammed full of information.

What seems more likely is that reading will become increasingly an elite activity, which it was through most of its history anyway. This would signal trouble for representative governments, which depend on an informed electorate. It would also lead to a society where the values of print-based thought would be devalued: we would see less abstract thinking, less science, more what we would today call superstition.

As a college teacher, I have had to deal personally and professionally with the increasing lack of literacy in my students. I must parcel out difficult readings carefully, in small doses, with much guidance. I cannot assume my students will have a large vocabulary. I must assist them in structuring their essays and papers. Gone are the days of "read this article and write me a paper on it."

For most students, college is the last time in their lives when they will read a large account of written material. This makes the culture wars over the "canon" so virulent, as Marc (1995) pointed out. Because overall reading time is shrinking in the lives of most of our students, this makes what they do read more important. We think. We hope.

I do not want to here endorse the dire predictions that television will produce a generation of brain-dead children. I have found my television-generation students quite able to think for themselves, if not always as clearly as I would like. Neither will I endorse the view that television and computers will be an improvement on our current book-based curriculum. Those writers who expect multimedia and hypertext to save our educational system will, according to medium theory, only abet the trend away from the cognitive habits of literacy they profess to admire (see Landow, 1992; Lanham, 1993).

My point here is that, sooner or later, the young must be instructed; and in an age of rapid technological change, their teachers must be instructed as well. Developing a critical vocabulary toward television should be high on the agenda of scholarship, as well as exercises to cultivate an awareness of the multifaceted ways electric media interweave with our perceptions, thoughts, conversations, and actions.

Here is the danger of the "text" metaphor applied to television. It collapses both sides of the *war between media* into one descriptive term. In fact, it tends to steer critical discourse away from recognizing the battlegrounds of the war altogether. It makes the *war* invisible. Watching television is "reading" a "text," we are told.

Why has this "text" metaphor proved so attractive? Why have academicians latched onto it, without giving it the critical scrutiny they lavish on, say, literature?

On a basic level, I think the "text" metaphor is reassuring to academics, and to writers generally. It describes the unfamiliar territory of television in familiar terms. It assures us that our job skills—heavily implicated with print—are not obsolete. Maybe some poor folks on assembly lines will be replaced by robots, but our skills are still relevant. No technological obsolescence for us.

This attitude, however implicit, is something like buying shares in the Titanic, before it sets off on its maiden voyage to hit the iceberg of electric media. The print ship is in trouble. It has taken quite a few hits, sprung some big leaks, and is almost dead in the water. We should no longer pretend that this is not happening, that watching television is just "reading" another "text."

SUMMARY

In this chapter, I advanced four main objections against the metaphors that identify television as a "text" and watching television with "reading." They mostly come down to this: These metaphors do not allow us to make distinctions in important areas that our theories should be examining.

My first objection notes that the activity of watching television is very different from that of reading a real text. When we read a real text, we must spend years in preparation, we must recreate an authorial voice, we must construct scenes and characters in our imaginations, we must concentrate and move through the still, silent text on our own effort.

By contrast, when we watch television, even very young children find it a rewarding activity with little practice required, voices and images are supplied so we do not need to construct them in our imaginations, and we do not need to concentrate on the process, so we may do many other things while watching television.

These and other differences between reading a text and watching television should be the subjects of investigation of our theories. The "text" metaphor will steer our theories away from such investigations by terminologically merging these activities that should be kept separate.

My second objection to the "text" metaphor is that it ignores the differences between very different kinds of sign systems. This is all the more strange because many writers using the "text" metaphor are also practicing some version of semiotics. I would think that this would sensitize them to the different properties of different signs. I used two vocabularies from two important philosophers to illustrate this point. Langer (1951) made a clear distinction between "presentational symbolism" (visuals) and "discursive symbolism" (words) in a book often cited but, I suspect, rarely read.

And Peirce (1932), one of the 19th-century inventors of semiotics, distinguished between *icons* (bearing structural resemblance to their referent), *symbols* (bearing only a conventionalized relation to their referent), and *indexes* (bearing an actual connection to their referent). Using Peirce's terminology, it is easy to see that a written text contains only one kind of sign, whereas a television show contains a moving mixture of all three—a kind of *supersign.*

My third objection to the "text" metaphor is that it has been overused, and is correspondingly vague. A "text" can be a pattern of electrical impulses on a television screen, it can be an indeterminate entity produced by the perceptual activity of an individual, the conceptual judgments made by a person, the activity of discussion with other people, the activity of reading publicity or advertisements, and so on.

In this regard, I suggested that the "text" metaphor once again merged activities that good theory-building should keep separate. I made three general suggestions about how we might replace the "text" metaphor. First, if one must use it, I suggest that it be placed in quotation marks, to make the metaphor visible and to indicate some conceptual distance. Second, it might be replaced with terms from ordinary language, as used by real people doing the activities being studied. Third, some other theoretical vocabulary and conceptual structure might be substituted. I advanced frame theory and schema theory as two candidates worthy of examination.

My fourth objection to the "text" metaphor is that it makes invisible a looming cultural crisis. It identifies watching television with "reading" a "text" at the historical moment when watching television is in fact replacing the reading of real texts, particularly for the young. This means that many young people do not get the practice needed in reading to become fluent, accomplished, easy readers. The associated cognitive habits of literacy are then more difficult to acquire. We face a decline in literacy, and it is a perverse logic that names one of the main causes for this decline—watching television—as "reading" a "text."

For these four reasons, I urge readers to be sensitive to the implications of the "text" metaphor. I hope readers will engage in efforts to discover and use theoretical language that will be more revealing and less misleading, which will not merge together activities and processes that should be conceptually kept separate.

ten

Hot and Cool Media—
Reworking McLuhan

Is radio *hot?* Is television *cool?* Is print *hot?* Do media have temperatures?

Yes, claimed media prophet McLuhan in his famous 1960s tract, *Understanding Media* (1964). I revisit these media metaphors here, with the perspective of more than 30 years. It is safe to say that McLuhan's use of *hot* and *cool* did not catch on. This is an interesting example of a use of metaphor that shines brightly for a moment, but that does not illuminate or convince over the long run.

I think I know why: The metaphors are used in a structurally inappropriate manner. It would have been better for McLuhan to claim that both radio and television were *hot,* and print was *cool.* Radio and television are active, they move around and come at us with a lot of energy. Print, by contrast, is still and silent on the page. If we are going to use a hot-cool spectrum, the active electronic media fit better at the hot end, and quiet print at the cool end.

* * *

I remember reading *Understanding Media* back when it first came out, and having trouble with McLuhan's *hot* and *cool* terminology. He claimed radio was a *hot* medium, whereas television was *cool*. He made his case using the Kennedy-Nixon debates during the 1960 campaign. These televised debates were widely thought to have been won by Kennedy, who came across well on television.

McLuhan thought that Kennedy's personality was better suited than was Nixon's to the medium. Kennedy was suave, urbane, *cool*. He fit the medium. Nixon, on the other hand, was intense, dark, *hot*. He did not come across well on television. However, later polls revealed that the radio audience listening to the debates thought Nixon had won. McLuhan took this to indicate that Nixon's *hot* personality fit radio better than television—radio was more *hot* than television.

From this example, McLuhan developed his definitions of *hot* and *cool* media. A *hot* medium gave high definition to a single sense. It assaulted your sense organs with a complete image, leaving little for the receivers to fill in on their own. A *cool* medium, on the other hand, projected its imagery in lower definition. It left more to the receiver to fill in, demanded more participation.

By this set of definitions, *hot* media were radio, movies, photographs, and print. *Cool* media were television, cartoons, manuscripts, and heiroglyphics.

I remember I experienced metaphorical misalignment when confronting these examples. With the power of television to involve the viewer being so great, the medium seemed hot to me. Both television and radio were *hot* in the 1960s, and getting hotter. Both projected energy, both involved people emotionally, both kept up a frantic pace of activity all the time. *Structurally, the frenetic activity of radio and television seemed hot, not cool.*

McLuhan's explanations of why television was *cool* were also not convincing. Because the TV image was formed by rapidly scanning lines, the picture was incomplete at any given instant. McLuhan claimed that this meant the viewer had to fill in the picture, requiring activity and making television fit his *cool* definition. However, the speed of the scanning lines on the television is greater than human persistence of vision, meaning that we do not see the incomplete picture, we do not fill it in.

And McLuhan's example from the Kennedy-Nixon debates also does not hold water. The most probable reason that radio listeners thought Nixon had won is that the radio audience was mostly Republican. This demographic held true through the 1980s, when Ronald Reagan gave weekly radio talks to the Republican faithful, even when avoiding all other contact with the press and public.

* * *

In the years since the 1960s, I have noticed how television has been described, and how it has described itself. Almost never have I heard the metaphor *cool* applied to television. We do not get a "*cool* new show," it is a "*hot* new show." Stars are *hot*. Critics tell us "who's *hot* and who's *not*." And when television goes to a still image—when it stops being television—we call it a *freeze frame*.

Likewise radio has its *hot* songs, *hot* new groups, *hot* tracks. The only thing *cool* is late-night jazz on an FM station.

I think public discourse has found there is a better structural fit between both radio and television and the *hot* metaphor. These electronic media are *hot* and they are heating up the society, making it more emotional, more aroused.

To take an example showing the heat of television: The widely played 1991 videotape of the Los Angeles police officers beating a Black motorist who had fled them. Now, this was really nothing new. Some police have been beating up on Black motorists for years, and there have been print newspaper stories, complaints, lawsuits, demonstrations, and so on. But none of these protests had the impact of the videotape. The medium conveyed an intense, involving image that can fairly be called *hot*. This image, loosed in society, "heated up" the debate over police brutality. It is clear that the event described in print would have had much less impact— would have been less hot. The verdict in the Rodney King trial unleashed rioting and burning in Los Angeles and other cities—a literal heating up of society by a videotape!

* * *

While McLuhan called television *cool*, he called print *hot*. Here again I experience metaphorical misalignment. Print seems *cool* to me. Structurally, there is not much of a fit between hot, frenetic activity, and the unmoving silence of print. Print also requires the reader to be still, it encourages attitudes of cool detachment.

Metaphorically, it is structurally more appropriate to say that *print media are cool, whereas radio and television are hot*.

Computers fall somewhere in between, but shading toward the hot side, as I discuss in chapter 22.

* * *

Hot and *cool* media—an example of a metaphorical insight that caught something, but that ultimately did not fly. The notion of a medium having a temperature is a provocative one. It does make sense to speak of the activity of a medium and the emotional arousal it produces in terms of metaphors of heat.

McLuhan was on to something, as he often was. Unfortunately, this particular metaphor was vitiated by his insistence on an overly narrow definition which led him to pontificate that radio was *hot*, while television was not. It is more metaphorically consistent to say that *both* radio and television are *hot*, and probably getting *hotter*.

eleven

Will the Media Create a Global Village?

Some years ago, McLuhan coined the phrase *global village*. It has stuck. I have seen network news people refer to the *global village,* communication scholars, futurists, newspaper headlines, all casually drop the phrase, assuming that everyone understands it. But the idea is actually more complicated than it first appears.

On the surface, the idea of a *global village* is appealing. It offers a utopian possibility—that we could know and relate to everyone in the world as if they lived in a small village with us. We could plug into a *global village* grapevine through the mass media, and know all the events and gossip. The "family of humanity" would be closer to recognizing itself.

The mass media, of course, are the stars in this scenario. This is one reason media professionals like the *global village* metaphor so much. Today's media are often accused of being invasive, predatory, violent, and depersonalizing. But these sins will be forgiven in the rosy community of the new *global village.*

Global village is a metaphor for an idealized future state of affairs. It is a bridge from the present into the unknown. Strictly speaking, it is a map without a territory—yet.

The metaphor of a *global village* speaks to a deep need in alienated industrial-urban society. It speaks to a need for connectedness and community. It suggests that we long to return, not to the womb as some psychologies claim, but to a cozy village.

* * *

The phrase *global village* is an oxymetaphor, an unstable combination of metaphor and oxymoron (see chapter 4). *Global village* is a metaphor formed through conceptual blending of two distinct concepts (Turner & Fauconnier, 1995). But it is something else also. A *global village* is an oxymoron—two words that taken separately would contradict each other. "Global" implies a planet-wide network, encompassing thousands of miles and billions of people. "Village" implies small, face-to-face communities. By fusing these opposites into a compelling image, McLuhan's oxymetaphor has a dynamism and memorability beyond that of the ordinary phrase.

I pay attention here to the oxymoronic aspects of this oxymetaphor to point out that the *global village*, however appealing, is probably impossible.

We know that a medium abstracts certain details from experience. So when we think we are seeing "events as they happen" on television, we are actually receiving a simplified abstraction from the complex actual events. It is not "living color," it is an electronic construction. It is not a real person we are seeing, but a series of dots on a glowing screen.

The kind of knowledge we get from television is very different from that of face-to-face interaction. In real life, we can look where we want to. On television, some unseen technical people do our looking for us. In real life, there is a totality, a gestalt, a whole situation with whole people, for us to immerse ourselves in. On television, we get small images out of context. The media cannot bring us "real people" in all their complexity and ambiguity, all media can offer are images and stereotypes.

Stereotyped knowledge of others does not lead to a personal understanding. Such knowledge can be easily manipulated by unseen hands, and complex people and situations get presented as one dimensional. Impersonal stereotypes only produce a sense of strangeness. The global media will only pile up more stereotypes for us to deal with. The close and meaningful contact of a small village will not happen.

* * *

There is an eerie sense, however, in which the *global village* metaphor captures something that is happening right now. Each day, television brings us a group of people, mostly the same—hosts, news reporters, actors and actresses. This group of people is like an *electronic village*, which we look in on daily.

The *electronic village* has its "wise elders"—old news people sitting on discussion panels. Then there are the brash Young Turks—lawyers, politicians, campaigners. During the day, mostly we see the squabbling young people on the talk shows. We keep up with the gossip of the soap opera neighborhoods. The *electronic village* has something for everyone, including cartoon communities for the kids.

The *electronic village* does cover the world. When the inhabitants decide to talk about something anywhere in the world, we all learn about it. And when the inhabitants of the *electronic village* ignore something, forget it. But when a topic gets onto the agenda of the *electronic village*, it gets on the political agenda of the country. Deregulation. Health care reform. Welfare reform. These start as talk show topics and interview questions, and soon migrate to Congressional bills, political campaign issues, laws and programs.

Who sets the agenda for discussion in the *electronic village*? Who are the tribal gods and oracles who decree that today Somalia is important and Bosnia is not? Who decides that date rape is hot, whereas incest is not? The inner workings of the *electronic village* remain inscrutable.

But I wonder what they will be talking about in the *electronic village* next year, or in 20 years? Will they casually be sitting around tables discussing scrapping the Social Security system, as so many baby boomers fear? Will the mediagenic newspeople then start reporting that advisory panels are recommending scrapping the bankrupt Social Security system? Politicians will start advocating it, there will be a "fight" of some sort, and a vote covered live in Congress, and then will we hear the results on the evening news?

And what else will they be talking about in 20 years? Perhaps how research has shown that people with a recessive gene in spot 148 in their DNA are carriers of antisocial tendencies and should be sterilized? Or perhaps to pay off the national debt we should sell Arizona?

The *electronic village* is a strange confluence of entertainment and power, image, and reality. It appears daily on our television screens. It would be nice to know more about it. We should focus on studying this phenomenon, not hoping for media to bring us an impossible *global village* sometime in the distant future.

twelve

Life is a Drama— The TV Generation's Metaphor

It is impossible to escape the drama metaphor when considering television. This chapter takes a close look at how the metaphor functions in the everyday lives of young people in the United States. Other aspects of the drama metaphor are considered elsewhere. In chapter 8, I concluded that the metaphor of life as a drama is the ultimate content of television. In chapter 3, I linked the forms of television symbolism with a bias toward dramatic presentations. In those chapters, and also in chapter 34, I discuss the common use of the term "like" in the discourse of the TV generations: "like" signals a new camera angle in an ongoing dramatic narrative, often accompanied with appropriate changes in tone of voice. Television technology is being internalized as a metaphor for how to communicate, and with it goes the metaphor of life as a drama.

Do we become what we behold? Every year, statistics tell us we watch more and more television. We are still struggling to define what "effects" this has on us. And what of the "TV generations," who have never known life without television? For them, TV is like electronic wallpaper—taken for granted, part of the furnishings. What effects will television have on them?

The contention here is that television magnifies a particular metaphor: the *life-as-drama* metaphor. To the TV generations, life will seem more like a drama than anything else (see discussion in chapters 3 and 8).

In two recent studies of the culture of the TV generation, the *life-as-drama* metaphor looms large. Moffatt (1989) an anthropologist, studied undergraduates at Rutgers University. He found students need to cover the "real self" with masks and performances. In a second study of new words from the 1960s, 1970s, and 1980s, I found a vocabulary of controlled performance emerging to describe current psychology (Gozzi, 1990).

Life as drama is, of course, one of the master metaphors of human culture. We might even call it a megametaphor—so large, so pervasive that it can order entire ways of viewing the world, seeming perfectly natural, even inevitable. We can easily muster bushels of quotations from all eras telling us that life is a stage, we all have our parts to play, the universe is tragic (or comic), and so on.

So what is new about the *life-as-drama* metaphor in the dramatic lives of the TV generations? Certainly no other generation has been so pervasively surrounded by drama from birth. Drama delivery systems have never been so sophisticated.

And perhaps never before have actors and actresses been accorded such widespread cultural acclaim. Many cultures do not trust actors and actresses—seeing them as too changeable, too able to create the illusion of personality. Yet what is a shortcoming in a culture that values stability, is an advantage in a culture that values change and mobility. We admire an actor who can be convincing in more than one role. In fact part of the fun is recalling what else we have seen the actor or actress in. We can then appreciate the performer's skill in playing another part.

Do we aspire to become what we admire? Have TV generations taken actors as models for their own personalities? Have the illusionistic skills of the actor or actress become part of the cultural repertoire of the normal adolescent in the late 20th century? Has the *life-as-drama* metaphor been internalized as reality?

* * *

Posing as an over-age freshman, Moffatt lived for a time in a Rutgers dorm in order to do ethnographic work among the college students of the 1970s. He also used questionnaires, interviews, and other observations to collect information on the students' worldviews. Moffatt's (1989) book, *Coming of Age in New Jersey*, uses drama as the appropriate metaphor to organize his findings.

Moffatt said that the students sharply distinguish between the private world of their true self and the real world of the manipulative social self. In public situations, you could not let your true self show, or risk being "busted" on, by joking peers. Real life involved, they believed, learning to play roles, wear masks, creating a more artificial social self. According to Moffatt:

> A well-socialized current American adult was neither inner-directed nor other-directed; he or she was both. Therefore, you had to come to know, or to construct, your "real" personal identity as you came of age. At the same time, you had to polish the practical skills of masking the same true self in the public world. You had to refine your ability to influence others if you wanted to get ahead in life. (p. 41)

Much of social life in the dorm involved rehearsing ad hoc performances that would teach students how to "operate." Students had to be careful to stage-manage their displays of intellect—being sure to appear neither too stupid nor too smart. The authentic self only was revealed to close friends and lovers.

Although the dramatic component of the Rutgers undergraduates' lives was certainly not unique, particularly in our "individualistic" culture, it seemed more pronounced, more extreme than life in the older inner-directed days. There was more emphasis on manipulation of others, less emphasis on discovering a "true" self. The very sharpness of the distinction between public and private self contributes to the necessity to perform.

* * *

This impression of increasing dramatism in the life of the young is reinforced by looking at the new vocabulary that has developed since the 1970s. Using a dictionary of new words, *12,000 Words* (Merriam-Webster, 1986), I studied the terms applying to psychological states. These results are more fully reported in *New Words and a Changing American Culture* (Gozzi, 1990).

The new vocabulary for psychological states stresses keeping control over performances. You need to "psych up" for performances, but "keep cool" during them. Don't "blow your cool" or you'll "blow your cover."

You need to "get it together" and "clean up your act" so you can "come on" strong and "come off" the way you want to. Don't get "bent out of shape" or become "unglued" if someone tries to "psych you out." You have to be ready to "play games" with the best of them and not "choke."

It is interesting that the term "together" here refers to one person, not more than one. It means, "composed in mind or manner; prepared, organized, balanced." If you can't keep from coming "unglued," you might go "borderline," or become downright "schizy." The term "schizy" is a diminutive version of schizophrenic, which popularly means having multiple personalities.

The problem of having many personalities will become, I believe, one of the central problems of the TV generations. Authenticity will become more and more difficult, as people "psych up" (get ready to perform) and "psych each other out" (make a show of confidence while undermining the confidence of opponents).

This is the era that added "identity crisis" to the language, along with "midlife crisis." However, there will be less identity to have a crisis with, as people will rely more on "identification" with others to produce a sense of their own self.

A new definition of the term "identification" in the ninth edition of the *Webster's Ninth New Collegiate Dictionary* (1983) is "A largely unconscious process whereby an individual models thoughts, feelings, and actions after those attributed to an object that has been incorporated as a mental image."

And where do those mental images come from? Many, if not most, must come from television, the most pervasive source of imagery in the lives of the TV generations.

We will see, in the future, one of the consequences of taking the *life-as-drama* metaphor literally. When the world becomes a TV stage set, and when we become actors on it, our roles will change as the set changes. We will not really know who we are, or who anyone else is. We will only know what lines are required by the current show.

thirteen

Is Childhood Disappearing Out Here in Televisionland?

I recall as a child in the early 1950s watching a big black-and-white television. Announcers would occasionally seem to address me, as one of the "kids out there in *televisionland*." I thought I lived in New York State. But it was also becoming *televisionland*.

Televisionland is an interesting metaphor, because it denotes the territory usually thought of as the real world. It contrasts with *Hollywood* or *filmdom* or *screenland*, which refer back to a (largely fictional) "reality" behind the screen. Everyone knows they have to travel to get to *Hollywood*, but *televisionland* comes to you.

Many years later, as I studied the media, I discovered some strange reversals in *televisionland*. For example, to me, the shows were the most important thing on TV. The commercials just happened to be there, to be endured in the days before the remote control and the "mute" button. But as I later learned, the commercials were the most important thing on television, because they paid the bills. The shows were just bait to round up an audience for the commercials.

And I had assumed that television shows were the product of the TV industry. Actually, I was the product of the television industry—as a member of an audience, I (or rather my attention) was being sold to advertisers.

So, living in *televisionland* was not quite what it seemed. I thought I was using television for my own enjoyment, which I was. But I was also being used by television for someone else's profit. Of course, it did not always work out that way. I remember Buffalo Bob, on the Howdy Doody show, pitching Ovaltine. Boy, it was a great drink that all us "boys and girls" would love. So I pestered my mother to buy Ovaltine. She told me I wouldn't like it. I insisted. Sure enough, when the Ovaltine came, I didn't like it. And so a skeptic was born in *televisionland*.

* * *

Since those early black-and-white years, *televisionland* has gone through many changes. In many ways, *televisionland* has come to look more and more like television itself. When I was young, and television was young, we weren't such slaves to fashion. We could look like kids, and wear whatever clothes we liked. We could have different haircuts. I look at young people today, and they look different—on the surface, anyway. They are much more likely than we were to have styled haircuts, and to wear brand-name clothes and sneakers. They look much more sophisticated and mature than we did as kids—although I am not convinced they are more mature. They still have a lot to learn. However, I see plenty of visual evidence for Postman's (1982) and Meyrowitz's (1985) arguments that childhood is disappearing, as television changes the information environment by presenting children with the same information available to adults.

Has childhood really disappeared in *televisionland*? In one sense, no—there are tons of products, shows, and movies marketed directly to children as a special group. Kids are still prohibited from working in most jobs and are required to go to school.

But in another sense, childhood is disappearing. Youth sports, for example, have become high-pressure career-related activities, with heavy family involvement and high-priced uniforms and equipment. No longer can you casually try out for the team. Schools have become more violent places, kids have to deal with guns and drugs—issues that used to be mainly on television.

I am sure that today's children must have to go through the same biological developments that children always did. (Although even this seems to be speeding up—for reasons that are poorly understood, children are maturing sexually at earlier ages, with the resulting much-lamented rise in teen parenthood.)

Perhaps what is really being lost is the idea of *innocence* in childhood. The information-rich environment of *televisionland* has shattered any notions of innocence that children used to possess, which is not to say that today's children are not naive—in many respects they are. They have not figured out today's complex society, and if they mainly sit and watch television, they never will figure it out. But there is some quality of freshness, openness, and trust that goes with the concept of innocence that seems to be on the wane.

* * *

So *televisionland* is actually a very strange place. We don't adequately understand it. It is like a transparent map overlay, superimposed on our everyday world. But the map overlay pushes you in some directions, and dresses you up in certain ways, and tells you what the rest of your world looks like. One problem with the television-inspired maps of our world is that they are distorted—toward violence and sensationalism.

Some of the most striking research I came across in my studies of the media is called "cultivation research" (see Gerbner, Gross, Signorielli, Morgan, & Jackson-Beeck, 1979). It asks people questions about what they think the real world is like. It also finds out how much television they watch. One consistent finding is that people who watch more television think the real world is more violent than do people who watch less television. This is especially true of younger viewers. Statistically, people who watch more television think they are in more physical danger than people who watch less television. These "heavy viewers" are more fearful, less trusting of their fellow humans, and more likely to think that people are just out to manipulate them. Among adolescents and children, these "cultivation effects" are magnified.

So *televisionland* is a fearful place. Hardly what we would have expected in those early days of Howdy Doody and Buffalo Bob.

* * *

We may be in danger of yet another reversal: heralded by the French media philosopher Baudrillard (1983). He claimed that television brings us a "hyper-reality," which will turn our ordinary lives into special effects. *Televisionland* may first take over our everyday lives and then make them pale in comparison to the dazzling light of the tube itself.

I am afraid this has already happened to many young people, with their color televisions, computer games, stereos, and widescreen movies. The real world has just become too dull by comparison. School has become an experience of exquisite and painful boredom.

How will such young people grow up into an appreciation of others, who may not be as beautiful or witty or quick as those electronic images in hyper-reality? How can they esteem themselves, when they know they have to rehearse and scheme to do what those media characters seem to do so naturally?

Perhaps childhood is disappearing in *televisionland*, to be replaced by eternal stage fright. If so, Howdy Doody and Buffalo Bob have a lot to answer for.

fourteen

Has Metaphor Collapsed?

It all started when I was reading *America* (Baudrillard, 1989). Baudrillard, a French philosopher had been traveling through the United States, waxing poetic on his favorite subjects of media, simulations, and, currently, the automobile and its culture, which he claimed he never fully understood the joys of until he toured America.

Then came an offhand remark which set my mind buzzing: "Astral America. The lyrical nature of pure circulation. As against the melancholy of European analyses. . . . Joy in the collapse of metaphor, which here in Europe we merely grieve over" (p. 27).

The collapse of metaphor! Why hadn't I heard about this before? Was I writing a book on something that had collapsed in France?

I scanned the rest of the book—no further mention of this momentous event. I was familiar with some of Baudrillard's other writings—but found no discussion of the collapse of metaphor in them. I was stuck. How to find out more information about this alleged collapse?

* * *

The usual ways of discovering information were not available to me. What did I think I was going to do, look in *The New York Times* Index and find a story from 1982:

METAPHOR COLLAPSES IN FRANCE
Thousands Panic—Humanities Departments Dissolve

Then there would be the follow-up stories:

Survivors Sought in Rubble of Collapsed Metaphor

and

Language Professors Thrown Out of Work

Perhaps more ominously:

Collapse of Metaphor Spreads to European Community, International Libraries Alarmed

A careful reading of the quote shows that Baudrillard felt that metaphor had collapsed in the United States, also, however Americans were joyful about it. I imagined the headlines:

"It's About Time" says Person-on-the-Street As Metaphor Collapses in Universities on East Coast; Midwest Alerted; Californians Ask, "Didn't Metaphor go out with Bell-Bottoms and Love Beads?"

But no, there were no such headlines buried in the microfilm records of the past decade. If this momentous event had occurred, it did not receive the coverage it deserved. This leads, inexorably, to the question of why—and to the postmodern conviction that nothing is as it seems. Has there been a coverup? One must take such possibilities seriously in this post-Nixon age.

Is it possible to imagine a conspiracy so vast, so powerful, that the collapse of metaphor could be successfully hidden? Kept from public discussion, while the entrenched interests of the status quo—publishers, newspapers, writers, academics—acted as though nothing had happened? All to preserve their privileged positions while in reality the basis for their elitism had disappeared?

Well, that might be taking it a bit far.

* * *

Still, this situation does raise the question of how one finds out about interesting developments of thought. It can be a very chancy affair. For all our high-tech information age equipment, we still must rely heavily on word of mouth, that ancient custom. I called various folks I know who keep up with developments in French thought—none of them had heard of the collapse of metaphor.

I went back to Baudrillard himself—back to the text. The passage quoted above continued: "The exhilaration of obscenity, the obscenity of obviousness, the obviousness of power, the power of simulation" (p. 27).

Here were some familiar themes from the philosopher—particularly his obsession with simulation. Perhaps here is a clue to his declaration of the collapse of metaphor. For a simulation has no original, although it seems to be the representation of something. It can even pretend to be an original in our media-based culture and nobody would know it.

Perhaps, in this age of simulation, the distance required by metaphor is closed. Metaphor is a bridge between different domains, asserting a structural similarity between areas normally thought to be separate. If, through simulation and the all-embracing simultaneity of the electronic environment, everything tends to blend together, domains melt into a gray continuum, then the distance necessary for metaphor is annihilated. Metaphor collapses just like a bridge across a canyon whose two walls suddenly move close together.

* * *

Perhaps this is what Baudrillard was getting at with his inscrutable epigram. Such are the joys of reading this philosopher, who strikes me as the French McLuhan, absorbed with the effects of the media and a master of the witty aphorism.

Has metaphor really collapsed? While pondering this question, I realized that the claim that metaphor has collapsed *is itself a metaphor*. It is a metaphor for the havoc electronic media have played on our language's category systems. How postmodern. In denying something, you must affirm it. In order to declare the end of metaphor, you must use a metaphor.

So I expect that metaphor will not go out of business soon, even though its nature may change as language itself changes in its relation to reality. Metaphor may not collapse, but it may transmute (see chapter 3). And we probably won't read about it in the pages of our newspapers.

fifteen

The Fable of the Electric Maps and the Mutating Territory

This chapter covers some of the same "territory" as chapters 2 and 3, but from within the famous metaphor proposed by Korzybski (1948). Korzybski wrote that "the map is not the territory." Although Korzybski was talking about the maps of language, I extend the metaphor to include media maps. In this extended metaphor, the map may not be the territory, but it can influence the territory, call its boundaries into question, and perhaps even take it over.

Once upon a time there was a territory. And people lived in the territory, quite happily. They had maps, oral and written, which described the different boundaries of the territory. They had time to study their written maps, and a representative government to legislate changes on the maps if necessary.

When a map adequately describes a territory, it is a very useful thing. It helps people know *where* they are, but also *who* they are, where they are going, and where they cannot go. If everybody is working with the same set of maps, they coordinate their behavior effortlessly—social harmony seems the natural state of affairs (see Korzybski, 1948).

But then one day a new kind of mapping technology arrived. It was called "electricity." At first it just provided small, very localized maps—but these electric maps were created very quickly, and gave some people advantages over others. Eventually everyone wanted access to the new electric maps, because the new maps were changing how certain people acted, which meant that the new maps were changing the territory. New things were possible, new regions of behavior and coordination were opening up, social harmony was becoming problematic.

* * *

And the electric maps just grew and grew. Soon they spanned the globe and entered everybody's home. The new electric maps had sounds and pictures, movement and characters. The old print and oral maps seemed pale, dry, unexciting by comparison. Plus the old maps took so much time and effort to study. The new electric maps were right there, right now.

In fact, some people said that the new electric maps were going to displace the old print maps completely. Young people stopped using the print maps, despite the promptings of their elders. All the action moved to electricity, it seemed.

And the electric maps got more and more sophisticated. Giant electric "brains" were developed, which "processed information" in volumes and at speeds incomprehensible to the naked brain. These "electric-brain" maps seemed to promise to make even the oral maps obsolete. People were becoming redundant, unnecessary in the new electric map-augmented territory. Humans were just inferior machines—slower, less reliable, more expensive.

* * *

There was a lot of violence in the electric maps. And people started noticing more violence in the territory as well. Could there be a connection, they wondered? Could a map actually recreate the territory in its own image? (The electric mapmakers discounted this idea. What, they asked, could be less substantial than an electric map? What power could it possibly have to shape material territories? Still, the debate went on.)

The electric maps provided all sorts of "information" about people and society. In fact, soon people started talking about "information overload," "information anxiety," the "information age." Even the print maps started piling up, nobody could keep track of them all.

With so much information out there, it was harder to control, harder to shape. So all sorts of institutions that depended on information control of some sort found themselves losing respect, if not also losing power. (Parents trying to control information for children; schools trying to control information for students; governments trying to control information for citizens, privileged groups trying to control information for the less privileged; image-makers trying to control information for various publics—all of these suffered a loss of status, a lessening of effectiveness. Suddenly it seemed there was less "respect" to go around. See Meyrowitz, 1985, Postman, 1985.)

Even the representative government of the territory found itself on shifting ground because of the new electric maps. The old mapping skills seemed suddenly useless, as the electric stage outshone all others in brilliance. Those who learned how to use the new electric stages were the new winners. (And it was a strange thing, but in order to use the electric stage to best advantage, to reach incredibly huge numbers of people, you learned to whisper, to understate, to keep it short, to give off quick impressions. The old maps were worse than useless, on the electric stage, they were wrong—telling you to shout so you could be heard, to make points boldly and repetitively, to extend chains of logic and reason. These did not map well onto the new electric mapping system.)

* * *

Strange things happen when a society's maps become outmoded. People don't know *where* they are as well as they used to. And they don't know *who* they are as well as in the past. They are less sure what their obligations are to each other and to the great abstractions of society: family, school, community, government, business. The social landscape is changing, the rules are changing, and people discover how much of what they thought was "themselves" was actually bound up with their understanding of society's maps.

And so what started out as an improvement in the maps wound up changing the territory. The old print and oral maps struggled to keep up. But the territory mutated under them, so even the same "words" and "concepts" came to mean different things.

It was as if, on the old oral and print maps, what used to be solid boundary lines became dotted lines, or shaded, indeterminate, disputed boundaries.

It was as if, on the old oral and print maps, big blank white spots appeared, uncharted territories emerging.

It was as if the projection grid had slightly altered, so the old oral and print maps still looked recognizably the same, but were distorted somehow, elongated in some regions and compressed in others.

* * *

And so the oral and print maps had to redraw themselves, resurvey the territory, calculate new measuring units, just to keep abreast of the electric transformations. This re-mapping took on something of the aspect of a fight for survival, also, since the new electric maps were claiming to be better than their older competitors, The electric maps took up ever larger portions of the time, money, and respect of the people, leaving less time for interacting orally with others, or reading.

But in order to redraw society's maps, a new kind of mapping had to be practiced. For the *maps themselves were now in question*, objects of analysis and dispute. The assumptions of the old maps were pulled mercilessly out into daylight and subjected to critical scrutiny. Maps of maps emerged— metamaps. "Interdisciplinary" studies were forged, crossing old boundaries. Discourse had to move to a new level of abstraction—metamapping. *What seemed to be "facts" on a map became "assumptions" on the metamaps.*

Once the old maps and their associated mapping systems became "problematized" objects for criticism, the ripple effects could be felt throughout society.

Some people reacted with fear, dug in their heels, and insisted on clinging to the old maps, and only the old maps, as the best way to deal with the future. Other people leaped joyfully into the breaches, producing all sorts of new maps, on all sorts of questionable grounds, which they claimed would answer the malaise of the times. Others turned the destructive techniques of metamapping on every map they could find, undermining anything they could think of with the new relativistic acids. Some people claimed that nothing existed but an infinity of maps— there was no territory, and never had been.

Through all the epistemological tumult, people wondered if the old maps had ever been "real" at all. Or had they just been "socially constructed" illusions, with no more validity than hundreds of other myths?

On a more pedestrian level, as people started using different maps, social harmony disappeared, like an image in a shattered mirror. Conflict and dispute became the subject matter of social life and discourse. Some people thought that social harmony had never really existed, it was just a fabrication of those with misplaced faith in old maps.

* * *

How to deal with this crisis in mapping? How could the mapmakers and meta-mapmakers even conceptualize their situation, much less structure the blank white areas on their maps? Here is where metaphor becomes crucial.

A metaphor is, etymologically, a bridge, connecting domains usually thought of as separate. Metaphor provides language and thought with the techniques and resources to expand, deform and reform, to map new territories. Metaphor keeps all sorts of maps flexible and adaptable.

And so we can conceptualize the dilemmas posed by calling our maps into question, by using the metaphors of maps, territories, and metamaps. These metaphors condense a complex situation and make it more accessible for discussion and thought. We can talk about conflict in the epistemological realm by tracing out the implications of our map and territory metaphors. Likewise we can use the map-territory-metamap metaphors to "fill in the blanks" on the new, contested maps, as we build out the entailments of these metaphors as bridges into the unknown.

And so metaphor spins beautiful webs, out into the blank unmapped territories, creating new maps and new understandings. Other techniques are used as well—just combining old words or syllables, for example, often produces surprisingly useful results. Making up new words—new symbols on the map—also helps fill in those gaps.

But metaphor provides systematicity. A metaphor has implications, which can lead to new insights, new bridges. Whole schools of map-building and map-reading can arise on the base of a powerful metaphor and its entailments.

This is the beauty, utility, and also the danger of metaphor. For one can get caught up in the system of the metaphor, and forget to check how well it corresponds with the territory it is supposed to be mapping. One can be dazzled by the illumination of the metaphor, and blind to the parts of the territory it leaves in the shadows.

And so our new mapmakers need to practice metaphorical criticism. They need to check the territory against the metaphorical mappings. They need to propose competing metaphors, and watch where the systems of entailments intersect and where they diverge. They must remember the map is not the territory, no matter how convincing or logical or beautiful the map may be.

Through the careful use of metaphor on all levels—mappers and metamappers may be able to develop maps which bear some tolerable and useful relation to the new territory we find ourselves living in. Perhaps our maps may be brought back into some "sane" relationship with the territory—even if not that perfect representation we might have assumed in the past. Perhaps our new, improved maps can help us define ourselves more clearly, can help us coordinate our behavior more harmoniously, can help us decide where we want to go more effectively.

Then maybe, just maybe, we can live happily ever after.

sixteen

The Technological Race as Metaphor

The news media loves a race. A race is exciting, you can measure who's ahead and who's behind, you can make predictions, you can bet on the results. But most of all, a race is simple. There is a clear-cut criterion for winning, there is an unambiguous winner, and when it's over, it's over. So it is perhaps understandable why media tend to create races where none really exist. Reality is usually more complicated than the *race* metaphor will allow.

But we are surrounded by metaphorical races. From growing up in the 1950s, I remember how vital the arms race was portrayed to be, with its companion on the racing form, the space race. I remember the national sense of shame when the Soviets put up the first satellite, the Sputnik, while our elegantly designed Vanguard rocket blew up on the launching pad, in full view of the TV cameras. This revealed to us that we were also in a race to produce engineers and mathematicians.

From a perspective of some 40 years later, it is still not clear what the results of the arms and space races have been. On the one hand, you could say that the United States won the arms race because Communism has (apparently) fallen apart, and because we never had to use the awful missiles and atomic weapons (after World War II, that is,) they did protect us. And we were first on the moon.

On the other hand, you could say that the arms race just locked us into an ever-escalating logic of producing more and more powerful weapons. These weapons will be used some day, some way, by some power. And the enormous expense could have been put into peaceful development projects that would lessen the likelihood of war in the first place. And the moon? So what? It may be that the arms race just produced losers.

And so even this race, which seemed so crystal clear in the 1950s, has its ambiguities. The real world is not a racetrack, countries are not runners, there is no finish line (we hope). More factors need to be taken into account than the *race* metaphor can allow.

* * *

There is another respect in which the *race* metaphor is misleading. Sometimes it is better not to win!

Botein (1993), an NYU professor made this point about technological "races." He criticized the race to be the first to develop an Information Superhighway. We might wind up, Botein argued, with an expensive system soon to be made obsolete: the "first-but-worst" syndrome.

As an example, he noted the development of television. The United States won the race, but still functions with 1940s standards, whereas the rest of the world gets clearer pictures from their 1960s technology. Of course, we are now in another supposed race to develop high definition television.

Botein said that the fiber optic technology on which the Information Superhighway depends will get better in the future, and it would not be wise to lock ourselves in to current stages of the technology just to be "first." On the other hand, it is possible that current technology is good enough, so we still see a headlong rush to develop the Information Superhighway.

Another critic of the race metaphor is McCloskey, an economist. In his book, *If You're So Smart*, McCloskey (1990) noted the widespread use of the race metaphor in economics. The loss of global prestige of 17th-century Holland or 20th-century Britain are often described as caused by losing the economic race of the time. Yet, McCloskey pointed out, these countries still benefited greatly from their economic growth—even if they did come in second, or third, or twelfth. It is not necessary to win—to be Number One—in economics. In fact, being Number One might put greater burdens on a country. In terms of national income and general prosperity, it might be preferable to be farther down in the pack.

* * *

The *race* metaphor can even get in the way of reporting on political campaigns. Patterson's (1980) studies of presidential campaign coverage show that media report on the "horserace" more than on the "issues." The latest poll results, who's ahead and who's behind, what strategies they are using to catch up or maintain their lead—these are the stuff of exciting media coverage, both in print and on television.

By contrast, positions taken about issues, which tend to be complicated, get reported less often, and are given less coverage when they are reported.

The media obsession with winners of races also plays a role in the primaries. In the 1970s, Morris Udall was running for the Democratic nomination. He came in second in several early primaries. Because of his second-place finishes, he was labeled a loser. In terms of the *race* metaphor, this is a logical conclusion. But reality is more complex than a simple race—even in this case. Udall could more accurately have been portrayed as a candidate with broad appeal, in many regions, and a possible unifying force. But the *race* metaphor has no room for such roles.

* * *

All around us are the remains of former races, which time has shown not to be races at all. The race to produce a "fifth-generation computer," for example, which supposedly locked the United States and Japan into competition in the 1980s, has disappeared in the 1990s. Likewise was the race with Japan to be first in producing computer chips. In the 1990s most U.S. chipmakers have signed joint-venture agreements with Japanese chipmakers—kind of like calling off the race, or agreeing to run with your partner's leg tied to yours.

Particularly early on, the *race* metaphor is appealing. It organizes a complex situation and orients us to what seems to be going on. And it does lend excitement to an otherwise dull subject like computer chips or flat-panel display screens.

But the *race* metaphor comes with high costs. It screens out more complex options than simply winning or losing. It obscures how desirable it may be to finish in second, third, or "lower" places. And it may proclaim a winner in the short run, who turns out to be a loser in the longer run.

seventeen

Virtual Reality As Metaphor

There is no quicker way to create an oxymetaphor than to put the word "virtual" in front of any other word. Is it real or is it virtual? We may never know. Although most discussions of this technology focus on future computers and software, this chapter takes another slant on the notion of virtual reality (VR).

VR has caught people's imaginations and has inspired fantasies far out of proportion to what the technology can actually deliver, now or in the foreseeable future.

Virtual reality technology promises to immerse you in an exotic computer-generated world. You put on the helmet-like headset, slip on the data glove, perhaps get on a treadmill, and connect up to a computer. (Ultimately you will wear an entire body suit.) Pick your reality-generating software—the planet Venus, perhaps, or a Wild West scenario with bad guys to shoot. As you move, the environment moves to create the illusion that you are moving around within it. Other people can also enter the environment, you can "interact."

To the virtual reality user, the experience is one of being "in" the new environment. To the outside observer, there is only the strange spectacle of a person wearing a bulky helmet waving a gloved hand around and moving in weird, unpredictable ways.

* * *

I have not yet tried VR technology myself, although I am told that the graphics are rudimentary and the illusion is partial. There is a slight time delay between your movement and the corresponding movement of the environment. The head-mounted display is bulky and heavy. And after a while, some users start to feel queasy and ill.

In fact, despite glossy predictions of VR in movies like *Lawnmower Man* and *Disclosure*, researchers are having difficulty reproducing realistic sights, sounds, and touches. The small TV sets in the eyepieces of the helmets do not have the same power to resolve details as does the human eye, so high-resolution images still look like they are composed of little dots (pixellated).

Realistic sounds are also proving difficult to simulate, despite the invention of a machine called the Convolvotron, which generates sounds that will vary with the movement of the subject. And it has proven surprisingly complex to simulate the touch of a real object by computer. Illusion is never easy.

As an article in *Technology Review* concluded, "it will be many years, if ever, before a computer simulation will be indistinguishable from physical reality" (Sheridan & Zeltzer, 1993, p. 27). Still, the article held out hope for useful applications in training pilots (where VR already has been used for many years), assisting architects and designers, training surgeons, and various forms of entertainment.

* * *

So why has VR technology become so glamorous, so seemingly full of promise? I had occasion to think about this while attending a conference in Miami Beach, Florida. Several panels were discussing VR technology (actually a more accurate name is VE or virtual environment, one panelist said). In VR there is the possibility of the virtual act, the act without consequences (Larson, 1996). We may blur the boundaries between real and illusion even further, and may import acts from VR environments into real environments, posing new ethical questions.

The panel presentations were interesting, but I had the nagging feeling that we were all missing something. And then I had an "aha" experience. The technology we call VR is a miniaturization, a model, of something that *already exists*. We have a massive VR machine already in place. We call it "the press," "radio and television," "the newspaper," "the news."

* * *

I had a perfect example right there. I had flown into Miami
Airport, which had been in the news lately. Some German
tourists had apparently been trailed from there, robbed and
murdered, by enterprising Americans. The Americans would
bump into their rental cars, and then rob them when they got out
to discuss the incident. In a couple of recent cases, this had led
to the murder of the tourists.

The "murdered German tourist" stories were spread all
over the world. And I was planning to fly into Miami Airport—I
wondered if I should put an American flag on my luggage. Added
to this, I received from the organization sponsoring the
convention a notice that had some helpful tips for survival in
Miami. These included not answering your hotel door if someone
knocked, and screaming out loud if you thought someone was a
pickpocket. Throw into the mix the regular diet of stories about
violence in Miami's streets, and I had quite a picture of Miami
built up in my mind. In fact, I was flying into a virtual Miami of
murderous thieves and dangerous hotels.

When I got to the real Miami, of course, there was no
violence, no discernable tension or fear, just a warm city with
people of many colors racing around to indeterminate
destinations. There were no mysterious knocks on my hotel door,
no pickpockets approached. The real Miami was considerably
more peaceful than the Virtual Miami.

* * *

"The news" creates for us a virtual reality every day. We assume
this reality, we talk about it with others, occasionally it might
even affect what we do. For us, it is "reality." But this media-
generated VR is an abstraction, a distortion. It centers on the
sensational, the gory, the exceptional. It leaves us thinking the
world is a more dangerous place than it really is, and that our
fellow human beings are more crazy and irrational than they
really are.

At least with VR technology, we know we have a headset
on and we have chosen to have this experience. With the VR of
the news, there is no headset and we get the experience whether
we choose it or not.

* * *

My realization did not stop there, with the insight that the news media apparatus is a gigantic VR generator. Our senses themselves, the very mechanisms of the body for constructing reality, create for us a sensory VR. We walk around in a VR all the time, and mistake it for "reality."

As pointed out by various teachers, including Korzybski (1948), there are no colors, there is no hot and cold, there are no sounds beyond our bodies in "reality." These phenomena are constructed by our senses. If our eyes could see heat, for example, the world would look quite different than we assume it "really" looks, as one can see in a photograph taken with heat-sensitive film, where many strange zones of color appear on "ordinary" objects.

* * *

So VR technology is itself a metaphor. It models a process that occurs on a sensory level, as we perceive "reality," and that also occurs on the social level as we get the "news" from afar.

What can we call such a metaphor? It is a *miniaturizing metaphor*, one that embodies and models a larger process in a smaller form. By examining and interacting with the *miniaturizing metaphor*, we can draw conclusions about the larger processes. As with any other metaphor, our knowledge is extended, our ability to see is enhanced. And, as most metaphors do, it structures the unknown domain, this new computer-human interface, in terms of the "realities" we already (think we) know.

If VR technology is used to help us appreciate the VR systems of our senses and "the news," then it will enrich our lives and our culture. If it is used as a further escape from our senses and "the news," it will just be another drug.

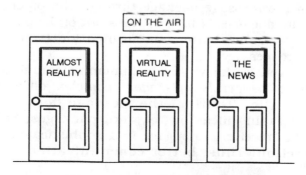

eighteen

The Conduit Metaphor and "Education Reform"

A powerful metaphor underlies many phrases about communication that speakers of English use every day. Reddy (1979) has called this metaphor the *conduit metaphor* because it models communication processes as if they involved shuttling packages (messages) through pipelines (or conduits). The conduit metaphor generates phrases like, "Have I *gotten my ideas across* to you?" and "Try to *put your thoughts into* words."

The conduit metaphor has many ramifications. It implies, for example, that the important part of communication is the sending of the message package through the pipeline. At the other end, all one does is take the idea out of the package to *get the message*. Thus, better communication is equated with sending more messages.

However, we know that in human communication, often the process of *getting the message* is complex, difficult, and far from automatic. "Getting" the message does not involve effortlessly taking ideas out of word packages, but instead requires the "receiver" to engage in a sophisticated process of reconstruction. Thus, better communication may not be enhanced by sending more messages, in fact, more messages may hinder communication.

These issues are more than intellectual exercises about a metaphor and its limitations. They go to the heart of the discourse about "information technology" and the kind of communication and education that are possible with these technologies. The conduit metaphor underlies much of the optimistic predictions made about the role of technology in society generally and in "education reform" in particular. The strengths and shortcomings of this metaphor should be examined, for they will reveal deficiencies in many of the optimistic scenarios extrapolated from conduit thinking.

Much of the discourse of education reform promotes increasing "efficiency" in the classroom by using information technology, which will convey vast amounts of information. The teacher, meanwhile, will become a "guide on the side"; and as the job is de-skilled, fewer expensive teachers will be required.

As a representative example of this kind of education reform discourse, consider the *U.S. News and World Report, 1993 College Guide*, an article entitled "The College of Tomorrow" (Elfin, 1992). It describes the "cutting edge" of a "revolution" in college teaching as "a rapidly developing computer technology called multimedia that combines text, graphics, sound, animation, full-motion film and video into educational programs capable of engaging the mind as well as dazzling the eye and the ear" (p. 110). This technology will "prevail," the article said, because it is like a "one-on-one tutorial." It "allows each student to create his or her own solutions to problems by interacting with almost limitless sources of information" (p. 112).

Note that simple access to information is all that is deemed necessary for the student. What really counts is to make it "dazzling" so the poor student will think he or she is at the movies and will pay attention. This prescription for education reform rests on the conduit metaphor's assumptions about communication, information, and learning. After we have examined the conduit metaphor we will be in a better position to understand how problematic these "reform" prescriptions really are.

In the next section, I outline the conduit metaphor and some of its corollaries, which have provided the scaffolding for much discourse about information technologies in education. I show how the current concept of *information* is closely linked to the conduit metaphor.

Next, I discuss shortcomings of the conduit metaphor, which gives a good description of communication technologies, but a poor description of human interpersonal communication. This leads to questioning the prescriptions for education based on the conduit metaphor.

I then examine a different family of metaphors for communication that have begun to emerge in the literature. I call these *resonance* or *reconstruction* metaphors because they model the processes of communication quite differently from the packages and pipelines of the conduit metaphor.

THE CONDUIT METAPHOR

The conduit metaphor was articulated most thoroughly by Reddy (1979). He examined many phrases about human communication from everyday language and found an underlying "semantic structure," which he called the *conduit metaphor*.

In this systematic structure, ideas are objects: We "have" an idea.

We can "put our ideas into words," which is like putting an idea object into a word container. Thus, a message that "contains" the ideas is created.

We then send the messages, which are word containers (which contain the idea objects) across pipelines, or conduits. We try to "get over," or "get a message across," or "get through" to someone. The words "carry" meaning, they "convey" thoughts.

The messages of word containers strike the receiver with some force. We are "struck" by an idea, a message can have an "impact" or at least "make an impression."

We take the idea-objects out of the word-containers. We "get ideas from" messages, we "see (or hear) a thought in" what is said, we "find ideas in" messages.

We then possess the idea that was sent to us. Can you "get this idea into your head?"

The conduit metaphor has some corollaries, which play a role in the discourse of the information age (see Turner, 1991, for a discussion). One is the age-old metaphor of "grasping" for understanding—we "grasp" an idea when we take it out of the message container.

Another corollary states that if we possess many idea objects, then we have a great storehouse of knowledge.

But perhaps the most far-reaching corollary of the conduit metaphor is that which equates ideas with information. We "put" information "into" messages, technologies "carry" information, and we "get" information "out." This process is unproblematic and relatively automatic in the conduit metaphor. If information is "delivered," the metaphor leads us to assume that it is "received."

The conduit metaphor is a conceptual metaphor in Lakoff and Johnson's (1980) terms. It provides a systematic organization for our thinking about communication. It then generates many assumptions and phrases that go unexamined in everyday language. The conduit metaphor provides a beautifully simple model for understanding human communication.

Furthermore, the conduit metaphor gains plausibility because it is embodied in actual communication technologies that we use every day. The conduit metaphor, shorn of its anthropomorphisms ("ideas," "grasping," etc.), provides a model of communication technologies like the telephone, radio, and television. A reliable communication technology does encode and package "inputs," sends them across conduits, and then decodes and extracts the "outputs" as closely resembling the "inputs" as possible. However, the inputs and outputs are not ideas, but specific bundles of electrical energy. "Encoding" and "decoding" are purely technical problems of matching wave forms. The "sender" is a device that transmits the encoded wave forms across the conduit, and the "receiver" is the device that picks it up at the other end. It is only the human being beyond the technological "sender" and "receiver" who deals in ideas.

Shortcomings of the Conduit Metaphor

I now detail some of the conduit metaphor's shortcomings when applied to human interpersonal communication.

Let's start with the receiver, who "gets" ideas "out" of messages rather effortlessly and automatically, according to the metaphor. But "getting" an idea is not like opening a package and "grasping" the contents. Words do not "contain" ideas. Only human minds "contain" ideas. Words are just marks on a page, or patterns of vibration through the air. When we receive words, we have not received any ideas. We have received some coded signals that give us directions as to how possibly to reconstruct the ideas that motivated the other person to speak or write the signals in the first place. This process of reconstruction is difficult, and requires our knowledge of the other person, our judgments about their intentions, our understanding of the contexts of the situation, and so on. Even after all this effort, the ideas we reconstruct from a message will not be the "same" as the ideas the other person has.

Note the implications of this difference for education reform. Under the conduit metaphor, "getting messages across" to students is pretty much a problem of constructing a pipeline. Once the message packages are delivered, "getting" the message's contents is relatively unproblematic. The students "grasp" the ideas in the message containers, and take them out. They then possess the ideas—and the more ideas they possess, the more they know.

Therefore, thinking based on the conduit metaphor assumes that education reform is just a matter of building bigger and better conduits, "dazzling" broadband displays, to carry more information to students. "Wiring the schools" and replacing teachers with "interactive" computer programs seem to be obvious prescriptions.

But if "getting" a message involves more than simply "grasping" an idea and taking it out of the message package, then this prescription for education reform may go amiss. If, instead, "getting" an idea is a process of reconstruction, difficult and fraught with false starts, then it is important to have a person there to assist learners in the process. If we replace people with technology that mainly delivers information, students may learn less, not more because they will have few cues to reconstruct the ideas that motivated the distant programmers of the technology.

Even if the technology is designed as an "interactive" and "one-on-one" tutorial, in reality, a student pushing buttons on a machine is in a "none-on-one" situation. There is no one to "interact" with, just a set of preprogrammed options, which may or may not have anticipated the confusions of this particular student.

There are other shortcomings to the conduit metaphor. People's ideas are often fragmentary, tentative, incomplete. Much of human communication involves the sorting out of confused and confusing half-starts toward saying something. It is much messier than the neat model of placing idea objects into message containers. And yet this messiness is characteristic of most learning situations—the students' ideas are half-formed or poorly formed. They may not know which questions to ask, or they may ask questions that were not anticipated by the distant technology programmers.

Also, in interpersonal communication, people are *simultaneously* senders and receivers. As Ong (1982) said, we are *in communication*. We are not sending packages across distances to each other, we are in a unified field where many "nonverbal" and "contextual" elements enter into the process of "getting the message."

Human communication, verbal and other, differs from the "medium" model most basically in that it demands anticipated feedback in order to take place at all . . . the sender has to be not only in the sender position but also in the receiver position before he or she can send anything. . . . I have to be somehow inside the mind of the other in advance in order to enter with my message, and he or she must be inside my mind. . . . This is the paradox of human communication. Communication is intersubjective. The media model is not. There is no adequate model in the physical universe for this operation of consciousness. . . . (Ong, 1982, pp. 176-177)

The final shortcoming of the conduit metaphor and its corollaries is this: it conflates "information" with "knowledge." More information is supposed to result in more knowledge. Yet this is not necessarily the case, as pointed out by Roszak (1986).

We may define *information* as separate bundles of "fact." We define *knowledge* as understanding of patterns and relationships.

With these definitions in mind, we can see that too much information may *obscure* the patterns we need to understand for knowledge to occur. *More* information may mean we know *less*. We get "information overload," resulting in "information anxiety." (This principle underlies the modern techniques of disinformation, where we become confused and unable to act because of a surplus of information.)

Thus, the conduit metaphor leads to prescriptions for education reform that may make our present problems worse, rather than better. The prescriptions amount to loading up schools with technologies that deliver "almost limitless sources of information," while de-skilling the job of teacher; and reducing the numbers of adults interacting with children.

But is this really wise? As it is, when a child graduates from high school, he or she will have spent more time watching television than time in school. Postman (1979) calculated that a high school graduate would have spent one-third more time watching television than attending school, and this was not including time spent listening to music and the radio.

Should we make school time mainly more media time? Should we set it up so students interact less with adults than they do already, with "latchkey kids" and single-parent families increasing?

And when we understand that the unexamined assumptions of the conduit metaphor may be false, we can see yet another problem with the technological replacement of teachers. "Getting the message" is not a simple or automatic process. Students need help from another person to learn to do it more effectively. And simply providing students with more information does not guarantee that they will know more—it might mean they wind up more confused and knowing less.

"RESONANCE" METAPHORS FOR COMMUNICATION

Many scholars have noted the shortcomings of the conduit metaphor when applied to human communication. They have proposed other metaphors, although the process is difficult, for, as Ong noted, there are no physical models that capture the complexity and intersubjectivity of human interpersonal communication.

I have given the name *resonance* to this other family of metaphors and models of human communication (following Schwartz, 1973), for they stress the shared property of communication, the "making common" that occurs. Carey (1989) called this a "ritual" view of communication.

> In a ritual definition, communication is linked to terms such as "sharing," "participation," "association," "fellowship," and "the possession of a common faith." This definition exploits the ancient identity and common roots of the terms "commonness," "communion," "community," and "communication." A ritual view of communication is directed not toward the extension of messages in space but toward the maintenance of society in time. . . . (p. 18)

In a resonance model of communication, ideas are activities that are formed within interaction with others. We are constantly modifying and revising our idea activities in communicative resonance with others. We use symbolic forms to communicate, but these forms never fully embody the "messages" that we construct and reconstruct. Symbols are not sufficient to carry the full burden of communication—we also rely on "nonverbals," "attitude," and various contextual cues.

Corollaries of this view stem from the observation that we are in communication, all the time; communication is not something that happens to us, once in a while, when we turn on a machine. Human communication is complex and difficult, involving imaginative reconstructions of persons, intents, images. The process of communication requires another person to resonate with, without this other person we are impoverished and learn less about others and about ourselves. Concepts are formed in this active process of communication, and are refined through use (see discussion in Turner, 1991).

When we view communication and learning from the perspective of resonance metaphors, a different set of concerns is brought forward than by the conduit metaphor. We become more concerned with using communication for maintaining the community over time, for example, rather than sending messages through space. And so the problem of developing social skills in young people is foregrounded. The conduit metaphor has little to say on this subject, and the resulting prescriptions have young people increasingly isolated from adults and other children, and involved in media. This proposed solution will only hinder the development of social skills that comes from face-to-face relationships.

The set of prescriptions coming out of a resonance metaphor of communication would highlight community, not technology. Although learning technologies can be useful in schools, they should not take over the main agenda. The resonance metaphor would prescribe adding more teachers, not fewer, and making classes smaller, not larger. It would stress the importance of students working together on projects, sharing notes and exercises with each other, and frequent contact with a variety of adults.

The resonance metaphor would point out that individuals reconstruct meanings differently from each other, so it would highlight the need for constant back-and-forth between teacher and student, and other students, in the active quest to acquire and refine concepts. It would also promote internships and "work" programs in the community, to provide context for learning and help maintain the community through time.

CONCLUSION

I hope I have indicated to the reader how a widely accepted metaphor for understanding communication—the conduit metaphor—contributes to making certain prescriptions for education reform. When we examine the shortcomings of this metaphor, we see that it hides the complex process of understanding behind a simple model of taking ideas out of messages.

When we switch metaphors for communication, to a more community-oriented resonance metaphor, we see another perspective that highlights the processes of active sharing that must go on for communication and learning to occur. From this perspective, we can see how the conduit-based prescriptions for education reform may lead to worsening education, rather than improving it.

section three

Computers and Metaphors

nineteen

The Chameleon Computer

I can think of no other object as difficult to describe as the computer. It is truly enigmatic, the classic "black box." Because it seems to have so few "instrinsic" qualities, the computer attracts metaphors, and fantasies, and seems to welcome them all. It is very difficult to answer the simple question: What *is* the computer?

It doesn't help that the computer is constantly changing its size and shape. The first computers, around World War II, were *mainframe* giants, taking up entire floors of buildings and requiring large numbers of people watching them around the clock. Thirty years later came the *desktop* computer, which one person could own and run. By the end of the century, the basic circuitry of a computer could fit on a microchip the size of a thumbnail, leading to *laptop* computers that can be carried around in cars and on airplanes.

And computers do not seem to have a limited territory of application. The computer seems to blend in almost anywhere. You can't tell it's there, but it influences the functioning of whatever it has blended with.

Computers, in the form of *chips*, are being put into all sorts of devices: tools, cash registers, CD players, windmills, telephones. The car engine already has computers in it that take over some of the functions drivers used to have, like increasing or decreasing the gas to the engine. And there are plans to give computers more control over the operation of the automobile. Bumpers could contain sensors that would detect other cars or obstacles, and that could relay back to a computer, which could then control speed and direction of the car.

The computer has already merged with the typewriter, giving us the ubiquitous word processor. Included in all the talk about the *Information Superhighway*, are plans to merge the television, the telephone, and the computer into an as-yet-unnamed device.

And there is reason to think that computers will someday be part of human bodies, implanted to perform certain tasks. A school of science fiction called *cyberpunk* has already envisioned the merging of computers with humans (see Barnes, 1996; Sterling, 1988).

So what *is* the computer? Most of us nonengineers can only comprehend this strange device through metaphors, and it has attracted plenty of metaphors. Most prevalent are the metaphors identifying the computer with a *brain*, saying it has *intelligence*, a *memory*, *languages*, and so on. But the computer is not a *brain*, at least not a human brain. We would benefit from having another metaphor.

This is why I suggest the metaphor of a *chameleon* for the computer. The computer has the ability to change its "coloration" to blend into its environment, which we have associated with the small reptiles called "chameleons."

As with any metaphorical mapping from one domain to another, there are significant differences between real chameleons and computers. The *real* chameleon does not become transparent, but rather has the ability to change the visible pigmentation in its skin to match its environment. It also has a long tongue to snap out and catch insects and other prey, and it has a prehensile tail with which it can hold on to branches or other objects. Clearly, in these respects, the computer is nothing like the chameleon.

But as the word *chameleon* has come to be used in our culture, it refers to a person who can blend in with his or her background, who can change opinions or personalities quickly, who can become difficult to see. Clearly, in these functional aspects, the computer is like a chameleon.

EARLY ATTEMPTS TO NAME THE COMPUTER

The *chameleon* computer is so slippery, so abstract, so difficult to grasp, that it was very difficult to find a name for it. Early pioneers came up with different metaphors. The 19th-century English mathematician Charles Babbage called his proto-computer an *analytical engine*—using, it is noted, a mechanical metaphor to describe a machine. Twentieth-century mathematician Alan Turing called his thought-experiment computer a *universal machine.*

In the early 20th century, dictionaries defined a "computer" as a person who computes. This term was metaphorically extended to the new computing machines, but "computer" was up against competition.

I looked at *The Reader's Guide for Periodical Literature* for the years 1945 through 1947. Articles about computers were listed under the heading of "Calculating Machines." In the article titles, *computer* was used five times, but so was the term *robot.* *Analyzer* appeared four times, *brain* appeared three times, *machine* appeared twice.

So in the early years of the computer, several metaphors vied for descriptive honors. Note that some of the terms relied on mechanical metaphors (*analyzer, robot, machine*), whereas some relied on organic metaphors (*computer, brain*). This indicates that two large metaphorical paths were open.

Ten years later, in the *Readers Guide for Periodical Literature, 1955-1957,* the choice had been made. The culture traveled down the road of organic metaphors. The articles were still listed under the general heading of "Calculating Machines." But *computer* was used 40 times, and *brain* appeared 22 times. These far outstripped *machine,* which appeared 9 times, *automaton* (4 times), and *robot* (3 times).

STRENGTHS AND LIMITATIONS OF ORGANIC METAPHORS

Why were the organic metaphors chosen over the inorganic mechanical ones? I suspect it is because the organic metaphors had a large cast of supporting metaphors to describe related aspects of the computer's function.

Although the computer is a machine, it works subtly and invisibly. It manipulates proto-symbols, and seems to produce intelligent answers to questions posed to it in proper mathematical form. So it creates a need for words to describe the symbolic aspects of its functioning. The *machine* metaphors were not subtle or sophisticated enough. The analogy with the human brain, however, proved irresistible.

Thus, we find the computer metaphorically described as having *intelligence*, able to *read* and hold *conversations*, possessing its own *languages*. All these organic metaphors fell into place with the choice of the organic master metaphorical path, describing the machine as a *computer* and a *brain*.

This choice of terms undoubtedly made computers easier to describe. However, I have my doubts that this metaphorical strategy has really enhanced our *understanding* of computers, because it invites us to project all sorts of human qualities onto and into these machines.

Thus, we expect to get computers that we can hold a real conversation with, as Turing predicted in the middle of the century. It has not yet happened, and I believe it will never happen, because computers lack the interior core of consciousness, that mysterious interiority that religions have called a "soul." Their circuitry is not illumined by the *light* of a soul or spirit, as the human mind is. (See Ramacharaka, 1905, for an explanation of the role of spirit in Hindu philosophy.)

This gets us into metaphysical depths that I cannot explore here. But that is precisely one of the interesting things about the computer—it pushes us to the limits of our understanding about human beings. I do not share the materialistic belief that humanity is simply a fortuitous collection of atoms and molecules, animated by some natural version of electricity, a random event in a meaningless universe. But mine is a personal belief, not something I wish to impose on others. My point in this context is this: If one does hold such materialistic beliefs, then one will not be able to tell the difference between a computer and a human being. The metaphors will fit too perfectly, too persuasively.

So far, the evidence seems to show that computers are really quite different from human beings. They need their "instructions" specified exactly, in advance, for example, whereas humans do not. They need electricity to run on, humans run on other fuel. They are composed of metal and ceramics and plastic, materials not found in great quantities in the human body. But our metaphorical language hides these differences, and has lead many people to expect that soon, very soon, the computer's intelligence will encompass so much that we will not be able to distinguish between computer and human.

REPLACING HUMANS WITH COMPUTERS

Meanwhile, we see businesses and engineers seeking more ways to replace humans with computers. This is dangerous because we do not understand either the limitations of computers or the special uniqueness of human beings.

The *chameleon* computer seems to fit in so well, in so many places. It seems to blend in, to enhance the functioning of so many things. We call it *intelligent*, it takes a stretch of imagination these days to realize that in many ways it is very dumb (see Sterling, 1992).

I know I would not want a computer system driving my car. It may be technologically feasible, but I would rather take my chances with the old-fashioned human system. Perhaps some day my attitude will seem quaint and misguided, but I don't think so. Computers have great difficulty assessing context. They are quick at the specific things you tell them exactly how to do. But when various vague situations arise, situations that require intuition and judgment to assess, computers do not do well. Unfortunately, most of life is made up of various vague situations, not clearly spelled out in step-by-step instructions.

Of course, the *chameleon* computer invites people to project their hopes and fears into it, and a couple of generations of computer visionaries have been seduced by the organic metaphors we use to "understand" the computer. The necessary breakthrough is always just over the horizon. "Neural networks," "fuzzy logic," and "bio-computers" today seem to promise that the metaphorical potentials of the computer will be fulfilled.

I do not doubt that the computer will have some surprises in store for us. But replicating a human being is not one of them.

The *chameleon* computer is an apt symbol for a culture that encourages chameleon people. Doubtless, the computer has partly caused and partly been produced by this situation. It is a lesson, however, in the symbiotic relationship between humans and their machines (see also Barnes, 1996). With the computer, there is more than the familiar question of control (Will the humans control the machines or will the machines control the humans?) We find posed the more intimate question of whether the human is a machine, or whether this machine is human. I take a hard line here. The human heart has reasons that the computer will never know.

twenty

Computer Metaphors That Undermine Human Identity

A two fold process, discoverable in our language about computers and about people, is subtly undermining our human identity.

This process involves, first, the *externalization* of human qualities onto machines; and second, the *internalization* of machine qualities into humans. Occurring through our choice of metaphors, the process has consequences for the debates in our culture over the nature of humanity, intelligence, mind, and machinery.

It makes a difference whether we speak of a computer as having a "memory" or "data-storage capacity." By attributing human qualities to machines, especially computers, we lose sense of what is human, have less understanding of how humans differ from machines, and construct an image of powerful machines and frail humans. The metaphorical undermining of human identity is only intensified by the careless use of language; it may be partly preventable by proper use of language and care with our metaphors.

Granted, the metaphorical use of human terms, such as *memory* for computer capacity, is a way to make complex technological functions more understandable. Although this is a desirable goal, serious confusion arises from such semantic practices. As a matter of personal belief, I do not believe that computers "think" or have "memories"; neither do I believe that humans are machines. Yet these common computer metaphors encourage us to make these assumptions.

Linguistically confusing people and machines amounts to a serious category mistake that has consequences for how humans regard themselves. To discover the tendency to externalize human qualities onto machinery, we can examine the changing definitions that lexicographers report.

As source material, I use definitions from the series of *Webster's Collegiate Dictionaries*, volumes 1 (1898) through 9 (1983). In particular, I pay attention to the appearance of new definitions from one edition to the next. In this way, semantic change can be observed historically.

* * *

I focus here on certain commonly used terms in computerese: *memory, machine language, words, intelligent, brain,* and *conversation.* Tracing new definitions of these terms in the dictionaries clearly exhibits the externalizations of human qualities onto machines.

As early as 1963, in the seventh edition Collegiate, a new definition of *memory* included "electronic computing machines." (By 1973, in the eighth edition, certain plastics were held to have memory, as well.)

By 1973, a new definition of *brain* was: "An automatic device (as a computer) that performs one or more of the functions of the human brain for control or computation."

A new definition of *conversation* in 1973 was: "An exchange similar to conversation, especially real-time interaction with a computer, especially through a keyboard."

These conversations could occur because machines were held to have their own *language. Language* itself took on a new definition in the 1963 edition, which referred to computer operations. *Machine language* appeared for the first time in the 1973 Collegiate, along with *machine readable* (directly usable by a computer).

Because the machine could *read language,* it is not surprising to see computer information described as *words* by 1973, as well.

In 1983, a new definition of *intelligent* appeared: "able to perform computer functions (an intelligent terminal) also able to convert digital information to hard copy (an intelligent copier)."

Intelligence is not just for people any more. Also in 1983, *artificial intelligence* appeared: "The capability of a machine to imitate intelligent human behavior." Although this latter term retains some differentiation between machines and humans, the former definitions do not.

* * *

This linguistic externalization of human qualities onto computers will probably only be intensified as robots come into more prominence. But this projection of mind into machines is already serious. For, although language does not completely determine thought, it can influence habits of thinking that shape our worldview in important ways (see Whorf, 1956). Any discussions of computers—or humans, for that matter—using the anthropomorphized vocabulary just cited will be subtly pressured toward certain conclusions.

Do computers think? Do they have minds, or can they someday? Are they conscious? Such questions are being discussed, and the language in which they are discussed can be crucial. If the computer is held to have a *memory,* and the ability to *read words* and translate them into its own *language,* thereby to make *intelligent* choices, the terms themselves will dictate a conclusion that computers are (or can be) conscious, thinking beings, with attendant rights and responsibilities. It will seem natural and unproblematic to increasingly replace humans with such *intelligent* machines.

But if we say that computers have data-storage capacities (instead of memory), that they can input and scan information in their own codes and perform mathematical choice-functions, then the conclusion will be instead biased toward a more mechanical view that computers do not really think, are not really conscious in the human sense, and so on. Then we might think twice before putting such a machine in the position of teaching children or making decisions about policy.

As the philosopher Searle (1982) pointed out, some thinkers conclude that because computers can simulate mental operations, they must have minds, awareness, and consciousness. Yet, he pointed out that computers can simulate almost anything. Nobody expects that a computer simulation of a five-alarm fire will actually burn down the neighborhood, or a simulation of an internal combustion engine will actually power a car. Why, then, the confusion about computer simulations and mind? The terminology being used to discuss the issue contributes immensely to the problem.

Here is a case in which real confusion can result in our thinking from the language that we use. We have a choice in this matter; we do not need to use anthropomorphized language to accurately describe computer operations.

* * *

This issue is not trivial, for it involves our definition of ourselves as human beings, which is somewhat uncertain at present. In fact, a new definition of "human" in 1973 betrays some problems with our human identity: "susceptible to or representative of the sympathies and frailties of man's nature (such inconsistency is very human)." Here humanity is seen as frail and inconsistent, as contrasted with the stronger, more consistent machinery that surrounds it.

Problems of human self definition will only become more acute in the future. For, as there has been a process of externalizing human qualities onto machines, there has also been a process of internalizing machine qualities into humans.

We can trace this internalization from the 19th century, when mechanistic terms started to be applied to biological phenomena (see Barfield, 1985). In the *Collegiate*, first edition (1898) we find as a definition of "machine": "Figuratively, any person controlled by another's will, or a collection of individuals working as an organized force."

The application of "machine" to humans thus had a negative connotation, which, however, is missing by 1963, when a new definition appears: "A living organism or one of its functional systems." This definition is an outgrowth of the philosophy of *mechanism*, which first appeared in the *Collegiate* in 1936 as "the doctrine that natural processes are mechanistically determined and capable of explanation by the laws of physics and chemistry."

A more recent application of mechanical terms to humans is found in the term *program*, which in 1983 took on the following new definitions: "to control by or as if by a program, to code in an organism's program, to provide with a biological program (cells that have been programmed to synthesize hemoglobin)," and "to direct or predetermine (as thinking or behavior) completely as if by computer programming (children programmed into violence)."

In addition, Merriam-Webster's dictionary of new words issued in 1983, *9000 Words*, lists deprogram:

to dissuade, from convictions usually of a religious nature often with the use of force (parents lure their children away from the communes so that he can deprogram them)

These new uses of the word *program* summarize many of the issues in the undermining of human identity. We see mechanistic biology *programming* cells, unnamed forces *programming* children and parents struggling to *deprogram* cult members who have lost their separate identities.

This application of mechanical terms to humans is just as momentous as the application of human terms to machines. It confuses our thinking about crucial questions. Are people machines? If so, they are clearly inferior to the faster, bigger models; and they inevitably will become obsolete. Are biological processes determined by the laws of chemistry and physics? If so, why bother giving people all those troublesome rights and freedoms, which are illusory anyway? How do you campaign for the rights of a population of mechanized automatons programmed in preordained patterns?

In discussing these issues, the language we use can crucially affect the conclusions we draw, or the research we conduct, or the laws we pass, or the moralities we enforce.

* * *

I believe that humans are not machines, computers cannot think. Each term may resemble the other in certain respects, but they should be kept conceptually separate. If not, we may wind up granting greater rights to computers and at the same time taking them away from humans. Ultimately we may not be able to tell the difference between humans and sophisticated machines.

This theme has appeared often in science fiction. The novels of Philip K. Dick (1968), such as *Do Androids Dream of Electric Sheep?* and the later cyberpunk authors (see Sterling, 1988) explore many issues posed by the merging of humans with their mechanical prostheses. Although Dick saw mechanical humanoids as amoral and dangerous creatures, later cyberpunks took more delight in proposing *cyborgs* that would exhibit occasional superhuman powers and also superhuman frailties. (See also discussion of the paradoxes of joining human and machine in Barnes, 1996.)

Some scientists and investors positively welcome the merging of humans and machines, looking for opportunities for profit. As *Wired* magazine editor Kevin Kelly (1994) said:

> Machines are becoming biological and the biological is becoming engineered. That's banking on some ancient metaphors. Images of a machine as organism and an organism as machine are as old as the first machine itself. But now these enduring metaphors are no longer poetry. They are becoming real— profitably real. . . . The apparent veil between the organic and the manufactured has crumpled to reveal that the two really are, and always have been, of one being. (pp. 1-3)

Kelly also described projects in bioengineering, cloning, and environmental manipulation. He ended, modestly, with a chapter on "The Nine Laws of God," prescriptions for designing a planet. Kelly agreed that the world resulting from the merging of machine and organism would be "out of control," but said that is a good thing. May he be released from his metaphorical prison before helping promote some catastrophe that affects us all.

This strain of late 20th-century thought, which accepts the metaphorical merging of computers with humans, and machines with organisms, fulfills some potentials of the dark side of Western Enlightenment thinking. A certain strand of "scientific" Western philosophy has identified the mind with "calculative reason," and proposed mechanical explanations for all biological processes. The problem is that mechanical systems are ultimately closed and uncreative, while living systems are open and creative (see discussion in Barrett, 1979).

The scientists in Kelly's book and the cyberpunks think that computers and feedback systems have opened up the closed mechanical systems *in the same way that living systems are open.* But this materialistic approach has just opened the door to chaotic and ultimately purposeless system behavior, and confused this with the purposiveness of life.

And the error is seen to be even greater if one believes, as I do, that humans have a mysterious interiority called a "soul" or "spirit," which illumines behavior with a moral *light.* No machine has such a spirit, regardless of how sophisticated a computer might run it. It would not be able to generate behavior seeking the *light,* but instead would grope around in unimaginable *darkness* (see Ramacharaka, 1905).

* * *

Pointing out a conceptual and linguistic problem is frequently easier than solving it, even if a first step. Perhaps all we can hope for in this situation is a widespread education into an awareness of the metaphorical nature of the anthropomorphized computer terms and mechanical biological terms.

If enough people are aware of the metaphorical language they use when describing computer *memories*, and so on, their thoughts may be less trapped by the implications of their terminology.

Instead of speaking of computer *memories*, we should say "data-storage capacity." Instead of *machine language*, "machine codes." Instead of *brain*, let's say the computer is a "processor." We don't have a *conversation* with a computer, we "enter" information. The computer doesn't *read* our inputs, it "processes" them. We "read" computer output. We are "intelligent," computers are "data processors."

These are simply suggestions; perhaps more accurate and euphonious terms can be found. Yet a linguistic separation between terms applying to humans and those applying to computers will greatly assist thought about the two, which currently is quite confused.

A change in terminology for computers may be impossible to "program," but if people who feel strongly about this issue change their own uses of the terms, that will be a start. The process of language change are anonymous and unpredictable but must start somewhere.

In this century, when so much of our reality-constructing potency seems taken away from us, we must try to maintain control over our own language. If we use it wisely, with full and articulate awareness of the dangers of metaphorically confusing humans and machines, we can take back into our own control some of the reality-construction process. And then maybe we won't be so ready to put computers to tasks that should be performed by people.

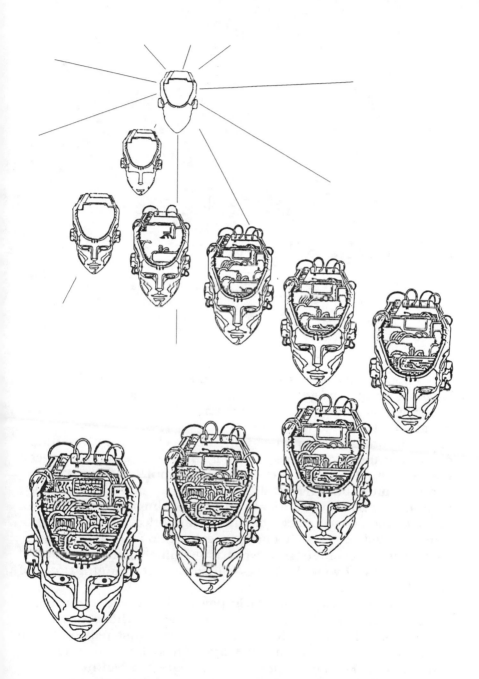

twenty one

The Cyberspace Metaphor: A Skeptic's View

As computer networks spread into more areas of our lives, our language has to struggle to keep up. We are faced with a new and unfamiliar situation, unsure of the potentials or implications. The situation cries out for metaphors.

In order to comprehend any new technology, we routinely describe it in terms already familiar to us. For example, we call the calculating power of the electronic computer *intelligence.* This is a metaphor, one that leads to a whole set of language-guided inferences about what these *smart* machines can do. I think many of the consequences of this metaphorical identification of human intelligence with machine calculation are unfortunate, leading to a devaluation of what is genuinely human. But the metaphor is powerful, it has captured the imaginations of specialists and laypersons alike.

We now have a similarly powerful and widely accepted metaphor to describe what is created when these *intelligent* computers link up over telephone lines into vast networks: the term *cyberspace.* In many ways, this metaphor is also unfortunate. For *cyberspace* is not space, as pointed out by Lippert (1996), but something much more abstract and potent that in many ways eliminates space. And the *cyberspace* metaphor invites a projection of all sorts of fantasies into it, which may not be possible or appropriate (see Gumpert & Drucker, 1996).

* * *

Cyberspace is the "space" behind the computer screen. *Cyberspace* is where telephone conversations occur—somewhere between the phones. *Cyberspace* is the "space" created by a computer network (see Sterling, 1992). The term was coined in the early 1980s by science fiction writer William Gibson in his trilogy of novels about futuristic computer users who are able to leave their bodies and ride through *cyberspace*. How they did this was not quite clear, but the imagery was sharp and powerful, as users floated by towering computer systems of the mega corporations, protected by shimmering walls of "ice," or computer security. In the Gibson novels, *cyberspace* was also populated by disembodied artificial intelligence systems with agendas of their own (see Gibson, 1984, 1986, 1988. My personal opinion is that *Count Zero*, Gibson, 1986, is the most thought-provoking of the novels, but it has received the least critical attention).

    Cyberspace is a metaphor because it identifies the region where electronic communication occurs as being a kind of space. It can be analyzed in several ways. First, Richards' (1936) terminology can be used: *vehicle* and *tenor*. The vehicle, or actual term used for the metaphor, is a combination of the morphemes "Cyber" (a trade name for computers that has become generalizable to all things computer related) and "space" (which covers a lot of territory: outer space, inner space, euclidean space, noncuclidean space, and others). The tenor, or underlying situation referred to in the metaphor, is the strange but real region created by an electric network of telephones and computers.

    Cyberspace could also be called a conceptual blend (Turner & Fauconnier, 1995). The metaphor blends features of computers with those of space to produce a new conceptual entity.

    Cyberspace can also be called an oxymetaphor: an unstable combination of metaphor and oxymoron (see chapter 4). Although *cyberspace* has some spatial aspects, one of its main functions is to annihilate space, and make distant computers instantly "present" (a point made by Lippert, 1996).

    Sterling (1992) highlighted the oxymetaphoric aspects when he referred to *cyberspace* as not exactly "real," but being a genuine "place" where things happen with actual consequences. Careers are made in *cyberspace*, thieves prowl in *cyberspace*, increasingly complete records of our lives are stored in *cyberspace*, and our money exists primarily in *cyberspace*.

The legal system is struggling to apply our notions of property and privacy—developed in the space of the external world—to the new world of *cyberspace*. What should we call certain crimes in cyberspace, for example, *breaking* in to a computer? Is this trespassing, theft, impersonation (see Sterling, 1992)? The *cyberspace* metaphor helps us talk about many real issues posed by computer networks. Yet the metaphors we choose will influence the results our deliberations have.

* * *

When we talk about *cyberspace*, we are dealing with a metaphor, which describes something we do not really understand. Therefore, the temptation is great to construct the meanings of that metaphor in accord with our preconceptions, our fantasies, or desires about how things should be. In the language of psychology, we "project" our desires into cyberspace.

Gibson projected his visions into cyberspace when he created the term for his novels. Gibson's cyberspace was a frontier where latter-day cowboys rode electronic steeds through a video game landscape to break and enter into the vaults of corporate computers.

This *frontier* version of the *cyberspace* metaphor migrated from science fiction to public discourse in the late 1980s. It was popularized by the Electronic Frontier Foundation (EFF), a group of computer professionals and others devoted to a certain vision of how "life in *cyberspace*" should be. The EFF name derives in part from the Gibson interpretation of the cyberspace metaphor. EFF members see *cyberspace* as a Jeffersonian frontier, peopled by many small freeholders, all with equal rights. They want to keep the *cyberspace* frontier open to all, and are lobbying to ensure universal access to the coming great electronic networks. May the force be with them (see Sterling, 1992).

Cyberspace as frontier appears in the title of Rheingold's (1993) book *The Virtual Community: Homesteading on the Electronic Frontier*. Actually, the book does not record any homesteads and records little in the way of lasting communities. In keeping with the *frontier* metaphor, *cyberspace* is held to create *virtual communities*. The *virtual community* is, I believe, an oxymetaphor, which uses an oxymoron as a metaphor. A real community may resemble the interactions in *cyberspace* to some extent, but it requires a physical "presence" and more commitment than simply sending messages back and forth. Online groupings tend to be shifting and ad hoc collections of people, where you don't know who is "there," hardly a *community*.

This *frontier community* vision of *cyberspace* leads to a set of predictions about the effects of computer networks on organizations and society. *Cyberspace* as a wide open frontier leads one to predict that computer networks will decentralize authority. Under this construction of the *cyberspace* metaphor, computer networks will flatten bureaucratic pyramids, empower individual employees, and reduce the role of centralized management (see Sterling, 1992). This interpretation of the *cyberspace* metaphor can be found hidden behind many of the predictions for the future of business and society being made today.

However, we also see the increasing use of computers to monitor workers, count keystrokes on computers, and keep track of time on telephones and computers, all of which produces less worker empowerment and more stress (see Kilborn, 1990). This aspect of *cyberspace* is hidden by the projection of a wild west *frontier* into *cyberspace*.

* * *

I sincerely hope that *cyberspace* can, in fact, produce a neo-Jeffersonian *frontier* of freedom for all. However, there is at least one other possible interpretation of the *cyberspace* metaphor. I call this the *skeptic's view of cyberspace*, and I am afraid it is all too likely to become fulfilled.

It is possible that computer networks will lead to *greater* centralized control, not less. Computer networks have the potential to place great power in the hands of a very few. Strate (1996) noted that computers can have total recall for all transactions, which can become "totalitarian recall" as it undermines privacy and individual rights. The computer network's ability to annihilate space also leads to the potential for *real-time* surveillance of all transactions on the network, what Gandy called the "panoptic sort" (see discussion in Strate, 1996). As computer networks spread to more places and handle more transactions, *cyberspace* could produce a total surveillance society. Under this scenario, *cyberspace* resembles Orwell's *1984* much more than a wild west frontier.

To describe this other potential effect of computer networks, I set aside the *cyberspace* metaphor and pose another metaphor: the *cyberfiber*. Here we combine the prefix "cyber" with the term "fiber," from fiber optics, the material that will be used in most computer networks. I know this term lacks the excitement of *cyberspace*, and I doubt it will widely catch on. But it does point out some aspects of the situation I think *cyberspace* misses.

A "fiber" is a much more enclosed region than a "space." It is not so hard to control what goes on to a fiber from some centralized vantage point. And the fiber can always be cut fairly readily.

In fact, a computer network is not a wide open, uncharted wild west. It is completely the creation of engineers and programmers. Furthermore, every action you take on a computer network leaves a trace. It's getting more and more difficult to "hack" your way around a network—the controls are becoming more pervasive, and automated. What appears to be a wide open *cyberspace* can quickly shrink into the *cyberfiber*.

So . . . is it *cyberspace* where the democratic explorer can roam freely and carve out a living on an electronic *frontier*? Or the *cyberfiber*, where an anonymous, all-seeing program keeps track of your every move, and some day may unplug you?

These two metaphors describe two choices for the future design and implementation of computer networks. They probably do not exhaust the possibilities, but may anchor the ends of a continuum. I myself would prefer to live in *cyberspace*, rather than be tethered by the *cyberfiber*.

But it is sobering to remember what happened in the real American west. Many of those frontier settlements grew up to become company towns. They were dominated by one large enterprise which exercised economic, political, and social control over the descendants of those Jeffersonian frontier people. A similar fate may await us on the electronic fiber frontier.

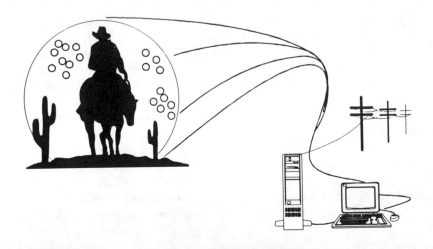

twenty two

Metaphors Converging on the Internet

The internet is a strange and wonderful thing. It inspires fierce loyalty in some of its users,who see it as a forum of free expression and vow to defend it against all who would misuse it. It inspires visions of profit in other users who are trying to harness its distribution powers for advertising purposes. Some observers see it as a vision of evil, where unscrupulous child molesters can lure innocent children away from their homes. Like the *chameleon* computers that make up its backbone, the internet seems to be a *blank slate*, or perhaps a *blank screen*. It encourages people to project their desires and fears into it, and it seems to do its best to conform to those projections. (For a discussion of the history and nature of the internet, see Krol, 1992.)

Just what *is* the internet? On the technical level, it is a network of networks, connecting different computer networks so that these systems, with different programs in different *languages* can communicate with each other. It was designed by the U.S. Defense Department to provide communications even if one of its nodes was knocked out in an attack. To do this, the system breaks up all messages into little pieces, called *packets*, which then are routed through different parts of the network, and reassembled at the destination.

Yet this technical definition does not tell us much about the cultural impact of the internet. U.S. culture is ambivalent about this network of networks. It has received a lot of media hype in the 1990s, but also much criticism. We can see this ambivalence in the changing metaphors used to comprehend the Internet.

Some metaphors imply that the internet is primarily a print medium. Thus, it has *electronic mail* (*e-mail*), you can *browse* with your *browser* as you would in a bookstore, you can set *bookmarks*, *post* messages on a *bulletin board*, and legal arguments have been made that each computer allows one to be a *publisher*. Many sites on the internet have also been described as *cool*, implying a low temperature, calmer experience similar to print (see discussion in chapter 10).

Other metaphors, however, imply that the internet is moving toward an electronic medium, that it is *heating up*. This is largely due to the web, which includes graphics, color, motion, and sound. Metaphors of heat are being applied more to the internet, implying a high temperature, more frenetic experience similar to electronic media. We have *hot* websites, and *hot links*. Even staid old *e-mail* has produced *flames*, and *flame wars*.

The internet is *heating up* because several technologies are *converging* on it, to use yet another metaphor. In fact, we cannot see the internet except through this screen of metaphors. This chapter discusses these metaphors. My theme is the shift from seeing the internet as primarily a print medium, and *cool;* to its present status as increasingly *converging* with television and other electronic media, and becoming *hot.*

E-MAIL

The *killer application* of the internet was unforeseen by its developers. *Electronic mail,* or *E-mail* proved to be the network's main use for scientists, not sending sophisticated computer programs and results back and forth as had been anticipated.

E-mail's popularity continues as the internet is being promoted to the general public in the 1990s. This powerful communication technology expands the scope and range of mediated interpersonal communication beyond anything available before (Gumpert & Cathcart, 1986). I use it myself, and find it taking up more and more of my day.

E-mail is a handy metaphor describing what we do when we send messages across the internet. It implies the internet is a print medium. But the *mail* metaphor hides some aspects of what is new in this process—primarily the ease and speed at which messages are sent and received. This ease and speed can lead to significant differences between the print mail medium and the electronic *mail* medium.

E-mail provides speed and ease approaching oral communication—we just type out a message, push a button or two, and the message is sent. When we get a message, we can simply use a reply function, and type out our response at once. (Interactive *chat* services allow us to send these messages to a *bulletin board* in *real time*, an even faster approximation of oral communication.)

However, we are at a distance from our mail correspondents—we cannot see them, and the nonverbal signals which help us adjust in oral communication are mostly absent. (Although there has been a proliferation of little *smiley* faces and other marks to try to add some of this dimension.)

This new communication situation, called metaphorically *e-mail*, can provide the worst of both oral and print worlds. It provides speed like oral communication, without the accompanying nonverbal messages or interpersonal adjustments that occur in real oral communication. It conveys the abstractions of print, but does not provide opportunity for reflection and analysis, which are the strong points of the print medium. The result is a greater ease of misinterpretation, leading often to bouts of angry, *hot* messages called, metaphorically, *flames*. Some people have taken *flaming* to an art form, and luxuriate in *flame wars*.

These *hot* metaphors remind us that the internet is an electronic medium, quickly changeable and emotional, as opposed to the *cool*, fixed abstractions of print. Even when using print, the electronic word takes on changeability and mutates into something else (see Lanham, 1993).

THE WEB

E-mail is primarily text, as were the first services available in the 1970s and 1980s: File Transfer Protocol, Archie, Gopher, and others. Looking at the internet during these years, it was easy to conclude that computers dealt with numbers and text, and that's what the Internet was about. The Internet was a print medium, and *cool* metaphors were applied, except for an occasional outbreak of *flames*. But, like the *chameleon* computer, the Internet is changing its coloration.

A new *generation* of software was developed, called *hypertext markup language*. Staid old "text" was going *hyper*. The system developed from this *language* was called the world wide *web*. (Did this imply a world spider? Weren't webs made to catch prey? Such implications were not considered in public discourse.)

With the *web*, the internet started carrying graphics, some of the graphics were in color, and some of them started to move. Then came *bitstreams* of jerky movies and TV images, or music and radio. Applications were developed to have telephone connections through the internet, overcoming the limitations of the internet *packet-switching* technology. By the late 1990s, there was talk that television would come over the internet, and cable and telephone companies were gearing up to provide access to the internet as part of their service packages. Computer companies were planning to put TV-receiving capacity into computers. And TV was going *digital.*

Suddenly we started hearing about *hot links* through *hypertext. Hot* websites appeared, with *Java* applications that set their color graphics in motion. The internet was metaphorically *heating up.*

CONVERGENCE

So how was all this confusing activity understood? How did the participants in this process conceptualize it? As is so often the case when we deal with new technology, the situation was understood through another metaphor: *convergence.*

Technologies were said to be *converging*, something like trains heading toward each other on the same track. When the *convergence* came, the television and the computer would crash together and merge into some futuristic appliance that also would include the telephone.

The *convergence* metaphor was sometimes mentioned explicitly, but more often floated to some *deeper* level where it influenced thinking and discourse in an unstated and implicit manner. "Technologies are *converging*," was the premise behind much of the deal-making and venture capital ventures of the 1990s. The metaphor made the process seem natural, physical, inevitable. Human agency seemed absent. Technology was following its own *trajectory*. There was no point in questioning the *convergence*, it seemed inevitable.

Yet the supposed *convergence* process was anything but inevitable. It faced significant technical blockages—not the least of which was the huge amount of *memory* required for a computer to store video images. *Convergence* also required regulatory changes, many of which were delivered in the Telecommunications Act of 1996, which the metaphor assisted in its passage through Congress. *Convergence* would also require economic and business realignments before it could be effected (see Baldwin, McVoy, & Steinfeld, 1996).

So a *convergence* process that seemed natural, inevitable, almost physical in its nature was actually a complex process involving many decisions by many different people and organizations. So complex, in fact, that it may not happen at all, or may only happen piecemeal.

Perhaps a better description of the technological process is that different technologies are acquiring the ability to *translate* data from one to the other. This *translation* metaphor makes the process seem less inevitable, and highlights the role of human decision making, for we may decide what to and what not to translate.

There is another ambiguity to the *convergence* metaphor. It is not clear whether this *convergence* of technologies will *converge* on the internet ultimately, or on a new system called by another metaphor: *The Information Superhighway*. Some press headlines confuse the two, but they should be kept separate. Whereas the first taste of *convergence* has been felt on the internet, a different system may supplant it.

HOT OR COOL?

As a metaphor watcher, I have been interested in the metaphors applied to the internet, particularly those old McLuhan favorites: *hot* and *cool*. I use these metaphors differently from McLuhan, however, as I discuss more fully in chapter 10. I think print is *cool*, while electronic media are *hot*. (McLuhan, for reasons I disagree with, thought print was *hot*, and TV was *cool*.) The history of internet metaphors bears out my point of view, I believe as the early text-based internet attracted cool metaphors. In the 1990s, with the world wide *web* using color, graphics, sound, and animation, *websites* start being described as *hot*.

In the late 1990s, the internet was described in discourse using both metaphors *hot* and *cool*. There are still *cool* sites, but also *hot links*, and *hot websites*, many of which contain *adult* material. I expect that as the internet moves more toward television, music, and telephone services, it will be described more as *hot*. As text services become less important, we will see the metaphor *cool* used less often.

This mixture of surface metaphors for the internet reflects deeper questions about the nature of the network that have been raised in court, as legal issues have posed the question again, of just what the internet is.

PUBLISHER OR *DISTRIBUTOR?*

As the internet spread more widely into society in general, some of its *hot* content raised legal issues. Young people were using *bulletin boards* (computers used for posting and receiving messages) to *download* images of naked women, strange sex acts, and so on. Were the operators of these *bulletin board* systems legally responsible for the content found on their systems?

The legal questions turned on a selection of metaphor—an analogy with a known domain, extended into an unknown domain. Was the new computer system's operator a *publisher*, or simply a *distributor* of the materials (see discussion in Wallace & Mangan, 1996)?

A publisher is generally protected from government censorship by the First Amendment. However, a publisher is expected to know the contents of what he or she publishes, and therefore can be held accountable for them in certain circumstances. A distributor is not presumed to know the contents of what is distributed, and should not be held liable for them.

The legal system has vacillated between these metaphors, and Wallace and Mangan proposed that the internet be understood as "a constellation of printing presses and bookstores" (p. 228). Wallace and Mangan used this pair of metaphors to justify applying First Amendment protections to *cyberspace* (the *space* created by the internet—see chapter 21).

I would like to see the First Amendment applied to the internet. However, if other metaphors prevail in the struggle to define the internet, such protections will not be extended. For example, if it is a *porn shop in your child's bedroom*, as one U.S.

senator called it, we can expect strong government regulation and interference (Wallace & Mangan, 1996).

A WORK IN PROGRESS

In 1999, the internet was still a work in progress. It is a magnificent collective achievement, involving the government, scientists and engineers, the computer industry, and ordinary people. For the first decades of its existence, it has been self-governing. It shows there is hope left for participatory institutions.

But for most of its existence, the internet has been considered a print medium—metaphorically described as *cool.* Now that its electronic media aspects are being emphasized through *convergence,* it is getting *hotter.* Whether society can take the *heat,* and apply appropriate metaphors to control this phenomenon, remains to be seen.

twenty three

The Information Superhighway as Metaphor

Every now and again, a metaphor becomes a media superstar. It drops easily from the lips of anchorpersons, it sparkles in the sound bites of industry leaders. "Experts" appear who elaborate on the metaphor by coining related mini-metaphors of their own.

Such a metaphor is the *Information Superhighway*. It is what I call a master metaphor, which organizes a group of mini-metaphors into a coherent cluster.

Thus, we could talk about different technologies as *on ramps* to the *Information Superhighway*. One television executive, concerned about possible negative effects on broadcasting stations, warned that there well be *drive-by shootings* on the *Information Superhighway*. Other companies worried about becoming *road kill*, as the new electronic networks could put many existing enterprises out of business.

The metaphor really took off in the media after the announced deal to merge Bell Atlantic, a large phone company, and TCI, the biggest cable operator on October 13, 1993. A PHONE-CABLE VEHICLE FOR THE DATA SUPERHIGHWAY, headlined *The New York Times* the next day, and the metaphorical sweepstakes was launched. For the next 4 months, the *Information Superhighway* or some variation of it seemed to be everywhere in the news. (The most common form to appear in AP news stories was *information highway*, according to a database search.)

Other companies rushed to announce mergers, afraid they would be left without a *lane* on the *Superhighway*. A kind of frenzy swept through the telecommunications, broadcasting, and cable industries as people wondered aloud what the future would hold for their particular niche in the business. Pilot projects were announced: *test freeways*. The future seemed to be almost here, bearing down on us at superhighway speed.

Then, on February 24, 1994, a funny thing happened. The heralded merger between Bell Atlantic and TCI fell apart. The deal was off, the future postponed. Other proposed mergers came apart soon afterward. AN INFORMATION DETOUR, *The New York Times* headlined on February 25, 1994. Most parties blamed as the culprit the FCC and its re-regulation of cable rates. But there were other stories too, tales of clashing corporate cultures between the uptight phone companies and the freewheeling cable companies. And then there was the pesky problem that much of the technology, and almost all of the software, had not been invented.

The industry seemed to breathe a collective sigh of relief. The future was not going to arrive quite so quickly. There was time to stop and ponder, time to head to Washington and fight over regulatory issues, which is where much of the superhighway discourse migrated.

Once in Washington, the metaphor aided in the passage of the Telecommunications Reform Act of 1996. When President Bill Clinton signed the bill, he used a pen from the signing of the Interstate Highway Bill in the 1950's.

* * *

Through all this, I had been teaching college courses on new telecommunication technologies. Textbooks became obsolete, as new developments appeared almost daily. My file of newspaper clippings overflowed my desk. There seemed no hope of keeping up with the outpouring of metaphors.

Then, after the "deal of the century" fell through, the pace slackened. The clippings pile slowed drastically in its growth. The media career of the *Information Superhighway* metaphor had peaked.

Some months later, the Harris Poll asked a national sample of adults whether they had heard of the *Information*

Superhighway and what they knew about it. Surprisingly, only 34% of those polled said they had seen, heard, or read about the *Information Superhighway*. Such is the oblivion of yesterday's media stars—how quickly people forget. I am sure if the poll had been taken during the period of media frenzy, the numbers would have been higher.

Still, that 34% who remembered hearing about the *Information Superhighway* did not exactly have a firm grip on what it was all about. Of this group, 59% said they did not understand it at all. (The article was entitled "Superhighway Hits Roadblock in Poll," 1994, showing there's life in the old metaphor yet.)

And so the work of the metaphor had not been as effective as I had supposed. I had thought that the *Superhighway* metaphor had fairly satisfactorily explained some of the implications of the new electronic network. I was, of course, concerned that the metaphor hid some basic assumptions, as all metaphors do. But this poll indicated that the *Superhighway* metaphor had not effectively communicated its subject matter to a large majority of the public.

* * *

Needless to say, the *Information Superhighway* will not actually be a superhighway. It will be a collection of wires, computers, and telephone-switching stations; which will carry video, audio, computer data, and two-way message capacity into the home. Eventually, it may hook together the telephone, television, and computer into one all-purpose device, yet to be designed or even named. People will be able to shop from home along the network, send video telephone calls, order movies "on demand," play video games, call up computer databases, watch 500 channels of TV, and so on. The promises are "blue sky"—anything seems possible, in this early stage of the rhetoric. Not all of these promises will come to fruition.

The idea to construct a "National Information Infrastructure" or a "broadband interactive network" has been around for a while. The Clinton-Gore campaign gave it momentum and the *Superhighway* metaphor became a durable sound bite in the campaign of 1992.

Already the *Superhighway* is reshaping the communications industry. This as-yet-nonexistent network has influenced the changes allowed by the Telecommunications Reform Act of 1996. Telephone companies now have the right to transmit television over phone lines. Cable companies can get into the local phone business. Corporations are merging, as they angle for access to the future broadband network.

A whole host of regulatory and engineering issues are posed by this huge initiative. The topic could be dull, abstruse, full of complicated jargon. But thanks to the *Superhighway* master metaphor and its host of mini-metaphors, public discussion of the network has been made more clear and accessible.

* * *

What will be the regulations governing this huge network? In other words, on the *Superhighway*, what will be the *rules of the road*?

How much access will the average home actually have? In the words of one observer, we don't want to build a *Superhighway* with *eight lanes* coming into the home, but only a *footpath* going the other way.

What will services cost on the network? On the *Superhighway*, what will be the *toll* at the *toll booths*? Can the average driver afford these *tolls*?

Who will control the network? Will the *Superhighway* be a *public road*, or a *private way*, which only the wealthy can afford?

There have been some problems getting the fiber optic cables into the *last mile* into the home. It appears coaxial cable is better suited to be the *on-ramp* onto the *Superhighway*. But the lack of new technology could put some *potholes* into the *on-ramp*.

The cable box is going to have to become "smarter" if it will function as the *steering wheel* to guide us along the *Superhighway*. How will customers get a *roadmap* displaying all their choices?

What chips are going to *pave* the *Electronic Superhighway*?

What computer systems will serve as *traffic controllers*?

How much *cargo-carrying capacity* will the *Superhighway* have?

How will *traffic jams* or *graphic jams* be avoided? What about problems of *gridlock*?

Although most of us will be happy to *cruise* the *Superhighway*, paying the *tolls* as we go, what about computer hackers looking to *hitch a ride* on the *Superhighway*? Who will be the *traffic cops* who will keep order?

Will the *Superhighway* just be filled with glitzy multimedia entertainment featuring instant gratification through sex and violence? Then, say some critics, it will truly be a *highway to nowhere*.

* * *

The *Superhighway* metaphor has served in yet another fashion in the public discussions over the broadband network. Just as the actual interstate highway system produced jobs, increased commerce, and provided new business opportunities for the country in the 1950s, 1960s, and 1970s; so also the *Information Superhighway* has promised to do the same thing for the 1990s and beyond (see Benhamou, 1993).

This use of the *Superhighway* metaphor goes deeper than simply finding mini-metaphors that describe some aspect of the proposed network. Now we are dealing with metaphor as predictor, what Schon (1979) called *generative metaphor*, which can structure an entire discourse along certain lines.

Will the *Information Superhighway* bring about the same economic stimulation that the interstate highway system did? Here we need to think carefully about our metaphors and their entailments. The *Superhighway* generative metaphor identifies information with cargo. It assumes that movement of electronic signals through wires is equivalent to movement of material goods over roads.

I have my doubts about this identification. When you move material goods along a real highway, you need drivers, trucks, gasoline, loading docks, warehouses, distributors as part of the job. When you send a message along the fiber optic cable, you need none of the above. I am skeptical about how many jobs the *Electronic Superhighway* will generate, once it is in place.

Still, the metaphor is attractive, and I find myself reluctant to write off this argument entirely. I am reminded of an example used by urban planners, and mentioned by Al Gore in a number of his speeches. A highway can be built out in one section of town that has nothing in it. The highway can look way too big—four lanes into empty fields. Yet, because of the highway, malls will be built, warehouses put up, and people will start to go to that section of town. Then they build houses and more stores, and so on. After a few years, the highway will need to be widened (see Tenner, 1991).

Something of the sort may happen with the *Information Superhighway*. I hope so—we'll need to provide jobs and ways to make a living in the electronic future. Maybe a new generation of *drive-in* businesses will spring up along the *Electronic*

Superhighway. We'll just have to *keep on truckin'* electronically. And hope our metaphors don't point us down the wrong roads.

twenty four

The Computer Virus as Metaphor

On November 4, 1988, computers around the ARPANET network (the direct ancestor of the Internet) began acting strangely. They filled up with extraneous data, became sluggish, and then clogged completely. The odd behavior spread, in a matter of hours, to about 6,000 computers across the country and overseas. The system, it appeared, had been attacked by an unknown intruder.

Engineers at SRI International in Palo Alto, the firm responsible for ARPANET security, at first thought the intruder was a *virus*, a software program that attaches itself to other programs. But the spread of the clogging behavior made it apparent that the intruder was a *worm*, a self-contained program designed to invade and disable computers. This second explanation was correct. In computer terminology, the rogue program that invaded ARPANET was a *worm*.

The *San Francisco Chronicle* headlined its November 4 story "Vicious 'Worm' Spreads Havoc Through Computers in U.S." (Petit, 1988a). The next day, its headline read: "How 'Worm' Was Defeated" (Petit, 1988b).

This was possibly the only newspaper, however, to use the correct term for the rogue program. In the wire services and at least 11 major dailies, the term of choice was *virus*. Even the *San Francisco Chronicle*, in its November 5 story, noted, "The attacking program, alternately called a worm or virus, had been cleared from most places by midday yesterday" (p. 1).

* * *

Why was this *worm* so quickly and painlessly identified as a *virus*? What we are dealing with here is a choice of metaphors. An analysis of these metaphors using the "interaction" perspective of Richards (1936) suggests a number of compelling reasons for the preference of *virus* over "worm."

Each metaphor, Richards said, results from the interaction between two parts: its "vehicle," which is the word selected, and its "tenor," the underlying situation. A powerful metaphor identifies two separate domains in such a way that we are able to explore one domain by tracing the implications of the other domain.

In the case of the computer intruder of November 1988, there was a choice of two major vehicles: the *worm* or the *virus*. If the *worm* was chosen as the vehicle, how would this illuminate the tenor, or underlying situation? Indeed, we have few systems of implications for "worms": They appear at night after rain, are good for fishing, and appear on putrefying food. Clearly the *worm* is not metaphorical star material.

The *virus*, however, provided metaphorical dividends immediately. With the *virus* as vehicle, many aspects of the tenor could be elucidated using related terms. News stories explained that about 6,000 computers were *infected* as the *virus* proved to be *virulent* and *highly contagious*. NASA *isolated* its computers from the *infected* network and *quarantined* them. Attempts were made to *sterilize* the network. Programmers struggled to develop a *vaccine*, and to *inoculate* against new attacks.

The *virus* proved to be a master metaphor that could organize mini-metaphors into a coherent field. It was easy to communicate using one-word mini-metaphors like *infect* or *inoculate*. This metaphorical system of implications described events in the unfamiliar domain of a computer network in dramatic, familiar, and structurally suggestive terms.

* * *

This system of implications of the *virus* metaphor partly explains, I believe, its instant adoption by most of the country's press, as well as its success against the competing *worm* metaphor. The endurance of the metaphor, however, can be traced to factors beyond the immediate entailments of the *virus* vehicle.

The computer *virus* had its way partly prepared for it by the spread of another virus, heavily covered in the media: the AIDS virus. As the story developed, parallels seemed to develop. Like the AIDS virus, the computer *virus* attacked the "immune systems" of the computers it invaded. Like AIDS, the computer virus spread through exchanges between individuals. Instead of bodily fluids being exchanged through sex, it was software exchanged through e-mail. This parallel was even drawn explicitly by the chairman of the Computer Virus Industry Association in an article in *The New York Times*: "The most stringent [protection] procedures—telling people not to touch other people's computers or to use the public domain software— is a little like telling people not to have sex in order to stop the spread of AIDS" (K. Weiss, cited in Kurtzman, 1988, p. F1).

In both cases, the entire society proved to be at risk apparently from the actions taken by a subculture. AIDS apparently spread through Haitian refugees and the gay male subcultures of the large cities. The computer *virus* originated in that subculture of computerniks known as "hackers." *The New York Times* November 8 article "Loving Those Whiz Kids," said, "On balance, the computer hacker appears to be both a national treasure and a national headache." It described "increasing friction between the eccentric wizards who design and maintain these systems and a society that depends on the machines to run everything from banks to hospitals to military forces." (Markoff, 1988b, p. 1).

The author of the *virus* proved also to be a graduate student, further cementing his status on the boundaries of respectability. On the first day of the "infection," a University of Illinois programmer guessed that its author was "very likely a bored graduate student" (Hilts, 1988, p. 1). This motif appeared in a later *The New York Times* story about the student, Robert Morris Jr., which described him as "unchallenged by many normal programming activities" (Markoff, 1988a, p. 1). Morris also turned out to be the son of a leading government expert in computer security, adding Oedipal overtones to the already convoluted metaphorical situation—for the father had helped design the UNIX system that the son attacked.

And yet another parallel: The spread of both the AIDS virus and the computer *virus* produced legal problems and threats to civil liberties, as draconian measures were proposed to curb future outbreaks (Markoff, 1988c).

These parallels between the AIDS virus and the computer *virus* surely aided the acceptance of the *virus* metaphor over that of the ill-fated *worm.* Other proposed terms, such as computer "letter bomb," as well as "rogue program," "renegade program," and "electronic invader," also lacked resonance.

* * *

The case of the November 1988 computer *virus* offers insight into the process of metaphor selection. The rich systems of entailments of the *virus* vehicle provided terms that quickly and dramatically communicated the structure of the situation through a series of mini-metaphors. However, we might say that the tenor, or underlying situation, also played a key role in the selection of the vehicle.

This master metaphor continued to produce payoffs even after the dust had settled from the original incident. In a letter to *The New York Times* on November 27, a computer science graduate student relied on a metaphor of biology infection to argue cogently for computer security through system diversity:

> In some ways, computer standardization is akin to the selective breeding of agricultural products, such as potatoes. . . . The breeding of a single genetic strain of potato in Ireland in the 19th century led to the potato famine of 1845. Because every potato in Ireland had exactly the same genetic material, every potato was susceptible to the same bacterial infection. . . . Computers are just as susceptible to infection as plants are. . . . In biology, successful species evolution preserves diversity and variation. . . . So, in computer systems, variation must be preserved. . . . The need for variation and diversity exists in computer systems just as it exists in nature. (Zorn, 1988, p. 14)

Here we see yet another ramification of the master metaphor of the computer *virus*. The metaphor's entailments allow us to systematically explore different aspects of a new and unfamiliar situation. Our language in this case does much of our thinking for us. Our conclusions are implicit in our choice of terms; all that remains for us is to follow the analogies down the paths they prescribe. Whether this is desirable in every case is, of course, another matter entirely.

twenty five

Artificial Intelligence—
Metaphor or Oxymoron?

The field of artificial intelligence (AI) is interesting to a student of metaphor, because it was explicitly founded on a metaphor—several of them, in fact.

In the 1950s, a group of scientists decided to try to provide the computer with *intelligence*. Their efforts gained plausibility due to a common metaphorical identification of the computer with a *brain*. Their efforts produced the field of AI. As I thought about the basic, or root metaphors of *AI*, I realized that these root metaphors took the form of a classical syllogism:

> Major Premise: The computer is a brain.
> Minor Premise: Thinking is computing.
> Conclusion:If we provide the computer with sophisticated programs, it will develop a mind similar to human minds.

Note how both premises of the syllogism are metaphors. Both have received widespread acceptance in popular and technical discourse. This underlying syllogism of metaphors generated a very persuasive discourse, which defined the field of *AI*. Once you assumed that the computer was a *brain*, and what it did was *thinking*, then it made perfect sense to expect your computer programs to generate a *mind* for the computer.

This persuasive syllogism can be seen at work in the predictions of MIT's Marvin Minsky, in *Life Magazine* in 1970:

> In from three to eight years we will have a machine with the general intelligence of an average human being. I mean a machine that will be able to read Shakespeare, grease a car, play office politics, tell a joke, have a fight. At that point the machine will begin to educate itself with fantastic speed. In a few months it will be at genius level and a few months after that its powers will be incalculable. (Darrach, 1970, p. 58d)

In the more scholarly confines of *Scientific American*, Minsky also made some predictions:

> Once we have devised programs with a genuine capacity for self-improvement, a rapid evolutionary process will begin. As the machine improves both itself and its model of itself, we shall begin to see all the phenomena associated with the terms "consciousness," "intuition," and "intelligence" itself. It is hard to say how close we are to this threshold, but once it is crossed the world will not be the same. (Minsky, 1966, p. 260)

Such assumptions have become the staple of science fiction movies and television shows, with cute little robots making clever quips to their human buddies. It is easy to write in a character and call it a robot. It has proved considerably harder, however, to actually build one.

* * *

Many of the optimistic predictions of early AI researchers have not been fulfilled. There seems to be a pattern of initial progress, leading to great expectations, followed by a leveling off, with no further gain. (For a discussion, see Dreyfus & Dreyfus, 1986).

Many of the stumbling blocks come when computers are set to doing "commonsense" tasks. Humans perform them routinely, but they necessitate programming huge amounts of background information into the computer. This background information, or "tacit knowledge," plays a crucial role in orienting humans to their world, and has proved almost impossible to duplicate in computers (see Polanyi, 1958).

Tacit knowledge is required to understand human language. Because computers do not have it, they have not been able to be adequately programmed to "understand" and produce natural human language. Computers are idiot savants when it comes to semantics—they can *look up* words in dictionaries for us, they can *scan* words into their *memory* files, they can even *translate* words into different languages. But when the task goes beyond relatively simple matching and rule-applying, computers do not function well.

After years of optimistic predictions, many researchers now feel the goal of complete computer comprehension of natural language is far off. "It's not in sight," Stanford Professor Terry Winograd told *Atlantic Monthly* in 1988. "I'm not saying it will never happen, but it's not something that can be done by improving and tuning up existing systems." (Wallraff, 1988, p. 71).

* * *

I think what we are seeing here is the expiration of the valid entailments of the founding metaphors of *AI*. Early on, the field needed definition, it needed a sense of direction. The syllogism of metaphors identifying the computer with a brain, and computing with thinking, provided that guidance. Researchers thought they were describing future computer programs and their potentialities, when they were actually just tracing out the entailments of their metaphors.

For a time, the metaphors proved useful. But then, as all metaphors must, they diverged from the realities they purported to describe. The persuasive conclusion of the syllogism of metaphors—that giving the computer sufficiently sophisticated programs would endow it with a conscious mind—turned out not to be accurate.

During these years, however, a professional field grew up around the founding metaphors—complete with professorships, expensive laboratories, grants, degree-granting programs, and so on. Many people in this field are so committed to the founding metaphorical syllogism that they attack any questioners as heretics or traitors (see West & Travis, 1991).

And yet it is possible that the founding metaphors will not turn out to be valid metaphors at all—they may be oxymorons instead.

This is an interesting situation to the student of metaphor, because we tend to assume a metaphor is a metaphor, and that's that. But that may not be that.

We may have a series of **oxymorons masquerading as metaphors.** Oxymorons are composed of terms that do not belong together, or that are contradictory in some way. Examples of humorous oxymorons are *jumbo shrimp, graduate student, standard deviation.* (see Blumenfeld, 1989). I have called these unstable combinations of metaphor and oxymoron *oxymetaphors* (see chapter 4)

The computer may be *nothing like* a brain. Identifying the computer with a brain may be putting together things that do not belong: creating an oxymoron.

Computing may be just a poor imitation of one small part of the vast and little understood process we call "thinking." *Thinking is computing* may be another oxymoron, joining opposites together.

Oxymetaphors are powerful and unstable compounds, that can explode propositions and dynamite discourse. They have the potential to produce positive or negative results. I suggest that they have done both in the discourse called "artificial intelligence." A case can be made that the mind is quite different from anything a computer could come up with. I turn to this topic in the next section.

* * *

It is worth pointing out that we really do not know much about "the mind." Our culture assumes that "mind" is associated with the brain, but we do not know just how. Most discussion in "scientific" terms assumes that a material base of brain operations is necessary for "mental" operations. Yet this may not be accurate, if we can credit accounts of "out of body" experiences, or "near death" experiences. The latter are most suggestive, for in some cases, people have been clinically dead, with medical instruments showing no brain activity. But the patients have reported being able to see their bodies, the room, the other people, and being able to think while in this state. Whatever position we may take regarding the validity of these experiences, the patients have returned with tales of thinking and perceiving while their brains have not been functioning (Morse, 1992).

Also, although our culture identifies thinking with the brain, other cultures do not. Some Amerindian and other tribal cultures and some Buddhist philosophies identify the seat of mind as the heart.

And the mind has an elusive, indeterminate quality. It can seem to take on many different forms. As Patanjali claimed in his

Yoga Sutras, the mind is like a crystal, taking on the colors of anything it is near to.

Our culture is very poor in vocabulary to describe states of mind compared with Hindu or Buddhist cultures. These have a long history of meditative practice and have bequeathed huge vocabularies to describe different mental states. The simple exercise of watching the mind can be an instructive experience. The mind is incredibly active, with all sorts of irrelevant thoughts and images floating through it, in fantastically small sections of time. When one sits and tries to concentrate on one thing for a period of time, the mind wanders in many directions before we even realize it.

Rather than assuming that we know what the mind is, we should humbly realize that the mind is largely an unknown domain. This is one reason it is so tempting to use the computer as a model for understanding our minds—it is an external object we can examine and tinker with. But what if our minds are fundamentally different from any external objects? Then any attempt to mimic its behavior with a computer will be doomed to failure.

* * *

It is significant that one of the real achievements of AI has been "expert systems"—where the "expertise" of some specialists has been programmed into computers. The *expert system* produces a series of questions, mimicking the procedures of the specialist. The computer follows a clearly definable procedure, and applies a set of rules and criteria which have been set in advance. Then it produces an answer, presumably similar to what the human expert would conclude. This computerization has worked for the most technicized, automatic and constrained thinking that humans do: an "expert" following a specific set of directions. However, most human thinking is much more open-ended and creative. Only a very little bit of human thinking is really like computing. As Dreyfus and Dreyfus (1986) pointed out, human understanding goes beyond simply knowing facts and applying rules.

* * *

This somewhat esoteric philosophical argument was brought down to earth for me when I saw a newspaper for union steamfitters and plumbers ("Machines compute," 1988). A

California utility had spent more than $300,000 developing a computer system to replace one worker, an engineer who had perfected the ability to diagnose and correct problems at one of the utility's massive dams. The programmers were not successful. The article asked:

> How would you possibly translate into computerese all that UA workers do? Our jobs entail a special combination of technical knowledge backed by years of training, on-the-job experience that helps perfect an inborn talent, plus plain old hard, physical work. You just can't duplicate all that with a machine. . . . There are also the intangible qualities of doing the job—such as knowing when it "feels" right. How can you program a computer—something with no thoughts of its own—to know when it "feels" right? (p. 1)

At first, giving electronic circuits the ability to reason like a human sounds simple. After all, reasoning is a matter of logical thoughts, one following the other in an orderly manner, right?

Wrong. Human thinking is not machine like. It includes logic, yes, but also emotions, conscience, experience, and individual preference. It turns out that much of human thought cannot be specified in symbols, cannot be crammed into the reductive confines of a symbolic system. This does not mean human thought is hopelessly irrational or uncontrollable. It just means humans follow a higher rationality than can be captured in machines or mechanistic systems of symbolism. Human symbol systems are ultimately open and creative, as opposed to the closed systems required by the computer (see Barrett, 1979).

* * *

The early *AI* researchers were pioneers, exploring uncharted territory. They needed maps, and metaphors provided them with those maps. The powerful metaphors equating human intelligence with computer computation paid dividends in conceptual clarity and fertility. It is completely understandable that these researchers should follow where the bright implications of their founding metaphors led them, as they ventured further into the dark confines of the digital labyrinth.

Indeed, the founding metaphorical syllogism still lives, as we hear predictions for speech recognition systems that will be used by *intelligent agents*, perhaps powered by *neural network* programming. The old dreams die hard.

The computer—and its potentials—force us to examine our assumptions about humanity, mind, and language. Metaphors and oxymetaphors are an integral part of this process. We should realize their limitations, and not follow blindly where they lead. Computers are not brains. Computing is not thinking. Confusing the two domains will just make us seem dumber and won't make computers any smarter.

twenty six

The Computer As Savior and as Spy: Superimposed Metaphors in the News

The headline in the Sunday *The New York Times* caught my eye: WORKERS USING COMPUTERS FIND A SUPERVISOR INSIDE (Kilborn, 1990). Was this a tabloid-style literal headline? Had some workers opened a computer and discovered the body of a supervisor impaled on the chip boards? No, the headline was metaphorical. Always on the lookout for computer metaphors, I read on.

The story was about the use of computers to monitor the work of telephone operators, data entry clerks, airline reservation operators, supermarket checkers, and others. Computers measure workers' keystrokes on the typewriter, amount of time workers spend handling calls and between calls, amount of time workers spend away from the console for lunch or restroom breaks. In addition, managers often listen in on phone calls unannounced. Not surprisingly, workers find this stressful. A study found 81% of workers monitored by computers and telephones reported symptoms of depression. Sixty-nine percent of workers in similar jobs who were not so monitored reported symptoms of depression. (That's still a lot of depressed workers, if you ask me.)

Metaphors that spontaneously occurred to people describing the situation included *electronic sweatshop, pressure cookers,* and *electronic taskmasters* (Kilborn, 1990).

However, there was an underlying, or root metaphor, that I noticed: the *computer as a spy*. It would pry into your every action and report on it. There were constant complaints of invasion of privacy.

At the same time, management defended this use of computers. "You're not getting trustworthy, smart people," one employee said. How else is management going to be sure they do their jobs? Thus, appeared a second underlying metaphor: the *computer as a savior*. The computer made it possible to manage untrustworthy workers in an efficient manner.

I was intrigued that the computer could carry two such different metaphors at the same time. This was explained by the different social positions of the observers. To the workers, the computer was a *spy*. To management, the computer was a *savior*. In the discourse of the news, this came out as superimposed root metaphors for the computer.

* * *

I looked through the rest of *The New York Times* that Sunday (for December 23, 1990) and was surprised to find other *computer-as-spy* and *computer-as-savior* metaphors. Sometimes they appeared separately, sometimes simultaneously.

In the business section, for example, there was a story about a commercial computer network that censored the electronic messages of some of its users, and closed some electronic "forums" that they deemed offensive (P. Lewis, 1990). In one, homosexuals were arguing with fundamentalist Christians. Did the system's managers have the right to read and censor other people's messages? Or was the flow of information over the computer network so important that this should override other considerations? Once again, the computer acted as a spy, reading other people's messages. But, at the same time, the computer acting as a savior allowed more interchanges than ever before, between people who may not communicate otherwise.

* * *

The *computer-as-spy* metaphor was highlighted in another article in the business section. This article dealt with companies that increasingly gather data on their competitors. According to the article, 10 years ago, the practice of "competitive intelligence—amassing and analyzing data about competitors—was considered a legal, but not very savory, version of industrial espionage" (Deutsch, 1990, p. 24). No more. Largely because of the proliferation of electronic databases and corporate computer networks, it has become possible for companies to conduct their own in-house intelligence operations.

The article featured a photograph of an executive at his desk computer, but typing on a laptop computer, captioned, "Gary B. Roush of Corning, which uses computers to collect information about rivals" (p. 24).

One person's spy is another person's savior. Who gets saved was made clear in a quote from the project manager of Ameritech, Inc.'s computerized intelligence network: "What we do is make sure our management is less surprised than the other guys" (p. 24).

The *computer-as-spy* metaphor also made a brief appearance in a page 1 story about Iraq's quest for nuclear weapons (Brooke, Protzman, & Wines, 1990). The article said that "American companies supplied some computers and electronics gear with nuclear-weapons application to Iraq in the early and mid-1980s with the Government's blessing . . ." (p. 4).

* * *

The *computer-as-savior* metaphor made its appearance in the news of the week in review with the teaser headline: ELECTRONIC NOMADS: TINY COMPUTERS MAY LEAD TO A WORLD WITHOUT WALLS. Inside, the story headline read: ANOTHER WAY TO GET TO THE GLOBAL VILLAGE (Markoff, 1990).

Right away in these headline metaphors we see miniaturized computers melting walls of all kinds and creating McLuhan's global village. This simplistic rhetoric is, unfortunately, all too common—a technological "fix" will solve all our social problems. However, we will need more than technology to get people to get along with each other and institutions to function responsively.

The article is about the "next wave" of computers, handheld computers that can decipher handwriting and that communicate with other computers via radio waves. People will be able to store and retrieve documents, send and receive messages and faxes, plug into databases or receive news on these computers almost anywhere cellular phone systems can reach. Eventually, satellite transmissions will allow such messages to "extend coverage to even the most remote wilderness areas," the article says, not questioning whether the person has gone to the wilderness to escape all this stuff in the first place (Markoff, 1990, p. 6). (And will someone back in New York be monitoring the keystrokes of our workers in the wilderness?)

Although these machines will truly be marvels of miniaturization, those in the grip of the *computer-as-savior* metaphor foresee vast social changes following automatically on the technology's introduction. A French theorist speculates that top-level bureaucrats and managers will be freed to constantly roam the globe, connected to their work only by the computers. An American inventor says "Large office buildings are a thing of the past." Apple Computer, Inc.'s chairman says "In the 1990s, what we're talking about is the complete reorganization of work" (Markoff, 1990, p. 6).

If this all sounds a bit familiar, it should. Similar predictions have accompanied every generation of computers. But the *computer-as-savior* metaphor is tenacious, it exerts a powerful fascination. And who knows, maybe this time the predictions will be right. So the impossibly optimistic forecasts keep on coming.

Another forecast from the article: It will no longer be necessary to have an address. "Addresses will become a single number that follows you wherever you travel" (Markoff, 1990, p. 6). Well, it should save on rent, but somehow I doubt that most people will embrace a portable computer and discard their addresses. And the *computer-as-spy* metaphor is always lurking in the background—do we want our address following us everywhere we travel?

* * *

The *computer-as-savior* metaphor was even spoofed in an article in the Arts and Leisure section. The article discussed media "jammers," artistic pranksters who parody mainstream media with fake ads, bogus billboards, and other hoaxes (Dery, 1990).

One "jammer," Joey Skaggs, tries to get journalists to cover his elaborate con jobs, then exposes the cons, to dramatize the gullibility of a sensation-seeking media. His latest: a high-tech vacation service called "Comacocoon." The promotional letter promised "complete relaxation while your imagination is guided to the destination of your choice" using a combination of anesthesia, subliminal programming, and computers. Clients would go into suspended animation, and go on dream vacations directed by a "pioneering BioImpression computer system" which would give subliminal commands (Dery, 1990, p. 36). This scheme could have been taken from a story by Dick (1969), "We can Remember it for you Wholesale."

This letter was sent out to 1,500 journalists in November 1990. Actresses played the role of secretaries answering the Comacocoon phones, and Mr. Skaggs became Dr. Joseph Schlafer. He received coverage in several magazines and on TV.

Here again we have the *computer-as-savior* and *computer-as-spy* motifs intermingled. The savior is a spoof, but the spy is real. Skaggs is on an undercover mission. Skaggs said, "Comacocoon has nothing really to do with dream vacations; it's about mind control. I'm making a statement about how easy it is for governments and big business to pull the wool over our eyes" (Dery, 1990, p. 36).

* * *

The *computer-as-savior* and the *computer-as-spy* metaphors are superimposed in the news. Perhaps we should expect such ambiguity regarding the computer, which is a protean technology, able to assume many forms, with simulation at its very core.

Conflicting contexts in the society lead to conflicting metaphors in the discursive construction of objects. Semantic blurring results. One person's spy is another person's savior, and vice versa. Our language is telling us we still don't quite know whether the computer is our friend or foe.

twenty seven

Why We Should Distrust Computers

General semantics is a set of ideas designed to clarify people's language and thought. It rests on Korzybski's (1948) work which has been elaborated by many thinkers (see the journal *Et Cetera: A Review of General Semantics*, founded in 1943, for examples of the variety of applications).

Two important principles of general semantics are first that the map is not the territory and second that we should avoid two-valued propositions.

The map is not the territory reminds us that the name is not the thing, that language is different from what it describes, and language can never describe something completely. For example, many unfortunate results can occur if we mistake a simplified name (say, "a Russian," "a teenager," "a Jew") for a complex real person.

Two-valued propositions divide the world into black and white, good and bad, with no middle possibilities. They conform to Aristotle's logical rule of the excluded middle, which states that something is either X or not-X, but cannot be both X and not-X at the same time. This kind of thinking can eliminate middle positions and support fanaticism and excesses of self-righteousness, while ignoring the shadings of gray that actual situations usually exhibit (see Hayakawa, 1954).

In this chapter, I attempt to demonstrate that the computer violates both of these maxims of clear thinking and communication.

WHERE THE MAP IS THE TERRITORY

A computer is a collection of circuits waiting for instructions. These instructions, or *programs*, configure the computer in certain ways so it will do certain tasks. Change the *software*, and you have changed the machine.

With one program the machine becomes a word processor, with another program it becomes a *photograph editor*, with another it becomes a *mathematical spreadsheet*, and so on. With one set of programs, the computer becomes "a Macintosh," with another set of programs, it is "IBM-compatible." There are even programs that will let a "Macintosh" work with programs for the "IBM-compatible," and vice versa. (In fact, one wonders how important these product differences really are, which we see promoted so incessantly by advertising. Is every computer able to simulate every other computer, as Turing long ago suggested?)

Here's my point relative to general semantics. To the computer, *the map is the territory*. The map is called the program—and the *chameleon* computer conforms to whatever program-map is fed into it. The territory of the computer conforms to the map, with no distance, with no metaphorizing. The program makes the computer become the image of the map.

If, someday, AI programs do succeed in giving the computer an *intelligence* sophisticated enough to function in the world, as science fiction predicts, we can expect that this computer would not know who or what it was. It would have serious identity problems. It would be constantly changing its "identity" as its programs were changed. We might even say that it would be insane.

EITHER-OR LOGIC

Aristotle's logic of the excluded middle sounds so reasonable. Either something is X or it isn't. That's it and that's all. But, in the real world, things are rarely so clear-cut. My favorite example from everyday life is the traffic light.

I am old enough to remember when all traffic lights had just two colors, and went directly from green to red. They were small little things, not like the huge multilight devices we expect to see over intersections today. This was digital logic at its purest. You were supposed to stop at the red light, and you could go at the green light. That was that. No middle ground.

But in the *real world*, the situation proved to be more complicated than this digital logic could effectively handle. At busy intersections, people would be in the intersection or just entering when the light would change to red. So traffic in the other direction would get a "green," but have to wait for traffic to clear out. Furthermore, people were driving at different speeds, it took time and space for a car to stop, and drivers needed some warning that lights would change. The actual dynamics of the intersection required a more complex logic than the simple digital "stop-and-go" or the red and green lights. And so a new category was added: the yellow light between green and red.

In real life, decisions usually allow for more than two choices. Sometimes it takes some imagination. Gandhi, for example, tried to settle disputes by finding a solution that would benefit all parties—turning a dispute into a "win-win" situation, instead of the usual "win-lose" one. In fact, when a situation truly comes down to a digital choice, we might call it war.

The digital computer relies for all its functioning on a binary number system of zeros and ones. It embodies the Aristotelian logic of the excluded middle. Can it ever transcend this limitation? Some computer theorists would probably assume that this digital limitation of the computer can be transcended by the simple speed and amount of calculations that a computer can perform. Pile up enough digital numbers and you get something that looks like a smooth analogue curve. (In fact, this is one of the procedures underlying integral calculus, where you take increasingly smaller rectangular measurements until you reach the curve as a limit.)

But does the underlying digital logic of the computer disappear when it is repeated many times? Or does the division and exclusion inherent in that logic reappear in new forms on new levels created by computer calculations? The new mathematics of fractals suggests that patterns tend to reappear at different levels of complex structures.

I suspect that both alternatives might be the case. Much of the crude limitation of digital logic can be overcome by repeating its operations many times. But I suspect that, like a fractal process, the same shapes at the base of the calculations will appear at the higher levels as well. These are the shapes of exclusion, intolerance of median values, and a highlighting of warlike oppositions.

This is just a hunch from an analogue human mind. But if it is true, then consider what it means. It means that computer models will have a *bias*, just like other technologies do (see Innis, 1950). For the logic of the excluded middle is a logic of division and exclusion, not one of unification and incorporation. Computers will be biased toward modeling situations and solutions in adversarial terms.

The computer models will produce sharper distinctions than the actual situation warrants, and will be biased against the shades of gray so often necessary for compromise. This does not mean that computers cannot model shades of gray in a situation, it just means that such gray regions will not be modeled properly, or sympathetically, and their potentials will be downplayed by the very nature of the modeling medium.

THE BIAS OF COMPUTERS

As computers are used for more decision-making processes, perhaps we can expect a persistent, unacknowledged bias toward divisiveness in their models. Is there any evidence for this? I can only point to the behavior of those institutions that have used computers the longest: the U.S. military, big multinational corporations, and what has been called "Big Science."

My argument would predict that computers would be a good fit with wartime, military applications, and they have been. Computers are used by the military for all sorts of war-related purposes. Computers have allowed *intelligence* agencies to spy on huge volumes of radio, telephone, satellite, and other messages. They have sped up the "response time" of all sorts of weapons systems. They have "enhanced" the performance of formerly dumb bombs, missiles, and other devices into *smart* bombs, and other wonders of the battlefield.

The behavior of multinational corporations has been guided partly by computer models since the 1950s. Has this behavior tended toward division and exclusion, rather than unification and inclusion? I think both processes can be seen in the behavior of these gigantic organizations, but which predominates?

If there is a main theme to corporate behavior in the second half of the 20th century, I would say it is "globalism." On the one hand, globalism gives us a rhetoric of unification, "one world marketplace." And globalism has provided justification for mergers and acquisitions into ever larger conglomerates.

But there are strong tendencies toward division, conflict, and exclusion exhibited as well. The very concept of a marketplace implies division and competition. But during the years of global expansion, the gap grew greater between the wealthy and the poor—both within countries and between countries. This has been partly due to corporate behavior guided by computer models.

Perhaps most telling is the readiness of these corporations to move factories and jobs from region to region, and country to country, chasing after a computer-generated *bottom line*. This *bottom line* thinking disdains loyalty to workers and regions. It looks on regulations to protect workers or the environment as burdensome expenses to be avoided, not negotiated. This *bottom line* logic seeks after the poorest and most desperate workers who will take the lowest wages and the most dangerous work. This logic also implies supporting dictatorial regimes that enforce an unequal economic order. This emphasis on policies requiring division and divisiveness may be enhanced by computer-generated economic models.

The third group, which has used computers for as long as computers have been around, is "Big Science." The representative group here would be nuclear physics, with its huge atom smashers set up to observe the smallest "particles" in the universe. This group remains committed to a scientific approach that assumes that knowledge will be generated only by dividing "atoms" into ever smaller pieces.

The "particle accelerator" works something like crash-testing cars, hurling relatively huge bits of matter at high energy into small "targets," causing collisions that spray around subatomic debris. This technology has produced a growing list of "subatomic particles" that may, in fact, just be artifacts of the violent technological approach. Nuclear physics may have produced an expensive junk-list of scrap parts after atomic collisions, rather than demonstrating any real entities. Certainly, the universe has seemed more puzzling as a result of this research. But my main point is that nuclear physics, which split the atom and gave us the atom bomb, has continued down this theoretical path of division as an approach. Yes, there is "fusion" research, but the main thrust of computer-guided theoretical physics has been toward division and fission.

DIGITAL DIVISION HYPOTHESIS

We are constantly told that computers can simulate anything. I wonder how accurate this statement is. I wonder if computers have a bias, due to their binary, digital essence. I wonder if our supposedly objective, mathematical models are not subtly, unobtrusively pushing us toward divisiveness, disunity, and war.

I would propose the digital division hypothesis, to be tested in various ways that I cannot foresee. The hypothesis states:

> Because digital computers are constituted by circuits embodying binary, off-on, two-valued logics, the models and other products of digital computers will have a bias toward emphasizing processes of division, exclusion, and conflict; and will have a bias against emphasizing processes of joining together, inclusion, and negotiation.

This is a hypothesis, not yet a fully supported conclusion. Yet I wonder if a computer built on a three-valued logic, or an analogue computer, would produce different models and strategies in certain important situations.

CONCLUSION

The computer is a strange device in which the map *is* the territory. It uses a simplified number system that is built on two-valued processes. To the average person, these may not seem to be important issues. But those familiar with general semantics will realize their seriousness.

We need to face the possibility of a bias built in to the supposedly objective modeling capacity of the computer. This bias may be toward divisiveness, exclusion, and war. We need to ask the embarrassing question: Is the computer insanely great, or is it just insane?

section four

Metaphors in Education and Knowledge

twenty eight

ᵍs Life a Game?
Notes on a Master Metaphor

The *life as a game* metaphor has been around for a long time but seems to have taken on an urgency previously unknown. Perhaps this is because we take our games so seriously. Big money, television contracts, endorsements, fame, groupies—all the accoutrements of success beckon the game-player of today.

Some of our more poignant philosophies of life have been expressed in game terms. "It's not whether you win or lose, but how you play the game" used to be quoted with approval to all school children. Today, the message seems to be, variously, "Winning isn't everything, it's the only thing," "A tie is like kissing your sister," and "Nice guys finish last." These sayings, originated by sports figures, have crept into the general language through many repetitions.

The *game* metaphor is what I call a *master* metaphor, one that organizes a whole field of mini-metaphors around it. Analogies from many different games spring easily to our minds and lips when discussing life: winning-losing, teammates-opponents, and so on. Whether from board games or field games, the choices, strategies, drama, skills, chances, and changes of the game-as-played apply to life-as-lived.

In fact, the *game* metaphor has become so pervasive that Weller Embler, the resident metaphor expert for *Et cetera* in the 1950s and 1960s, wondered if life was really a game in our civilization, if, indeed, the metaphor has turned out to be the reality (Embler, 1966).

This points to one aspect of metaphors that applies to words in general—their self-fulfilling quality. If we describe life as a game often enough, life will take on more and more aspects of games. Eventually, we will not be able to see any significant differences between life and games. We will seek out guidance from games in the living of our lives, perhaps at the expense of other sources of guidance that might be more appropriate. Here we catch a glimpse of the awesome, unsuspected power our language can have over our lives.

* * *

The *game* metaphor is so compelling that we tend to use it without reflection. It helps us communicate in vivid and dramatic terms some aspect of life we want to talk about. It does just what the metaphor should do—enlivens our conversation, enriches our thought, and presents strategies for coping.

In many social situations, there are indeed *rules* that we are expected to follow, common *moves* that mark off the beginnings, middles, and ends of encounters, and significant *choice points*. We find people who will *cooperate* with us in society, and also those who will *compete* against our interests. We *practice* our social skills, often under the *coaching* of another. We make *game plans*, put them into effect, and revise them as we go along. We frequently use our checkbook to keep a kind of running *score* of how we are doing.

We routinely apply the *game* metaphor to politics. Campaigns are reported as *horse races*, with the election as the *finish line*. We have *dark horses, stalking horses*, and candidates *quick out of the gate. Winners* and *losers* are clearcut. The *stakes* are high. We have *favorites* and *long* shots.

The team aspect of games is often referred to when discussing politics. There are *first-rate players* and *second-rate players* on the president's *team*. Parties have to *move the ball* (see Blankenship, 1976).

Game metaphors have also crept into business and economic life. In any situation you need to know the *name of the game*. We hope for a *level playing field*. You must guard against an opponent's *wild card*, and be careful with the more *dicey* aspects of the situation. When the *crunch* comes, you just *let the chips fall where they may*. You hope you won't blow the whole *ball game* (see Gozzi, 1990).

Even the study of language has embraced *game* metaphors. In Wittgenstein's (1953) fertile formulation, language is seen as a game, with a few simple rules and many possible moves. In this view of language, you don't find out what a word means by asking for a verbal definition, you find out what the word means by learning what it does. A statement is a move in a language game (see chapter 43).

* * *

However, with any metaphor that maps a structure of implications from one domain to another, there will come a point when the map no longer fits the territory. We need to be alert to such appearances of incongruity in our metaphoric mapping.

Lest we become prisoners of our *game* metaphors, it will be worthwhile to explore some entailments of the *game* metaphor, to note the difference between games and life.

Behind the *game* metaphor there is an idealized vision of society in which all players start from the same line, the same rules apply to all, and the score is 0 to 0 at the beginning of the game. Perhaps this is a comforting vision, but a moment's reflection shows it to be deficient.

Rarely in life do all people start out with the same initial situation. A child of wealthy parents faces one set of rules, a middle-class child faces another set of rules, a working-class child yet another, and a ghetto child still another. The playing fields will be different for each, and the score is already weighted in favor of the advantaged children. The scoreboard does not read 0 to 0 at the beginning of the *game* of life (see Pratt, 1987).

Of course, keeping score in life is more problematic than in a game. People may choose many criteria for *scoring*: sexual encounters, money, good health, short flashes of ecstasy, long mellow retirements, personal fulfillment, or successful offspring. How do we count up these scorecards? How do we compare different players? The radical simplifications of the *game* metaphor obscure the differences in style and types of successes possible in life.

Indeed, an obsession with *scoring* and winning can rob gameplayers of much that is valuable in life and limit their vision of how to live a satisfying life. We can benefit if we use the *game* metaphor thoughtfully, but we will ultimately *lose* if we let the metaphor use us.

twenty nine

Hardball and Softball as Metaphors

On a hot, green summer day a few years ago, I was sitting on a park bench in my home town of Amherst, Massachusetts. On my right, there was a boy's league baseball game in progress. On my left, and farther away across the playing fields, there was a softball game being played. As I sat relaxing, I was struck by the difference between the two games, which are, of course, played by almost exactly the same rules.

The hardball players had on their uniforms, their spikes, their expensive mitts. But what I really noticed was the demeanor of the players: tense, controlled, intense.

A ball was hit to the shortstop. He fielded it and threw the runner out. A few players said "yeah," "how to go," but the shortstop was for some reason not satisfied with his play. He looked angry at himself, kicked at the dirt, talked to himself as if he were correcting himself. Then it was all concentration on the next batter.

Every player in the field was this same picture of intensity. Every one was focusing on himself and on the pitch. There was no comraderie, no easy kidding. There were a few spectators on the sidelines—parents, I supposed. They were mostly quiet except for applause or cheers in the proper places.

Maybe it was a big playoff game in the youth league, I didn't know. But I can't say it looked like a lot of fun.

By contrast, even though the softball players were farther away, I could hear them shouting and cheering. On one cheer, I could see the ball had gotten past one outfielder, who was running after it as the batter raced around the bases. She got the ball and threw it in, but far too late. But nobody went into an orgy of tense gesturing, the game went on.

It was a coed game, I saw, with picnic baskets lining the sidelines. Babies and little children were playing nearby. The mood was relaxed, good humored. It didn't look like the quality of play was that high, but nobody seemed bothered by it. The noisy softball players were having a good time in the sun.

It was one of those moments when a comparison, a contrast, strikes you with a fateful sense of appropriateness—a metaphoric moment. *Hardball* and *softball*—two ways to approach life. Two types of personality. Life is not a game, as I pointed out in chapter 28. However, some aspects of life are wonderfully symbolized by games. The *hardball-softball* metaphor was just too much fun to ignore.

* * *

The term *hardball* received a new dictionary definition recently, referring to "the use of uncompromising or forceful methods." It is used to describe the tactics of business people involved in "hostile takeovers," that unsettling phenomenon of the 1980s. I have also heard *hardball* used to describe the methods used by organized crime.

In business or elsewhere, *hardball* players go by the cold numbers. For them, the *name of the game* is usually money, or power. Anyone who cares about relationships is considered to be out in *left field*. Being softhearted can cost you the whole *ball game* (see Gozzi, 1990).

There is a fascination with *hardball*, both in business and on the baseball diamond. A pitcher can brush a batter back with a close pitch, sometimes sparking a dugout-emptying brawl. It's a game of inches, between a sport and something more physically threatening. So also with the business world, as people gamble with uncounted millions of dollars in their wheeling and dealing. I have often wondered what keeps people from threats of physical force, or on the right side of the law. As the stakes get higher, the temptations to use force must escalate. The line between legitimate business and crime going legit must get awfully blurry.

Perhaps because of its on-the-edge quality, *hardball* has great crowd appeal. They play *hardball* on the *fast track* (see chapter 26). Television constantly portrays *hardball* business and crime dramas, perhaps giving us misleading impressions of the real business world. And the *hardball* World Series is broadcast to an audience of millions.

* * *

Softball, either on the diamond or in the boardroom, does not get such attention. *Softball* is more relaxed, less focused on the results and more concerned with the fun of playing the game. *Softball* players do not have the drive and inner tension of *hardball* players. *Softball* players are performing less. *Softball* may be less exciting to watch, but it is more fun to play.

We don't yet have an officially sanctioned metaphorical use of *softball*, as a complement to *hardball*. But maybe we could use it to describe those of us who also *play the game*, but are not out to manipulate, destroy, or take over our fellow players.

Just as in business, I suspect there are *hardball and softball* styles in interpersonal relationships. I like to think of myself as a *softball* kind of person—fair-minded, easygoing, able to relax. I have known numbers of *hardball* types, both male and female—driven, competitive, Type-A types.

I hope that being a *softball* kind of person can be maintained even when times get hard—in business or interpersonally. But you never know, in these uncertain times you could wake up any day to discover it's a whole new *ball game*.

thirty

From The Road to The Fast Track—American Metaphors of Life

Life is a journey is one of the most ancient and venerable of metaphors. It is a core metaphor of the mystical Chinese philosophy of Taoism: The Tao is The Way, The Path, which is constantly changing.

In the English language, we have a series of metaphors that rest on the root metaphor *time goes past us from front to back*, as pointed out by Lakoff and Johnson (1980). We *face the future*, *the time will come*, we *look ahead* to next week.

In the United States, in the second half of the 20th century, we have fashioned our own variations on this universal theme, focusing on one of the most conspicuous elements of our landscapes: the road. The road has been a powerful metaphor for independence and freedom from the constraints of ordinary life, ever since *On the Road*, by Jack Kerouac (1957/1976), became the Beatnik Bible in the 1950s. Kerouac saw beauty in gas stations, and freedom on the road. The metaphor caught the imagination of a generation. Many of the key phenomena of the 1960s developed in coherence with this metaphor.

* * *

Ken Kesey and the Merry Pranksters, for example, traveled around the country on a bus driven by one of Kerouac's buddies, Neal Cassidy. The Beatles piled a bunch of people into a bus for their Magical Mystery Tour. And getting high on psychedelic drugs was called *taking a trip.*

And what was at the end of *the road?* California, celebrated in song and story by the Beach Boys as a land of endless beaches, tanned girls, surfboards, and hot rod cars.

In a way, the road took over the task historically assigned to the frontier in U.S. history—it was an outlet, an opening, a way for the disaffected and disenchanted to pick up stakes and move on. It offered hope and adventure, mixed with uncertainty and danger. The 1960s was also an era of hitchhiking, when people would give each other rides and share life stories. I remember many days hitchhiking on both coasts during those years, meeting all sorts of people, never quite sure where I would wind up, but often being pleasantly surprised by the knowledge and insights of ordinary people.

* * *

When the *Sixties* faded into dissension, paranoia, and the Me Decade, the beatnik-inspired *road* metaphor relaxed its grip on people's imaginations. But it did not go entirely away. Instead, it transmuted into another metaphor, the *fast track.* From being a relaxed, hang-out *road,* the metaphor became a high-stakes, corporate, competitive *track.*

Two variants of this metaphor are common: the *fast track,* which one finds in schools, law firms, and corporations; and the *fast lane,* which seems to be open to anyone willing to take risks.

On the *fast track,* one finds driven, competitive, overachieving children, men, and women. People on all levels of the *fast track* get extra homework, demanding crisis problems to solve, short deadlines. The *fast track* wears people down. You get lots of money, but have little time in which to enjoy it.

Lately, we have been hearing about alternatives to the *fast track:* In the mid-1980s there was controversy over the *mommy track,* where women having children would be shunted onto a side track a bit less fast. By the 1990s, the *mommy track* was looking more desirable to both men and women who needed to raise children. That led to the *local track,* which allowed women to work part-time but still advance in their firms (Deutsch, 1991).

Life in the *fast lane* has in it a considerably greater variety of characters. The ways of earning money in the *fast lane* are often borderline legal or downright illegal. Gangsters, hipsters, con artists, hustlers, and drug dealers set the tone. It is a world of high stakes, high status, beautiful women, beautiful lies, fast money, fast cars, fast talk, fast women—at least so goes the mythology. The *fast lane* is a kind of terra incognita—no one is sure of the rules. One imagines road signs: FAST LANE, LEFT: POOR PEOPLE EXIT RIGHT (Baudrillard, 1989).

But sooner or later you arrive at the *toll gate*. What is the *toll* for living in the *fast lane*? We are rarely told, beyond the formulaic endings in the movies and on TV where the denizens of the *fast lane* demimonde get gunned down by the wholesome representatives of law and order. Despite this, there are always plenty of recruits, it seems, for life in the *fast lane*. Is the *fast lane* a death trip? Or can people escape it to find rewarding lives in a quiet suburb? We don't really know. In a way, it may not matter—most of those in the *fast lane* don't seem to care.

* * *

I have noticed occasionally popping up, another metaphor that is coherent with these fast track-fast lane metaphors: the *rearview mirror*.

McLuhan (1964) made this metaphor famous by talking about the way at first a new medium is made to do the work of the old media—looking at the future through a *rearview mirror*.

But the metaphor emerged unexpectedly in the conversation of Deming (1992), the total-quality management guru, talking about management by results. Managing a company only according to its results, he said, is like driving a car by watching only the *rearview mirror*. His point was that managers need to pay attention to the processes that produced the results if they wanted to make lasting changes.

The notion that we are going inexorably ahead and yet refusing to look through the windshield, but instead concentrating on the *rearview mirror*, provides a powerful critique. It conveys the senselessness and dangers of attitudes that refuse to face the unsettling future.

And *rearview mirrors* can be tricky. I am reminded of the lettering on many such mirrors: "Objects Are Closer Than They Appear"—an appropriate epigram for the *fast lane*.

So our leisurely beatnik *road* has become a high-pressure corporate *fast track* where even wishful looking in the *rearview mirror* won't shield us from unexpected buffeting by other denizens of the *fast lane* who might overtake us at any time.

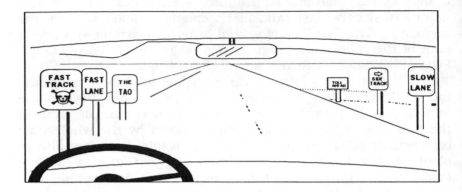

thirty one

The Fast Food Franchise as Metaphor

It was the first hot day of the year—sunny, not too humid—summer definitely on the way. I didn't feel like fixing myself the same old boring lunch at home, so I went out to my favorite fast food franchise. A new branch had just opened nearby. They served vegetarian subs and salads, and I had been waiting for this branch to open.

Inside, the color scheme and architectural formula was definitely the same, but the new folks had not gotten the kinks worked out. Two young girls in tee shirts proclaiming them "sandwich artists" were slowly putting together subs, opening containers of cold cuts to restock the bins, and looking for large-size cups to give customers. The line of waiting customers grew steadily, and the young ladies occasionally glanced apprehensively at it, probably wishing for less business.

I was lucky and got through fairly quickly. As I watched people patiently waiting in line, I reflected on this miracle of modern life—the franchise. I realized how much I expected of it, by noticing how strange it was to see the system not quite up to speed. We want smooth, efficient service; an affordable product that is the same every time. (The "same" every time? Did I actually think that, after just reading Korzybski, 1948, again last night where he vehemently denies the "is" of identity because nothing is the same as anything else? Even the "same" thing is constantly changing on the atomic level.)

Well, not exactly the same, but close enough to be recognizable. We want the predictability. That's what keeps us coming back. The franchise is this little system, that functions predictably (most of the time), and that gives us something to eat with which we are familiar. A fast food franchise is an embodied metaphor for the *perfect repeatable system*—that dream of gamblers everywhere. We put down a small bet, according to the *perfect system*, and it pays off every time.

For the customer, the small bet is the price of the submarine sandwich. The payoff is the tasty, fresh, concoction to eat. For the franchisee, the original bet is larger, but still relatively small. The franchisee buys the rights to the name and the system, rents a store and puts up a sign. If the *perfect system* works (as it should, site and traffic surveys having been taken as part of the sales process), it pays off in steady business and growing profits.

Starting a business is a gamble. We want everything going for us we can get. The franchise promises us a *perfect system*— we can't lose. We hope.

* * *

After I finished my fast food meal—"fast" refers not only to preparation time but also to eating time—I had another errand to do. Time for an oil change on my aging but reliable car. Off to another franchise.

Once again, a familiar routine—quick, smooth, efficient. Some guy in a hole in the floor reaching up under the car and draining all that messy oil into a nice neat container. Another guy checking the air in the tires, and the levels of the car's different bodily fluids. Kind of like a pit stop in a race, but slower.

Another *perfect system*—cars were lined up waiting to get in. A few minutes and you're out the door. The system is so smooth, the people become interchangeable parts. The system is so smart, there are no special skills needed, so "labor" can be low paid and unskilled. If anything really wrong with the car shows up, "sorry, we don't handle that."

I continued to think about the *perfect system* as I drove away, my car humming contentedly with its new oil. The oil change franchise was located on a "strip" of franchises—all winning systems in the competitive game of small business. Every "strip," ugly as it may be, is a monument to the variety of *perfect systems* we have been able to come up with.

Every one of those franchises was filled with low-paid workers, generally low skilled as well. We have made our systems smart so that people could get dumber. I wonder if that is a good idea.

* * *

As I write (mid-1995), franchises are supreme. They dominate the roadways and scoop up ever larger shares of the economy. Today, the franchises look invulnerable. McDonald's has set up shop all over the world—an empire larger than that dreamt of by Alexander the Great (see Chapter 32). I would probably buy a franchise myself, if I weren't otherwise gainfully employed. The siren song of the *perfect system* is hard to resist.

And yet there must be limits. Any system will sooner or later fall out of adjustment with contrary and ever changing reality. Tomorrow, some shock to the system—perhaps in one of the vulnerable supply sources—perhaps in changing public tastes and consciousness—perhaps in the fluid and mercurial currency system—may bring the mighty franchises to their knees.

* * *

All of which raises the question, is the *perfect system* really possible?

Today, the answer seems to be "yes." We live in a culture that hopes and dreams and schemes for the *perfect system*. Every time we patronize a franchise, we are affirming the existence and functioning of a *perfect system*.

But like any gamble, you have to wonder if the system is really that good, or if it has been riding on a streak of luck. Any system must be tied to a specific context. We know the context is always changing. Sooner or later the changes will add up so much that the *perfect system* itself will have to change as well. Yes, McDonald's has added salads, and breakfasts, and so on. These are incremental changes, absorbable by the *perfect system*. I am wondering about the fast food apocalypse, the crash of the franchises.

At present, this crash seems far off, merely an image from a soon-to-be-produced movie. (Actually there was a science fiction movie about this already—*Demolition Man*—where a war between the franchises had been won by Taco Bell, and all franchises were now Taco Bell.)

But I don't share in the gambler's mentality, and I doubt there really exists a *perfect system*. I am reminded of a remark made by Gandhi, who said there is no such thing as a government so perfect that humans do not have to be good.

There's no system so smart that it can long survive dumb humans. We design perfect systems and imperfect humans at our peril. I would rather wait a little longer for my food or my oil change, and know that the people involved were well-paid, skilled, and able to make adjustments to fit the needs of someone who might not fit perfectly into their almost perfect system.

thirty two

McMetaphors

We usually think of a metaphor as a word or a phrase. However, a single syllable has recently taken on the power to create metaphors. I am referring to the powerful syllable "Mc," a pair of phonemes, two units of sound, with no intrinsic meaning at all.

When used as a prefix, the syllable "Mc" has the ability to transform a word into a metaphor for the great American institution of McDonald's— itself a metaphor for a whole approach to service and marketing. So close is the connection between "Mc" and the hamburger chain, that when a hotel chain tried to market a series of "McSleep" motels in 1988 they wound up in court.

Quality Inns wanted to name its new motels "McSleep" to connote the idea of a motel that is "basic, convenient, inexpensive, standardized," they told the judge (Ayres, 1988). In other words, the syllable "Mc," when added to the word "sleep," created a metaphor for McDonalds—as McDonald's is to fast food, so McSleep is to motels.

McDonald's did not want to be the implicit term in Quality Inns' metaphor. They argued that their trademark needed a high level of protection precisely because it described nothing in particular and had "no inherent link to goods and services." They were afraid that the public would be misled about the ownership of the new motels. McDonald's wanted to claim the syllable "Mc" as its own property.

Ridiculous, claimed the lawyers for the Quality Inns. They pointed to a list of more than 60 words using the prefix "Mc," culled from newspapers, magazines, television, and so on. (McReading, 1988). A look at some of the words on that list will illustrate the metaphor-creating power of the mighty "Mc."

* * *

We probably are all familiar with "McPaper," the description of *USA Today*, the slickly packaged, easy-to-digest national newspaper put out by the Gannett chain. It contains "McNews," small, individually wrapped morsels, tasty at the time but leaving you hungry 10 minutes later. Often it reports on "McPresident."

Other words on the list: "McFashion," "McArt," "McFuneral," "McTelevision" (I don't know what that would be—it's hard to find any television that isn't already McTelevision), "McLaw" (not a bad idea), "McTax," and "McWhatever" (whatever . . .)

My favorite "Mc" word is "McJobs." "McJobs" are part-time, low-paid, low-skills jobs that proliferated in the 1980s. They are better than nothing, but not as good as a real job.

McDonald's and Quality Inns had been discussing the possibility of putting McDonald's restaurants and the new motels onto "McStop" Highway Plazas, along with gas stations ("McGas?")

Apparently the lawyers in the case got a little giddy with all the "Mc" words and started claiming that McDonald's sought a McMonopoly on McWords.

* * *

The prefix "Mc" obviously gains its power to create metaphors from the ubiquity and success of McDonald's and its marketing concepts. The McDonald's formula is perfect for the television age—quick small bites, convenient and cheap, tasty at the time with the illusion of wholesomeness. Interchangeable people, parts, restaurants, food. Standardization worldwide—which means reliability but also the fear of boredom.

McDonald's itself has become a metaphor for this successful mass marketing style, so the power to suggest that style, and linguistically link a word with that style, gives the syllable "Mc" deep metaphorical resonance. But did that mean "McSleep" was an infringement of copyright? Could McDonald's lay claim to this syllable in the language?

On September 19, 1988, *The New York Times* headlined: "'McSleep' loses to Big Mc." The judge called "McSleep" a "deliberate attempt to benefit by the good will and reputation of the giant fast food chain." He ruled that the term could not be used.

Quality Inns named their new chain simply "Sleep Inns," and "McSleep" was dead. But the powerful symbol "Mc" lives on, irrepressibly creating metaphors in our everyday language.

* * *

Several years later, in 1992, the mighty "Mc" appeared again in *The New York Times*, this time in a discussion of "McSchools," the planned, for-profit private schools being designed by Whittle Communications (Jacoby, 1992). The metaphor fit. These schools were supposed to hire fewer teachers and load children up with electronics—a computer, monitor, printer, VCR, fax machine, paintboard, stereo and telephone, according to plans (Chira, 1992). Instead of teacher interaction, McSchools would offer standardized "interactive" Mclessons on this fancy electronic assortment. Personally, I had my doubts. (Note: these doubts were borne out by subsequent events—the plans for Whittle Schools were abandoned.)

Here, the metaphor-producing "Mc" was able to convey not only the essential approach of McSchools, but it also conveyed a value judgment—similar to that in McPaper—that raised questions about the quality of this mass-produced, mass-marketed product. That's a lot of semantic work accomplished by one syllable.

Where will the mighty "Mc" strike next? Will it be hauled into court again—a repeat offender? Will it be imported into other languages—becoming a cultural imperialist?

Whatever its future, the syllable "Mc" has proven to be one of the simplest and most straightforward ways discovered since Aristotle to create McMetaphors.

thirty three

Confessions of
a Metaphoraholic

In the spring of 1993, I was sitting on a bench in a hotel lobby in Lexington, Kentucky, waiting for a van that would give me a ride to the airport after an academic conference. Next to me on the bench was a man I had never met, but who, like me, was still wearing his conference name tag. I recognized his name (James McCroskey, a communications professor at University of West Virginia), and we started talking. Academic conferences, whatever their shortcomings, are still places where you can talk to strangers and not be considered a potential mugger.

I asked him what he was working on. "We're studying *talkaholics*," he replied. Right away, I spotted a new metaphor, and, compulsive sleuth that I am, I started quizzing him about it. Where had it come from? Actually, one of their subjects had coined the term. But it was so clear that the researchers had put it on their survey, which they sent out to 800 people. Everybody knew what it meant.

This chance conversation pointed out to me the power of the suffix *-aholic*. It has the power to create metaphors out of ordinary words, simply through the chemistry of combining with them. In chapter 32 I noted how the prefix *Mc-* could create

McMetaphors, like *McSchool* and *McPaper*. Now, I glimpsed the power of the suffix *-aholic*, and realized, with a shock, that I might be a metaphoraholic.

* * *

A cluster of *-aholic* metaphors has started to creep into our everyday language. We have the *shopaholic*, who just can't stop shopping. We have the *workaholic* who devotes too much time to work, and not enough time to the rest of his or her life. Then there's the *chocoholic*, addicted to chocolate. Lately, we've been hearing about *sexaholics*, or sex addicts; and *foodaholics*. I don't know if *talkaholic* will catch on or not, but it fits into the genre.

The tenor, or underlying ground, for all the *-aholic* metaphors is, of course, *alcoholic*. It describes a complex of compulsive behavior, including loss of control over one's choices, denial that there is a problem, increasing lack of ability to cope without the supporting drug, and deception and abuse of others. Various self-help regimes have arisen to combat this syndrome. They themselves provide elements of the metaphorical territory— the need to confess, "hitting bottom," and surrender to a higher power.

This cluster of *-aholic* metaphors is but one in a series of drug-related and addiction-related metaphors that have crept into our language since the 1960s. We humorously speak of being *junk food junkies* or being *turned on* by someone. Yet all these terms carry with them a sense of dependency, a need for escape, an aura of compulsiveness. Perhaps they are saying something about the quality of life in our current consumer culture (see Gozzi, 1990).

* * *

And so I had to wonder about my own compulsive behavior when it came to metaphors. I search for metaphors everywhere. On the plane, I look at a catalog showing products you can order by phone from the plane. It is called *Sky Mall*—a metaphor. I start thinking about malls as metaphors for contemporary life—maybe I'll do a piece on that someday. I notice one of the sections of the catalog is called "Jetcetera"—only further fueling my compulsive hunt for metaphors.

Has my search for metaphor interfered with my rational perception? I notice a mental restlessness, an inability to see a thing for what it is, only for what it might be like. I scan *The New*

York Times, cutting out metaphorical references. I correspond with other metaphoraholics, trading articles and pointing out new coinages. Have I become addicted? I tell myself I am not addicted—but perhaps I am in denial. I think I am happy—but maybe I'm just rationalizing my addiction. Perhaps I need counseling.

Well, I have a confession to make: This isn't really a confession. But the metaphor-making suffix *-aholic* requires one, so I felt obligated to supply one when writing about it. And it is a means to explore the strange mind *trips* you can launch when you start to apply the categories of addiction and recovery to your own behavior. Just what is addiction? Just when are you addicted? And how do you know you are not in denial? The answers to these questions are by no means clear, and becoming blurrier all the time.

* * *

Of course, we all love to hear "confessions"—a quick scan of the magazine rack will prove that. We are eager to get a peek backstage of other people's lives, to discover whether or not they are prey to the same quirky needs and desires we are.

One writer, whose name I do not recall, said that the main problem of our time was "impulse control." I wonder if this problem is not the inevitable result of a consumer culture that puts so much energy into advertising. Countless times every day we are urged to "see-want-buy," in the words of an advertising textbook.

Studies have shown that people shop more when they are depressed. So our *shopaholics* are probably depressed people who, instead of dealing with the causes of their depression, try to escape from the symptoms temporarily by shopping. Perhaps similar dynamics are at work with our other *-aholics*.

In any case, the satisfactions provided by such compulsive behavior are only temporary and partially satisfying. We will have to shop again tomorrow. I am reminded of the Buddhist warning that desire is an enemy, leading to attachment and pain. Is our consumer-advertising machinery a giant apparatus for producing pain? Then all our *-aholics* will need to search for some higher power that does not advertise.

thirty four

The Generation X and Boomers Metaphor

Generation X: blank, unformed, unknown, "whatever." The media uses it to refer to people born in the later 1960s and the 1970s, who are young adults by the 1990s. *Generation X* is a metaphor, referring to an age-cohort of North Americans, giving them perhaps a spurious unity. Many of my college-age students object to the term. It makes them feel labeled, stereotyped, unappreciated in their diversity.

As far as I can discover, the first use of the phrase *Generation X* was in the 1970s as the name of Billy Idol's band in London (Mazzarella, personal communication, 1995). Then it became the title of a book by virtuoso Canadian writer Douglas Coupland. It got picked up by the mainstream media and seeped into the consciousness of the culture.

The *Generation X* metaphor is explicitly vague. It allows us to project our own experiences with young people into it, and then classify them as confirming the existence of a *Generation X*. But some themes recur in descriptions of *Generation X*.

Xers feel they were born too late. They missed out on all the fun of the 1960s: protests, sex, drugs, and rock 'n roll. All the good jobs are gone—taken by *Boomers*. They are facing rising

225

costs, a declining standard of living, a polluted planet. Oh yes, they whine and complain a lot. And they are supposedly less smart and talented than the older *Boomers*—declining SAT scores "prove" that.

I have encountered many of these attitudes among *Xers*. One young man was bemoaning missing out on the fun of the anti-war demonstrations. I informed him that those demonstrations were not fun. They were serious and were extremely dangerous—you couldn't tell what the police forces would do nor could you count on demonstrators to act reasonably. At the anti-war demonstrations I attended, I always made sure I knew the way to the nearest exit. The young man was surprised. No, it didn't sound like much fun, after all.

* * *

The *Generation X* metaphor exists in inevitable polarity to the *Boomer* metaphor, which has its own story. The *Baby Boomers* were born after World War II, up through the 1950s. There were a lot of them, and they rode into the world swept along by an economic boom and chastened by the atomic boom. They had all the advantages consumer culture could give them. They took rock music to new heights, refined the art of protest, and had a lot of fun. So the story goes.

But then what happened after the *Sixties* (which actually spread well into the 1970s)? Now the story takes on a darker cast. The *Boomers* "sold out." They quieted down, became yuppies, and forgot about social change. And they left the next generations, the Baby Bust generation, and then *Generation X*, facing a world of diminished expectations with fewer opportunities.

Such, in broad outlines, is the narrative of the North American generations. It contains enough truth to be interesting, enough distortion and stereotyping to be infuriating.

My reading of the fate of the *Boomers* is somewhat different. They did not sell out, they won. They kicked up such a fuss about Vietnam that the foreign policy of the country had to be changed. This action was almost without parallel in modern history. When the war disappeared, the draft disappeared also; and one of the main external forces uniting the age cohort dissolved. People then went on living their lives, and seemed to melt into the faceless crowds of suburbia. However, very few of them became "yuppies," and most of them encountered the age of diminishing expectations before *Generation X* discovered it. The

Xers can thank the *Boomers* that they did not have to face the draft or endure long foreign wars.

I also read the *Generation X* story differently. These young people live in the richest nation in the world, are well-educated, and still have tremendous opportunities. They are being told that their lives will be constricted and cramped. I wonder how much of this is true, despite the avalanche of readily cited statistics that show it is harder to get a single-family home, for example. So what? There are plenty of creative ways to live, the single-family home is not the only possibility for a satisfying lifestyle. We may, in fact, be facing a long-term economic contraction, but we still have tremendous resources, not the least of which is our imagination.

* * *

I am neither a *Boomer* nor an *Xer*. (I am slightly pre-*Boom*, having been born during World War II.) But I do wonder about *Generation Xers*—just how different are they? On the whole, I tend to see more similarities than differences between *Boomers* and *Xers*. Common to both, there is an idealism and a hope that the planet can be put right. However, as an observer of language, I have noticed some differences between the generations.

The main linguistic marker of an *Xer* is the use of the word "like." *Like* I should say "overuse." They, like, use it all the time. I have wondered about this verbal tic. It seems to me that "like" is used to set a stage, a scene, like television. I notice "like" appearing in stories in conversation, where one person is describing what happened. "I'm like, 'why'? He's like, 'well, I don't know.' So I'm like, really upset, you know?" Each scene can require a different tone of voice as well.

Plat (1995) presented an excellent discussion of "Like." He also noted the similarity of "like" discourse to a television show, and said the use of "like" in a conversation signals a new camera angle, with the storyteller impersonating a camera. Perhaps it would be more accurate to suggest the storyteller is impersonating a TV director. In any case, it looks as though TV technology is being internalized and is functioning as a metaphor for discourse (see discussion in chapter 1, and Ong, 1982).

* * *

Another change in the language I notice is a change in diction: "la parole" of Saussure (1916/1969). Voices seem to originate from farther back in the throat, words tend to be softer, blurrier, pronunciation is less crisp and exact. Does this contribute to the impression that *Xers* are lazy? I recall a line from F. Scott Fitzgerald, where he says a character has the "sound of money" in her voice. What sound is in the *Xers* voice? Is it the sound of a consumer culture, used to being served with material goods?

The other big language-related difference I notice is that Xers do not read nearly as much as *Boomers* did. They have had television available to them all their lives, whereas many *Boomers* can remember life without television. As a result, many intelligent Xers can't spell, and even those who spell well are caught by homophones—words that sound alike but are spelled differently. Correcting college essays, I am constantly encountering such mistakes, because computer spell checkers miss them. Forget "there," "their," and "they're"—even *Boomers* have trouble with them. But there is a surprising number of homophones one encounters. Here is a list from recent student papers: "buy" and "by," "tale" and "tail," "mist" and "missed," "bear" and "bare," "seen" and "scene," "waste" and "waist," "proceeding" and "preceeding," "fair" and "fare," "peak" and "pique," "basis" and "bases," "were" and "where," "compliment" and "complement," "real" and "reel," "discrete" and "discreet," "scores" and "scours," "manor" and "manner," "signal" and "single," "wear" and "where," "alter" and "altar," "weather" and "whether," "principal" and "principle," "click" and "clique," "than" and "then," "morning" and "mourning," "session" and "secession," "prospective" and "perspective," "wary" and "weary," "verses" and "versus," "sweet" and "suite," "site" and "sight," "bow" and "bough," and the list goes on. And in a few years, a new acceptable spelling of "lose" will be "loose."

I think that many years ago, when writing and print were just becoming established, literate elitists set homophonic "traps" so they could tell if a distant letter-writer was educated or not. Proper spelling would indicate good breeding. Spelling errors, especially on homophones, would signal an undereducated person, probably trying to claw their way up the social ladder. Well, even today's college educated people fall into these homophonic traps. This experience is evidence to me that we are moving away from a print-dominated culture and back toward an oral culture.

Is this evidence of decline? Are the *Xers* harbingers of a cultural loss of standards? I must confess, at times I suspect so, but the feeling does not last long. Our language is changing as our culture changes also. The main job is to preserve what is good, and not insist on keeping extraneous relics from the past in the name of "standards."

* * *

It is fashionable for *Xers* to assume that the *Boomers* got all the good jobs, and the *Xers* are stuck living at home. But returning home to live as an adult is an experience common to both generations. I did it myself for a time as an adult, and it was very positive. Recently I heard a term for such *Boomers* who come home to live: *Boomerangs* (Cogan, personal communication, 1995). As time goes by, I believe the continuities between the two generations will become more visible, and the *Boomers* and the *Xers* will probably share the same fate, whatever that may be.

thirty five

The Nineties—
An Empty Metaphor Waiting
to be Filled*

"These are *the Nineties*" people will say, as if they are saying something meaningful. The phrase *the Nineties* creeps into conversations in odd moments, vanishing as quickly as it appeared. Ads, of course, are ready to sell us the styles of *the Nineties*. Consultants are ready to prime us for the job market of *the Nineties*. We are told that education will have to change in *the Nineties*.

But what does *the Nineties* really mean? As of this writing (in early 1993), I have to be honest and say I don't really know.

The Nineties is a metaphor, a phrase standing for a decade; but more than that, a mood, a characteristic set of attitudes, some important events. But, as of early 1993, *the Nineties* had not really crystallized yet, and the decade was almost one third gone. We have here an empty metaphor, a container waiting to be filled.

---

*I originally wrote this chapter in 1993, and decided to let it stand as written, even though I think it still holds true in 1999.

* * *

The Nineties sounds like a plausible concept, I think, largely because of the success of the metaphor *the Sixties*. We all know about *the Sixties*: the love generation, the Beatles, the anti-war protests, long hair, marijuana and LSD, blue jeans, civil rights, Black Power, urban riots, and moon walks.

Actually, it took *the Sixties* a while to get going, and they continued into the 1970s. The "I Have a Dream" speech by Martin Luther King was given in 1963, the Free Speech Movement at Berkeley occurred in 1964. the Beatles arrived in New York in 1964, But it wasn't until 1967 that the "Summer of Love" became a "happening," to the tunes of "Sergeant Pepper's Lonely Hearts Club Band." The Kent State shootings took place in 1970. Some of the biggest anti-war and anti-draft demonstrations occurred after that. It wasn't until 1973 that the Vietnam War ended and the draft was suspended—announced on the same day, I recall.

Since that time, *the Sixties* have been packaged and sold to younger generations as rock 'n' roll oldies, funny fashions, and peace slogans. I recall hearing some college students in the late 1980s talking about a "Sixties Party" they had been to: Everyone wore tie-dyed tee shirts and flashed the "V" sign and said "peace" to each other. This was *the Sixties* to them. Gone was the sense of critique of the culture, the protest against foreign entanglements, the sense of the culpability of big corporations for planetary war and ecological destruction, the visibility of the "military-industrial complex."

The Sixties may return, however. Some bold prophets of *the Nineties* are predicting that the social protests in this decade will outdo *the Sixties* as they take environmental and world peace issues as their focus. Is this just wishful thinking on their part? Are they merely projecting their fantasies into the empty metaphor, trying to give it form? Stay tuned.

* * *

Once *the Sixties* had happened, it was easy to see that there had been a *Fifties* as well, a period of conformity, optimism, big cars, and suburbia. And we moved on into the *Me Decade* of *the Seventies*, where people became self-absorbed and withdrew from public participation. This gave way to the "Go-Go Years" of the deregulated *Eighties*, the Reagan Years, where the rich got richer and the poor got poorer and the middle class got squeezed.

Such, at least, have been the media stereotypes of the past decades. Of course, they contain inaccuracies—any generalization of such magnitude must. But their repetition has given them a legitimacy, a sort of self-fulfilling prophecy in reverse, so we remember the *Seventies* as the "Me Decade," forgetting that this was also the beginning of widespread environmental awareness and the recent organized women's movement. We remember the Reagan Years for their renewed bellicosity in foreign affairs and the excitement of the takeover wars, putting aside thoughts of the painful and enduring economic shrinkage that may be the decade's most important feature.

* * *

And so we come to *the Nineties*, a very large metaphor that is mostly empty. We are adding shovelfuls of time and events to try to fill it up. I have been noticing some of the ways the metaphor *the Nineties* gets used, and I think I detect some nervousness.

A typical use of the metaphor comes from a TV infomercial. "In the Nineties, time and convenience are becoming more important to us . . . and I think the trend is moving toward the home." This social forecast comes from a 30 minute commercial for a home exercise machine: "a machine for the Nineties." It has an "on-board monitor that calculates calories burned," because "feedback is a very important feature" of the machine.

A number of themes are struck here that often appear in *Nineties* predictions. "Time and convenience are becoming more important to us . . ." Why is that? Perhaps because we have less time? Maybe we are working two part-time jobs to make ends meet? Maybe we have to put in overtime to fill in for the people who have not been replaced?

Another theme of *the Nineties* is high-tech gadgets for the home. This "machine for the Nineties" even has an "on-board" calorie monitor. We are constantly being promised more services available through our telephone lines and TV sets, symbiotically linked by our home computers. We will be able to shop, bank, pay bills, order up entertainment—and never have to leave the house. Technology will replace human contact, fleeting though that contact has become.

Why is it desirable to do everything from the home, and never venture out to deal face-to-face with other people? We have a need for human contact that this high-tech future will leave

unfilled. It sounds to me like *the Nineties* may be a lonely time—
at least this theme is implicit in the imagery of the isolated, high-
tech suburban castle.

* * *

High technology—the replacement of human contact with
machines—continued downsizing of corporations so those with
jobs will have to work harder. These themes also often appear in
discussions about job hunting in *the Nineties*. Ackaway (1991) in
his book, *The Devious Decade*, insisted that lying on a resume is
necessary in order to get a job.

Ackaway offered helpful tips on how job seekers can
inflate their claims about past responsibilities and cover their
tracks with a friendly reference person. He justified such tactics
by pointing out that executives do this anyway, and in the tight
job market of *the Nineties* with so many white-collar workers laid
off, job seekers need to inflate their resumes to stand a chance of
landing a good job. Perhaps. There will always be justifications
for deception, and some deception is probably necessary in any
job hunt; but I would still like to think that one's resume should
be a relatively accurate map for the territory it describes.

Still, I myself have predicted that the United States is
headed for a period of increased stereotyping of others, deceptive
communication, and combative attitudes toward others. I came
to these gloomy conclusions after examining the new words for
communication that had entered the language from 1961 to
1986. Over half the new words described deceptive, combative, or
socially pressured communication practices: "psyching out" your
opponent, "shooting down" a proposal, taking "cheap shots" at
others, "hanging tough" in the face of pressure. As these new
words become part of our working vocabulary, helping us think
about our experience, they will shape our thoughts and
communication into plans for deception, mystification, and
verbal combat (see Gozzi, 1990).

So *the Nineties* are here. As we peer into the dark caverns
of this empty metaphor, we try to discern shapes in our future.
We project our fears and our fantasies into *the Nineties*, but we'll
just have to wait for some "defining moments" that will light up
the metaphor and give us a glimpse of what we are in for.

METAFOUR   MEGAFOUR

thirty six

The Metaphor of the Market

The marketplace holds a fascination for people of all cultures. It is a place where folks come together for all sorts of purposes, not just economic. It is an arena in which they test their wits, bargain and barter, exchange news. The market day marks off the calendar. And, of course, it is the location for the exchange of goods that sustain life. According to an ancient Chinese saying, "At a market all things find their places."

Americans have grown up with "super" markets, which are *embodied metaphors* of the abstract market concept. These establishments seem to be growing bigger every year, more industrialized and less personalized than corner stores. There we do not expect to haggle over prices with the manager of the store; we go by the posted prices. This habit puts us at a disadvantage in many traditional markets in other countries, where customers are expected to haggle over prices, sometimes off and on all day. When an American comes in and pays the asking price right away, he or she may be branded as a rich fool.

Yet even within our own country, markets have changed. Eighteenth-century and 19th-century markets were more wide open affairs, closer to the Third World markets of today. Particularly on the westward-moving frontier, markets served as focal points for social events and political speech-making. Candidates for elective office often found a tree stump in a newly cleared field near the market, mounted it, and started to speak, drawing a crowd and giving us the phrase "on the stump," which is still used for campaigning politicians.

Because stumps were plentiful, there was not much of a problem in being heard if you wanted to speak. Next to the market for goods, there grew up a market of speakers and ideas. People could listen, discuss, and choose among several alternatives, often vociferously making their opinions known on the spot. It was this process that political thinkers and jurists have in mind when they use the metaphor *marketplace of ideas*.

* * *

The *marketplace of ideas* was frequently invoked as a guarantor of freedom of the press, of democracy itself, and it even found its way into legal opinions (Bosmajian, 1984). The heart of this metaphor was the notion that in a democratic system people needed to be able to choose among ideas and political programs as they did among goods at a market. They needed to be able to question the quality and sources at both markets, and to be assured of getting real value for their commitment.

Underlying this concept of the market was another metaphor, voiced by the 18th-century economist Adam Smith, which spoke of the invisible hand of the market. This *invisible hand* embodies rationality, Reason with a capital R, which transcended the short-term goals of each buyer and seller in a market and which allocated goods in a wise fashion.

Thus, the *marketplace of ideas* was a metaphor that implied that the processes of democracy and of Reason were at work. Not only did the marketplace provide democratic access to all, allow productive discussion to take place, and facilitate informed decisions, but the market also provided an overarching framework of rationality that mitigated the shortcomings of those who functioned within it. Like any powerful metaphor, it rested on a common experience held by all—going to the market—and applied it to a different domain: social and political discourse. Like any successful metaphor, the *marketplace of ideas* metaphor used key elements of the familiar experience to structure experience in the unfamiliar domain.

* * *

Because the *marketplace of ideas* metaphor so successfully fused the experience of a free-access marketplace with that of a free-access democratic discourse, it has diverted attention away from its shortcomings as a metaphor. Are ideas really bought and sold like commodities? Does every idea (or politician) have its price? Some would answer these questions in the affirmative, yet they point out that the market may not always be the best measure of the profundity or correctness of an idea. What sells in the market is not always the top-grade item.

Furthermore, markets may behave in a deceptive or irrational fashion. Particularly if a market is dominated by a large monopoly interest, its prices and offerings will not reflect supply and demand. The metaphor of the *marketplace of ideas*, within which the *invisible hand* allocated goods wisely, was based on a marketplace consisting of many small sellers in competition with each other, and many buyers free to go somewhere else if they were not satisfied. It did not envision a captive market with distorted prices.

* * *

The reality of markets has changed in 20th-century America, although the language describing markets has not. We still hope for a *marketplace of ideas* to be functioning; we still look for the market to make rational decisions for us. "Let the market decide" has become a rallying cry for deregulation of all stripes. Unfortunately, the kind of market called for in this phrase has long since disappeared.

When we stroll through the supermarket of the 1990s, we might get the impression that there is still much competition. After all, look at how many brands we have to choose from. In detergents, for example, we can choose among Biz, Bold, Cheer, Duz, and Ivory. Only when we look closely at the box do we see that they are all made by one company, Procter and Gamble. How about coffees like Maxwell House, Yuban, Maxim, Sanka, Brim, and General Foods International Coffees? Yes, they are all made by a subsidiary of Philip Morris and Kraft, which also produces the following products: Marlboro, Benson & Hedges 100s, Virginia Slims, Parliament Lights, and other cigarettes; Miller, Miller Lite, Lowenbrau, Meister Brau, and other beers; Jell-O, Post Cereals, Tang, Minute Rice, Stove Top, Shake 'n Bake, Ronzoni, Miracle Whip, Parkay, Oscar Meyer Franks and meats, Philadelphia Cream Cheese, Velveeta, and other grocery items; Light 'n Lively, Breakstone's, Sealtest, Breyers, and other dairy products (Stevenson, 1988).

Here we have a classic example of language creating a false map for the territory—in this case, more accurately, the labels preserve a false map, as the territory is rapidly changing underneath it. The labels preserve the memory of a day when many products came from many producers. The underlying reality is changing almost daily, as we are swamped by mergers and takeovers, buyouts and selloffs.

The same processes of consolidation can be seen in the press, that traditional *marketplace of ideas*. Independent dailies are disappearing rapidly, being absorbed by chains like Gannett, which in 1989 owned 90 daily newspapers, 35 weekly or semiweekly papers, a news service, a satellite information network, 10 television stations, 16 radio stations, the Louis Harris & Associates research firm, and other properties (*Editor & Publisher Int'l. Yearbook*, 1989).

Time merged with Warner in 1989 to form the world's largest media company. This megacorporation controls *Time, Life, Sports Illustrated, Fortune, People, Money, McCall's, Working Woman, Southern Living, Progressive Farmer*, and other magazines, as well as Time-Life Books; Book-of-the-Month Club; Little, Brown; Scott, Foresman; Warner paperbacks, and other publishers. In addition, it controls the world's second largest record company and the second largest cable operation along with HBO and Cinemax (F. Norris, 1989).

* * *

Just as our physical markets are becoming dominated by a few large corporations, so also our *marketplace of ideas* is becoming an oligopoly. Access is no longer free or easy. Discussion of issues is limited. Choices are increasingly constrained.

When we say, "Let the market decide," we must remember that it is a far different market, with fewer sellers and more buyers, with many more goods but less price flexibility, than the market of the past. Thus, the invisible hand of rationality will work differently—and the market is no longer a guarantor of either Reason or democracy.

Metaphors in Education and Knowledge

thirty seven

Economic Metaphors for Education

We are increasingly obsessed with money and *the bottom line*. We look for *the bottom line* in everything—importing this metaphor from accounting into many other situations. Often, this helps us cut through the details of a complex and confusing world. But when it comes to education, the obsession with money may not make sense.

In the past several years, we have seen an increasing tide of criticism of education in the press. Much of this criticism argues from an implicit assumption that *schools are businesses*, which have been turning out inferior products at ever-increasing prices. This economic metaphor needs to be confronted directly: Schools are not businesses.

A business exists to create profits for its owners and managers. That's the business *bottom line*. Don't be misled by the public relations about serving the community. A service may be needed; but no profits, no business.

A school, on the other hand, exists to create educational benefits for its students and the community. Many of these benefits will only appear in the long run, indirectly. Schooling on a large scale has rarely made a profit and has always needed subsides from governments, churches, or some other source.

Schools and businesses are fundamentally different types of institutions. One seeks short-term profits for a few, the other seeks long-term benefits for the many. They have, of course, some similarities, which lends credence to the economic metaphors applied to education. But when we use economic metaphors to prescribe remedies for the problems of schools, we are importing a number of assumptions that are not supportable, when examined in the light of day.

* * *

The economic metaphor is often applied to schools implicitly, unstated, where its assumptions can work unexamined. Take, for example, a graphic illustration in the September 14, 1992 *Business Week*. Two charts were given: "The U.S. keeps spending more on students . . ." caps the first chart, with the inevitable rising line; "but their performance has declined" headlines the second chart, with the downward-sloping SAT scores illustrated (Braiman, L., Sept. 14, 1992, p. 73).

Here, with the compression and brevity of true metaphor, we have summarized an entire argument for the inadequacy of our educational system. The accompanying article describes various "private-enterprise solutions" to reforming the schools.

Yet let us consider our graphs, seemingly so simple and clear, and reflect on their unstated, hidden assumptions. The pairing gets its force because the statement violates a commonly held set of assumptions—about the *bottom line.* These are economic assumptions—if we spend more on something (students), we expect the product to be better (higher test scores). If we spend more, but get less, then we are being ripped off. (I will not enter here into the vexed question of the relationships between real learning and test scores. For a critique of tests of all kinds, see Postman's *Technopoly,* 1993.)

The underlying metaphor at work is, of course, that *the school is a business,* with student test scores as its product. This root metaphor fuels much of the outrage over escalating costs in all levels of education. There must be something wrong with the company—costs are up and the product is shoddy.

The *school-as-business* metaphor has grabbed many minds forcefully, as powerful metaphors will; and suggested many "solutions" to the problems. Obviously *the business* has to cut costs, and one of the obstacles is an intractable workforce. It follows that adding technology—usually computers with "interactive" features, and downsizing teachers and faculty, making them more "productive," is one solution.

If *a school is a business*, then such steps seem reasonable, even prudent. But if a school is not a business, and operates on different principles, then these "reforms" may be retrograde. For example, if we think of *a school as a miniature neighborhood*, where miniature people learn the skills of getting along with each other, then reducing their opportunities for interaction with each other and with older people will hinder the successful functioning of the school.

* * *

I would like to return to the graphs for another journey through the metaphor "The U.S. keeps spending more on students, but their performance has declined." Let us fall into the economic metaphor and explore it for a bit. If *a school is a business*, say a manufacturing business, it gets its raw material (unlearned students), processes it, adds value to the raw material by shaping it, and produces a product (students who test well).

But what if the raw material comes in worse shape each year? What if the raw material, formerly ready for processing and tractable to reshaping, has become obdurate? Perhaps we have run out of the best lodes of raw material and can only get inferior strains with many impurities. Or, perhaps the material has been polluted, producing unwanted side effects making the material more difficult to process.

Then our *school-as-manufacturing business* needs to add pre-processing steps, (which can be done in the form of preschools and remedial classes). Our *school-as-manufacturing business* will need to slow down its processing speed because of the intractability of the new raw materials (which occurs when less subject matter is covered in a school year).

A strong case can be made that the raw materials for our schools-as-business have been polluted and are more difficult to "process." We know, for example, that too much television (more than two hours a day, says the U.S. Academy of Pediatrics) impairs reading skills and school performance. Yet most children watch much more television than this. We know that supportive families where children are encouraged and assisted in their schoolwork are crucial ingredients for school success. Yet one in two marriages currently ends in divorce.

The metaphor of *the school-as-business* directs our attention away from the quality of the raw materials. Even within this metaphor, one could say that the rising costs of education are, in fact, rational responses to the increasingly difficult job of "processing" social and television-impaired "raw material."

* * *

The fundamental weakness of *the school-as-business* metaphor lies in its inability to comprehend the most important processes that occur in a school—socialization and learning.

Children need to interact with other children and with adults to become healthy, socially functional people. But how does this contribute to the *bottom line* of test scores? Doesn't "social time" seem unproductive? If we view schools through the filter of *the schools-as-business* metaphor, these vital aspects of growing up will be systematically devalued and reduced. In the name of "efficiency," the social growth of our young people will be stunted.

The *school-as-business* metaphor suggests learning is like manufacturing—taking raw materials and shaping them. Or perhaps learning is like "information processing," something businesses can do with an assist from technology. Clearly, the metaphor implies that with some added computers and perhaps year-round schooling (longer manufacturing runs) we will improve test scores.

Yet learning is an organic and social process. The learner must be persuaded to some degree to participate. Ideas take time to germinate. What if learning is not like a manufacturing process, but more like planting a garden, caring for it, and allowing it to grow? The machine in the garden will only trample the delicate fruits and flowers.

* * *

Our choice of metaphors has consequences. Every metaphor has points of illumination and blind spots. The structure of our metaphors suggest plans of action. We have seen a growing tendency to apply economic metaphors to education. It behooves us to wonder if we want our young people treated like raw material in a manu-factory.

thirty eight

Structure:
The Intellectual's Metaphor

I remember when the metaphor of *structure* arrived across the ocean from France. I became aware of it in the late 1960s, mostly from remarks from professors who dismissed it, and from books displayed in the new books sections of intellectual bookstores. The "structuralists" were the academic-intellectual equivalent of the lively spirit of questioning that permeated the era now thought of as *the Sixties*.

What excited me most about the structuralist program was its ambitious attempt to unite disparate fields of knowledge. I had come to feel that the disciplinary separations between fields of study was artificial and actually a hindrance to progress. At the time, I was interested in the links between psychology and history, but it seemed to me that there might be a unifying approach to studying humanity that would go beyond those disciplines.

I remember being excited to discover that others shared this vision, and furthermore that they thought they had discovered a method for promoting this unity of knowledge. I was excited by Piaget's (1970) book, *Structuralism*, which explicitly tried to tie together psychology (Piaget's own area of study) with anthropology (drawing on Levi-Strauss, 1966), mathematics, sociology, and other areas under the structuralist umbrella. At least the right questions were being asked, I felt, and by "respectable" academics at that.

* * *

There was one problem, however. The structuralists definition of *structure* was barebones—in fact, too narrow by far, I felt.

Following Levi-Strauss (1966), structuralists defined *structure* as a pair of polar opposite terms, mediated by a third term. Thus, you could take almost any pair of opposites and call it a *structure*. Levi-Strauss analyzed myths using pairs of opposites like "the raw" and "the cooked," "nature" and "culture." This was a simplification of the more general definition of *structure* as a set of elements and relationships in a mathematical group. Yet *structure* remained very abstract, negating much of the power of the metaphor.

To me, the beauty of the metaphor of *structure* is that we are all familiar with architectural structures because we live, work, and play in them all the time. We can be complex and sophisticated in our discriminations, yet because we are so familiar with architectural structures we will not become lost in our metaphors. I elaborate this expanded structural metaphor here by equating different cultures with their respective houses.

* * *

Let us say that a culture can be described in *architectural-structural* terms—for example, a strange culture we are unfamiliar with but trying to get to know. Clearly, we need a way in—a doorway. This can come in the form of a friend or "informant." Once inside, we will only see the public areas of the culture at first—the parlor, reception area, or living rooms where everyone is on their best behavior.

Yet a culture has to deal with all the aspects of human function, just as does a house. If we can get to the kitchen and dining areas of the culture they can provide us with many important clues to the ways the culture approaches its environment and its resources. Compare, for example, the Chinese kitchen with an American kitchen. The Chinese kitchen has many people helping prepare the food, the American kitchen has few people and many gadgets. A Chinese meal involves cutting up many different vegetables and combining them in many different ways. An American meal is often a chunk of meat, some bread, and maybe some potatoes or salad. Does this comparison tell us something about the cultures as a whole? I think so.

The comparison tells us that Americans rely more on technology and less on people. We prefer a few large tasks to many tiny ones. Chinese take a more labor-intensive approach to things, and prefer to break tasks down into many small pieces.

* * *

Every *structure* must have a foundation. What is each culture's material foundation? Is it village-based agriculture, as in China, or is it mechanization as in the United States?

Every *structure* must provide a roof, to protect against the elements. The *structure* must have walls, to shelter its inhabitants from heat or cold. How does a culture shelter its inhabitants? Physically, of course, we can compare buildings in different cultures. But metaphorically, the roof and walls could be the sustaining beliefs and rituals that provide the members of the culture with a sense of purpose and certainty in life. In ancient Chinese culture these were rituals centered around the family and the state—the goal of a good state was to produce good families, according to Confucian doctrine.

Modern cultural *structures* are more open, with thinner walls and roofs, only bare support beams in some areas—some would say that modernity provides little or no shelter against many of life's crises.

Every *structure* has corners, and boundaries. Some people and behaviors fall outside the boundaries. But if the walls and roof have holes, then it becomes harder to tell who is really outside the structure and who is inside.

And what is the energy source that keeps the *structure* humming? Animals, wood fires, gas, electricity?

Of course the *structure* has different levels—different *floors* with stairs or elevators connecting them. Is life very different on the different *floors*? How far apart are the *floors*? Do people in the cultural *structure* easily pass from *floor* to *floor*? Or are the *stairs* and *elevators* scenes of pressure and conflict? Are guards posted to keep too many people from getting *upstairs*? How easy is it to fall *downstairs*? It's easy to see how one person's *floor* is another person's *ceiling*.

These are just a few suggestions about how *architectural structure* could be used as a powerful metaphor for culture. I think it is an incomparably richer approach than simply looking for pairs of opposing terms and claiming you are illuminating *structure*.

* * *

So what has happened to the Structuralist dream of unifying knowledge? It seems to have disappeared behind a mountain of paper, arguments over the accuracy of Levi-Strauss' anthropological observations, disputes with Piaget's stages of growth of children: based as they were on observations of White, European, generally upper middle-class children—how generalizable can they be? And so on. It is an age of specialists and specializations, hostile to the generalizing impulse, which always needs to be received with an open mind. The specialists have again taken the ascendancy in this fragmented "post-structuralist" period.

Yet I believe that the metaphor of *structure* cannot be counted out so early. It does too many things for organizing our thought and observations, it is too familiar yet complex at the same time, to be discarded on the scrap heap of yesterday's intellectual fashions.

After all, every culture we know of actually builds and lives in some form of structure. On the face of it, this should make the structural metaphor a likely candidate for unifying and organizing information about all of humanity.

I have suggested here that one problem was the overly restricted definition of *structure* used by the structuralists. Perhaps a more expansive, rambling, and architectural treatment of the metaphor will provide us with more capacious results.

thirty nine

The Projection Metaphor in Psychology

I was looking through my books recently when I came across a remarkable passage in a volume of Carl Jung (1960), which, about 25 years ago, I had taken the trouble to copy.

> . . . we still go on naively projecting our own psychology into our fellow human beings. In this way everyone creates for himself a series of more or less imaginary relationships based essentially on projection. . . . A person whom I perceive mainly through my projections is an "imago" or, alternatively, a carrier of imagos or symbols. All the contents of our unconscious are constantly being projected into our surroundings. . . . All human relationships swarm with these projections. . . . Unless we are possessed of an unusual degree of self-awareness we shall never see through our projections but must always succumb to them. . . . (pp. 264-265)

This passage caught my eye because of its fundamental metaphor: *projections.* Apparently, this metaphor was suggested to Freud and Jung in the early days of moving pictures, by the action of a projector throwing an image onto a screen (Metcalf, personal communication, 1985).

Certainly *projection* is a factor in many unsatisfactory relationships today, especially, I think, between men and women. Too often, accurate interpersonal perception is difficult, and ambiguous situations encourage *projection*. Women's styles of tight and revealing clothing, bathing suits, and so on, often invite *projections* of sexuality, yet the actual women involved may not welcome such attention. Men's behavioral styles of self-assuredness, "managerial macho" decisiveness, often invite *projections* of a father figure, or wise person, which the actual person may discover is a barrier to true friendship or intimacy.

Many people in the mass media are there because they are "photogenic" or "mediagenic." This elusive quality, I think, partly comes down to the fact that their images in the media are very receptive of *projections*. Our media "stars" carry around a huge baggage of *projections*, which partly explains why people get so involved in the stars' supposedly "private" lives.

* * *

But what are these *projections*? Do we actually shoot across space images that land on the target screens of other people, and then perceive these *projected* images as coming from outside? How do people become "carriers" of such *projected* images?

When we start to look at the *projection* metaphor closely, such questions become puzzling. So, although the *projection* metaphor is tremendously vivid and dramatic, it has serious limits—as any explanation based on metaphor must.

Although every metaphor illuminates, it also hides some aspects of what it illuminates. What does the *projection* metaphor hide? Simply this—we do not "project" anything out onto other people, in the manner of a movie projector sending beams out across space. All our perception is internal to our body (at least I think so now in early 1997). Our nervous systems construct a holographic image that we experience as space-time, and within which we live. I would substitute a *construction* metaphor for the *projection* metaphor if we want to stay away from facile assumptions about *projecting* across space.

* * *

Our senses construct a sort of "virtual reality" for us. We wander through the world with our sensory-virtual-reality "helmets" on, blind to anything not picked up by the apparatus, unaware that the world outside has no color, or sounds—just waves of energy.

This is described well by Korzybski (1948), in his discussion of the first stage of abstraction:

> . . . the events outside our skin are neither cold nor warm, green nor red, sweet nor bitter, but these characteristics are manufactured by our nervous system inside our skins, as responses only to different energy manifestations, physico-chemical processes, etc. (p. 384)

Korzybski did not use the construction metaphor, but he saw something of the sort was going on with the psychological phenomena of *projection*. Korzybski saw *projection* as a reversal of order in the abstracting process. Instead of abstracting from the lower orders of sensation into the higher orders of ideas, people sometimes have ideas first, but experience them as lower order sensations. "This reversal transforms the external world into a quite different and fictitious entity" (p. 170). Korzybski saw this reversal or confusion of orders of abstraction as potentially threatening to survival. On a less drastic level, he said "This reversal of order, but in a mild degree, is extremely common at present among all of us and underlies mainly all human misfortunes and un-sanity" (p. 170).

The *construction* metaphor would claim that, as we construct our images of people, we use the materials from our unconscious mind. Thus, the resulting image is a compromise between information coming in from our senses and fantasies and desires in our unconscious.

The *construction* metaphor correctly locates the *projection* process within ourselves. Therefore, I think it is possibly more accurate in describing the process than the *projection* metaphor, which requires an unlikely *projecting* of images across space.

* * *

However, I think it is very important to "date" such knowledge, as did Korzybski himself. This is how it looked, as of early 1997. I have started to wonder, as I have studied communication more, if we are really as isolated and separate as our individualistic virtual reality assumptions make us out to be. Does all our perception and cognition occur "inside our skin" as Korzybski so clearly put it? Or, do we in fact share in something larger than ourselves when we perceive and communicate with others?

I am coming to feel that we do share in something larger than our bag of skin and bones when we communicate. I call it a shared perceptual field. This field has properties greater than the sum of the individuals involved.

So perhaps we do *project* something out to others, and they *project* onto us as well, through the refracting lenses of the shared perceptual field. Then our *projection* process would include both *construction* and *projection*.

It is an important issue, implicated in much of the misery of humankind. Who knows where the next insight into it will come from?

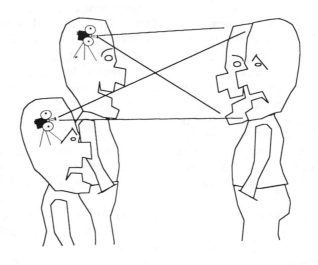

forty

The Jigsaw Puzzle as a Metaphor for Knowledge

We commonly say that something is a *puzzle*, or we are *puzzled* by something. A *puzzle* can actually be a very large and indeterminate situation, which stops us dead in our tracks because we don't know what to do. Sometimes I think that nature itself is a large *puzzle*, which we can put together in various ways, achieving different lifestyles for ourselves depending on how we *solve* the *puzzle*.

It is useful to have a metaphor like *puzzle* to describe such an indeterminate situation. *Puzzles* are indeed important things. They played a role in many ancient myths, which involved having the protagonists figure out some riddle or puzzle before being allowed onto the next stage of their journey.

And so when I was putting together a series of jigsaw puzzles, at one point in my life, I took the opportunity to think about puzzles in general. The jigsaw puzzle itself, the cardboard-and-paper collection of differently shaped and colored pieces, was an *embodied metaphor*. It embodied, in physical form, a large metaphorical concept. Within limitations, it provided fruitful material for thinking about the process of solving puzzles of all kinds.

* * *

You start, of course, with a huge pile of randomized pieces. Thousands of them. It looks hopeless. Disorder reigns supreme.

But you do have a couple of things going for you. First, there's the picture on the box—you actually know what the answer will look like, in a large sense. You can get hints about the general groupings of the differently colored pieces—those blues will represent water, these blues are the sky, these buildings are brown and tan, and so on. The result will be a Mediterranean seashore scene, with boats and buildings under a blue sky.

Is this an accurate metaphor for our situation when faced with puzzles in life? Sometimes, yes. We often have a general sense of what is going on, what should be happening—we just don't know the details. We don't know how it can be brought about, brought under control. We don't have *all the pieces filled in* yet.

In life, our fantasies, theories, ideologies are the pictures on the box. We try to put together the pieces of our lives so they will match these dreams.

So in an important way, in solving puzzles, we work backward from solutions. This goes counter to our expectations of moving logically, step by step, from premises to conclusions. Logically, we are supposed to work forward from premises, not backwards from solutions. But in real life, as in the embodied metaphor of the jigsaw puzzle, we often do not proceed logically.

* * *

We have another thing going for us as we tackle our jigsaw puzzle. The boundaries of the puzzle are straight lines. We can separate out the edge pieces because they are usually the only ones with straight edges.

Is this an accurate metaphor for solving puzzles in life? It can be, if we assume that our conceptual boundaries are like the straight line borders of our puzzle. We understand certain concepts up to a limit. That limit is the edge of our puzzle.

And so we work in from the edges of our puzzle. As we do, certain outlines appear, and we search for pieces which will fit them. We work in from the context, try to *fill in the blanks*.

Again, this is different from how we conceive "logical" "problem solving" to work. We usually think of going to the "heart of the matter," and "building on what we already know." This might be analogous to finding a bunch of pieces that are the same color, and that obviously belong together. We put them together into a tan building, say. They are then a "subassembly" ready to be "plugged in" when the rest of the puzzle is ready. But the main action is working in, bit by bit, from the edges.

* * *

Early in the puzzle-solving process, there are lots of pieces lying around. The job is to classify them, group them together. Broad categories are formed—edge pieces, blue-sky pieces, blue-water pieces, and so on. This is similar to the taxonomic work that occurs at the start of any endeavor to increase knowledge.

Slowly, patiently, you move from disorder to different stages of order, from randomness to regularity. The *frame* is put together. Certain prominent "subassemblies" get assembled.

It is interesting to watch as individual pieces disappear when they are fit into place. At first, there is a clear shape waiting to be filled. We search for a piece with a good *fit*. Many are close, but do not fit. Then, when we find the right piece, it goes in effortlessly, and blends in so quickly that a gestalt is formed. We no longer see the piece that a moment before we were so glad we found. It has become another part of the growing context, as we work in from the edges.

This phenomenon of the disappearing pieces is similar to what happens to many subsidiary discoveries after a general puzzle is solved. Who now remembers those experiments on gravity or optics that preceded Newton's laws? They have faded into the background, as it were, and all we see is the completed puzzle.

* * *

As we progress in our puzzle-solving venture, we increasingly experience the pleasures of closure. "Aha," "That's it," "there you are, you little bugger." And we are rewarded with a growing unity, a clearer picture, increasing order, decreasing random piles of pieces. We are working against entropy, against randomness, a process which is necessary for life itself and inherently rewarding.

As we get farther along, we go faster. Whole subassemblies can be put into place, increasing our coverage in large chunks. The remaining tasks become sharper, more clearly defined. The pesky ambiguous pieces start to be put into their places.

At this later stage of puzzle-solving, the broad taxonomies of the early stage are less useful. We are now down into the details, into the local questions.

We still must rely on trial and error. Sometimes we get a piece that almost fits, but not quite. The problem is this is the last one like it. That means some other piece is in the wrong place. We have to find it, and then all the earlier fits off that wrong piece have to be moved as well. There is magnification of errors, although the jigsaw puzzle usually stops you before you get too far.

* * *

Finally, the puzzle is completed. The last piece is ceremoniously put into place, even though the end has been apparent for some time. The big picture is before us: a Mediterranean seashore with boats and buildings under a blue sky. All the individual pieces that so occupied our time have vanished, all the piles of pieces have disappeared. Instead we see a unified whole.

This is the hope of everyone who needs to solve a puzzle in real life. That, through patience and trial and error and luck, we may come to understand a larger process, a more comprehensive whole. When the puzzle is solved, we will know what to do, how to act, how to overcome whatever is stopping us.

And what are the puzzles of everyday life that we need to solve? I would say that language is probably the most common. We have lots of words and pieces of language lying around. We need to put them together into the proper shapes, so they will help create the big pictures we desire.

Whether it is as simple as asking for something in a store, or as complex as asking someone to marry us, language provides the pieces for a puzzle which, if we put it together properly, can make our lives a whole lot better. Or, if we never do solve the puzzles of language, and how they are related to social and natural "realities," our lives will be the poorer for it.

Language Describing Itself

forty one

Our Inflationary Language

We use language, that marvellous technology, every day, to talk about our lives, our past, our future—we can even use language to talk about language.

But what happens when language changes its role in our lives—when we start using it differently, or when *it* starts using *us* differently? How can we get a handle on changes in the role of language, when we must use language to discuss them?

I have been wondering lately if the role of language in our lives has changed from, say, the 1950s, that era of Ozzie and Harriet, Beaver Cleaver, Eisenhower, and Casey Stengel, to the 1990s. What do I mean by the changing role of language? Let me illustrate with another example—that of television.

In the 1950s, television was relatively new and special, and when people watched, they often turned out the lights, sat quietly, and watched shows as if they were movies. By the 1990s, television had become electronic wallpaper, left on for hours as people did all sorts of other things. The lights are on, people talk, cook, and so on, paying attention only sporadically to the set. Now people don't watch shows so much as they watch TV.

So the role of television has changed since the 1950s, even though we still refer to "television," as though television (1950) is the same as television (1996). We still refer to "watching television," although the activity itself has changed since the 1950s. What if the same thing is true of our speaking and listening, our everyday uses of language?

If we are using language differently, and if our changed language is using us differently, what resources does language itself offer us to discover and conceptualize this change and reflect upon it? Here is where metaphor comes in.

* * *

Metaphor allows language to transcend itself, to extend its categories, to examine the unfamiliar in familiar terms. But which metaphor to choose? On the one hand, practically anything can be pressed into service as a metaphor for something else. On the other hand, only a few metaphors have resonance with their associated areas such that we learn accurately about the "target" domain by exploring implications of the "familiar" domain. Aristotle thought that choosing the right metaphor is an unteachable gift. It is also something of a crap shoot.

While thinking about the changes in our language and language-use from the 1950s through the 1990s, it occurred to me that the metaphor of *economic inflation* might be useful. Certainly we are all familiar with the paradoxes of inflation—we have more money but it buys less, we think we are getting a raise but it turns out to be a pay cut. Might the same things have happened to our language?

* * *

Words have been metaphorically compared with money before: we *coin* a phrase, both money and words *circulate*, have *value*, and so on. Korzybski (1948) remarked that money was a symbol of all human time-binding activities. So on the face of it, metaphorically equating the circulating money systems with the circulation of words, to discover what has occurred to our language-in-use—*la parole* of Saussure (1916/1969)—seems promising.

One parallel is clear, and well-documented. We have more words circulating, just as we have more dollar bills. Our dictionaries have been expanding rapidly as lexicographers struggle to keep up with new words. The English vocabulary has been expanding as fast in the second half of the 20th century as at any other time in its history.

At the same time, there is a pervasive feeling that "communication" has become more problematic. We may have more words, but they seem to purchase less meaning. I studied the new words for communication that emerged in the 1960s through the 1980s, and found that more than half referred to deception, mystification, "psyching out" of various forms, social pressure. Verbs like "do a number on," "stonewall," "lean on," "put down," and others tell a story of communication becoming more problematic (see Gozzi, 1990).

What is it we are trying to "purchase" with our words? To follow our metaphor further, if the economic exchange leads to the purchase of "goods and services", what does the language exchange lead to? One answer is: meaning. There is a pervasive sense that our words mean less, even as we have more of them. The new words themselves speak of "playing games," "doing a number on," "code words," "bureaucratese," "academese," "educationese," "psychobabble," and other endearing terms.

In the imagery of Postman (1993), meaning has *drained out* of many of our culture's important symbols. Postman attributed this to their repetitive use and trivialization in advertising and the media. So in the purchase of meaning, our language seems to have followed a similar inflationary path as our money. Prices are up, it takes more money and words to purchase goods and meanings, but the resulting acquisitions seem thinner, flimsier, less reliable.

* * *

There is also an important "service" we are attempting to purchase with our words: other people's attention. When we talk with others, we want their attention—without it we cannot get anything worthwhile from them.

An extended study of people's conversations has shown that the pursuit of attention has become epidemic—"conversational narcissism" is widespread. People try to direct conversations back toward themselves constantly, seeking attention like starved children (see Derber, 1979). Perhaps there is less attention to go around because, as people become more preoccupied with themselves, they have less attention to give to others. Or perhaps they are spending so much time with media and fantasy characters that they have less to give to each other.

Our language-economic metaphor would then work like this: Attention ("quality time") is becoming more scarce. Therefore, the "price" goes up—more words are necessary to "purchase" it. But the more words in circulation, the less value they intrinsically have.

What results is an inflationary spiral—we speak more words in an attempt to purchase scarcer attention, but only succeed in aggravating people more so they are even more reluctant to pay attention, requiring more words still.

* * *

Clearly this is not the last word on this subject. But the notion of an *inflationary* language, with all that implies for cheapened communication, is thought-provoking. How do we get "price stability?" How do we maintain our standard of communication? Tight words? Restrictive sentence-formation policies?

Maybe we need a reverse "supply-side" approach—everyone should vow to talk less, thereby making words more valuable. (Good luck on that one, just like the other "supply-side" economics.)

Maybe we need a return to a "gold standard" of sorts, where our words are backed by our honest intentions. We could start with our government. Maybe some of the honesty would "trickle down."

forty two

Stalking the Wild Metaphor

There are times I think of myself as a hunter—not a hunter with a gun out to kill wild game, but a hunter with a camera, seeking to "shoot" pictures that capture the wild game in their hiding places. The wild game are metaphors. The jungle where they live is the language of everyday life.

* * *

A wild metaphor, untamed, undomesticated, is something like an animal that takes on the protective coloring of its surroundings. It looks like any other part of the jungle of language at first. We are tempted to pass over it without comment, allowing it to perform unnoticed its subtle work of implication.

Even when we think we have spotted a metaphor, and taken its picture, we often cannot be sure what it is. Is it a metaphor, or some other species of figurative language, perhaps its close cousin the simile? Or its truncated relative the synechdoche? Or the contrarian oxymoron?

Here, some of the standard collegiate guides to wild metaphor will be of some assistance. However, their examples, ripped from the context of the jungle, impaled on exhibit slides, do not do justice to the subtleties involved in detecting and trapping the species in the wild.

When we do spot a previously unnoticed metaphor, we can have an exhilarating "aha!" experience. I call it a metaphorical moment. Things fall into place, make sense in a new way. Often we see familiar territory in a new light, are able to draw a more sophisticated map through part of the jungle of language.

* * *

After a while, the metaphorical metaphor hunter learns more about the behavior of his or her prey. It helps to study the snapshots of other hunters, who have found metaphors in the unlikeliest of places. It is something you have to get a "feel" for, something that takes intuition, experience, and time. It will never be an exact science, formalizable into precise rules.

Metaphors often travel in herds—called *clusters* by some students of the species. If you spot one little metaphor and then start to look around that section of the jungle, you will often find its relatives nearby. The trick is spotting the little metaphors— minimetaphors that blend into the scenery. They rush by so quickly they are easy to miss.

Once you have spotted a couple of minimetaphors, if you look carefully you will often find the master metaphor lurking in the vicinity. Like an alpha baboon male, the master metaphor keeps the rest of the herd in line and determines the direction the group as a whole will take.

* * *

Once you have captured a metaphor on "film" and have identified it and held it up to scrutiny, what do you have? A lively conversation piece, no doubt, but something more than a stuffed animal or a home-viewing slide?

Here we start to reach the limits of our jungle animal master metaphor. We need to stretch our imagination about the relations between the animals and the jungle a bit. For the animals are part of the jungle, and their behavior shapes the jungle to some extent. Where they commonly go, for example, leaves trails, easier paths that humans can follow.

A herd of metaphors, then, has probably grazed around the jungle of language in certain well-defined ways, leaving definite paths of implication for people to travel along.

When we have spotted the metaphors, we have spotted the agents who have helped make the map of the jungle what it is. When we understand the map better, we may realize that certain paths which lie wide and inviting ahead of us are simply paths of metaphorical implication, and not, as we might have hoped, paths out of the jungle altogether into the bright tropical sun of unvarnished truth.

* * *

Herds of metaphors—the master metaphors and their accompanying minimetaphors—are in some ways the easiest to track down. There is another variety of metaphor that blends into the jungle of language even more than the small, quick minimetaphor. This variety of metaphor, in fact, has become so identified with the jungle that it is usually not thought of as an animal at all. Its common name is *root metaphor.*

A root metaphor has taken root like a tropical plant, and a whole section of the jungle of language has grown up according to its genetic pattern. A root metaphor is enduring, like the jungle itself. Although herds of minimetaphors come and go, the root metaphor germinates, takes root, grows, flourishes, withers, and dies over the course of centuries.

The earnest metaphor hunter stalking through the jungle with his or her metaphorical camera may not realize it, but may be clambering through the structure of a huge root metaphor the whole time. It is a clear case of not seeing the forest for the trees.

To find the root metaphors, we need the larger maps, we need the historical accounts of early travelers, we need the folklore of the natives as guides. We may need to act more like gatherers, and less like hunters. For root metaphors set out the paths and the jungle, the whole structure of what we know and can communicate about.

Is the entire jungle set out according to the genetic imprint of root metaphors? This question is debated, some claiming yes, other observers claiming no. The best cases for root metaphor dominance have come, it seems to me, from examining specific traditions in philosophy and science. When we move from these relatively orderly sections of the jungle of language, however, into the more varied and twisted byways of everyday language, I would suspect that root metaphors must share their influence with many other factors.

* * *

So the wild metaphor is a strange beast indeed. The species runs from the tiny minimetaphor flitting through the jungle of language, to the herds of metaphors carving out a living space in the jungle, to the immense, plantlike root metaphors that undergird whole sections of the jungle itself.

Hunting the wild metaphor can be frustrating, and exhilarating. The moment of discovery—the metaphorical moment—is an "aha!" experience to be savored. Reflection on the metaphors can lead to insight and understanding of new territories, or redefinition of familiar territories.

And yet there are times when the metaphor seems to disappear in front of your eyes, melting into the background of language, making you wonder what you were looking at. And at other times the metaphor seems to grow and encompass everything in the jungle, making you wonder how you could distinguish the metaphor from anything else. A strange quest, indeed, requiring constant efforts to keep it all in focus.

forty three

Is Language a Game?

Is language *a game*? Can a metaphor—a part of language—encompass the whole?

The *game* metaphor for describing language has an interesting double life. In one incarnation, it is discussed in philosophy, sanctioned by the authorship of Ludwig Wittgenstein. But it also has a street life, in ordinary language, where "playing games" refers to dishonest, deceptive, and malicious uses of language. Both lives tell us much about the metaphor, without yet exhausting it.

* * *

In philosophy, the name of Ludwig Wittgenstein is one to be conjured with. His name drops heavily into philosophical arguments, tending to end them with an air of finality. Whether he deserves it or not—or whether he wanted to be or not—Wittgenstein has become a kind of "heavier than thou" reference of final appeal.

This is strange enough in itself, where we might ask why any philosopher should be treated as the Bible once was—maybe we need Bibles of some sort, profane or sacred?

But it is even more strange considering the nature of Wittgenstein's later works, which are mostly collections of loosely connected observations on various things. Readers are left to puzzle over enigmatic statements, and given very little assistance. Wittgenstein fans have even published his notebooks, in the hopes that some of the enigmatic jottings there will illuminate the other enigmatic pronouncements (see Barrett, 1979).

The phrase "language game" appears in Wittgenstein's later work (see Wittgenstein, 1953). He came up with the concept to illustrate his theory of meaning, which had changed from his earlier work. The "later Wittgenstein" rejected the "early Wittgenstein's" view that language was a mirror to reality. The early Wittgenstein held that *a proposition is a picture of reality.* Rejecting the *mirror* metaphor; the later Wittgenstein proposed the *game* metaphor. How could we tell what something means? Watch how it is used. Meaning as use—this is the philosophical core of the *language game* metaphor.

Wittgenstein's examples of *language games* were all very simple, modeled on children's games. They involved one or two word directions being given in the context of specific activities like building a brick wall. The language can in no sense be understood as a mirror, or picture, of reality. But it can be understood as *a move in a game.*

The *language game* metaphor as used by Wittgenstein has many useful aspects. It ties language closely to its context. It emphasizes the shifting circumstances and uses to which language can be put. It allows for flexibility in making and interpreting "rules," and for conformity and originality in making "moves."

Like playing a game with someone, in order to use a language there must be some shared understandings between people. We often have teams of *language game players*, and occasionally *compete* with other *teams*. But we can have cooperative games as well, in order to build something or just *play language games* for pleasure.

Language games can exist at various levels of abstraction. We can even have "families" of *language games*, Wittgenstein suggested. Thus, learning a field of study such as law, would involve learning the related *language games* of interpreting legislation, courtroom procedure, drafting of complaints, and so on. These *language games* might be considered part of the larger family of *language games* called "the justice system."

Wittgenstein does not go much beyond the embryonic formulation of the *language game* metaphor. The metaphor is much richer and suggestive, but philosophy has not yet explored it to anything near its potential. Meanwhile, the metaphor has migrated into "ordinary language" (which was also an interest of Wittgenstein's), with a slightly different twist.

* * *

In my study of new words in American dictionaries in the 1960s, 1970s, and 1980s, I often came across the metaphor of *game playing* (Gozzi, 1990). People were described as *playing games*, or playing *head games*, if they were trying to deceive others through language. A number of new speech act verbs participated in the game metaphor, describing speech acts like *psyching out* an opponent, *doing a number* on them, *downplaying* their strengths, hoping they will *choke*.

I also found the *game* metaphor in expressions commonly used by business executives. They want to know the *name of the game*, whether to play *hardball*, how to come up with a *game plan*. They don't want to be in *left field*, they want to be on the *money*. They might have to play *it by ear*, and hope that no *wild card* will send them back to *square one*. You're only as good as your last *ball game*.

The world of the *hardball* executive is a world of unprincipled competition, full of threatening gestures and unforeseen pitfalls. This life is a hard *game*.

And so the *game* metaphor, in ordinary language, loses the grandeur of philosophical abstraction; and takes on the dirty job of describing dishonest, deceptive, threatening uses of language. We may admire *language games* in the abstract, but we don't want people to *play games* with us in real life.

* * *

These two uses of the *game* metaphor—the philosophical description of meaning-as-use, and the street games of deception and mystification—do not exhaust the *game* metaphor. The metaphor is extremely rich, and I would like to see it explored more than it has been.

But does the *game* metaphor encompass language? Does it adequately describe what is going on when we use language? I puzzled over this question for a long time, unable to come to a firm position. Then, one day I had an "aha" experience while reading, of all things, an article about interactive computer games (Platt, 1995).

The article was describing the new, interactive computer games that are being designed today for the arcades of tomorrow.

With advanced graphics and storage capacity, these computer games are capable of creating complex stories, realistic-looking characters and situations. But the game designers were running up against a problem.

If you allowed for too much interactivity, if you allowed the user to control much of the ongoing action, you lost control over the story. In fact, the story and its characters tended to disappear in a haze of options. And so you were pressured into simplifying the story, simplifying the characters, so you could ensure a satisfying resolution. But then you lost the complexity that made the story attractive and made the characters interesting in the first place.

Some designers were convinced that there was an unbridgeable gulf between story and game. *Story* involved complex characters, many options, involved plot lines. *Game* involved one-dimensional characters seeking clear-cut goals in a simplified environment.

Here was an insight I could apply to my question about the limits of the language game metaphor. Although doubtless story and game shade off into each other, they are different enough to effectively critique our language game metaphor. A *game* is a simplified situation, and *game players* are correspondingly simplified characters. That is a large part of games' appeal. They provide us with limited and clear alternatives, they give us an unambiguous outcome. Unlike the "real world," where alternatives are usually fuzzy and outcomes may never be known for sure.

When we *play games* with someone, as the street version of the metaphor has it, we are, indeed, working in a circumscribed universe. We are after some goal, we must deceive in order to get it. Perhaps the goal is only to humiliate the other person—in any case there is a relatively unambiguous outcome, and we can feel like "winners" for a short time, at least.

But there are times when we do not *play games* with others—at least I hope so. Then we put our language to other uses—telling stories, for example, but doing many other things as well. We make requests, we offer excuses, we make promises, we simply acknowledge someone, we get information about useless topics, and on and on.

Jumping up to the philosophical level, we could, I suppose, put all language behavior into the category of *game*. But taking our cue from "ordinary language," as Wittgenstein advised, I think we should restrict the applicability of the *game* metaphor to situations where we have a more or less clear goal, where we will know whether or not we have "won."

Thus, *language games* would involve different uses and behaviors than language stories. Because in a story situation, if it is sufficiently complex to be interesting, we often face competing goals, no clear strategies present themselves, and the outcome, if there is one, is often ambiguous and bittersweet.

"Real life" seldom achieves the clarity and decisiveness of a game. We need language to function in the ambiguous worlds of our lives. Simplifying life or language down to a *game* will only help us some of the time. Maybe Wittgenstein's opposition of the *game* metaphor with the *mirror* metaphor was not as productive as it could have been. Maybe the better contrast is between game and story.

So, is language a game? The best answer seems to be— only some of the time, when there is something we want. In a positive sense, a *language game* allows us to make *moves* and get results. In a negative sense, a *language game* implies we can't be open about getting what we want, so we must *play games.*

forty four

Metaphors by the Seashore

A vacation at the seashore is a time to relax, unwind, and maybe get a new slant on life. On two recent stays at the shore, I found myself reflecting on metaphor in new ways: once when contemplating the bridges of the Chesapeake Bay, and once when I collected seashells on the beach.

* * *

The Chesapeake Bay looks small on a map, but it has more than 7,000 miles of coastline, due to the many rivers and inlets that make its coast so jagged. When driving around the Bay, my wife and I were struck by how many bridges have been built, over marshes, grasslands, and water.

Not only were there a lot of bridges, but they were long, often traversing acres of marsh and wetlands before even reaching the water. The most famous long bridges are the Bay Bridge near Annapolis, and the combination bridge-tunnel that crosses the opening of the bay near Hampton, Virginia. But there are plenty of other long bridges in the area, unheralded yet sleek and lovely.

These bridges are relatively recent, however. A woman who has lived on the Chesapeake all her life recalled for me when there were ferries everywhere. These ferries, often very small, little more than a flat raft, carried a few cars or wagons from the farms and fishing villages on the Bay, traveling a couple of times in the morning, and again in the afternoon. Life was slower then, geared to the pace of the ferry, at the mercy of the weather.

When the huge bridges were erected, life sped up. Vastly more traffic rushed across the bridges, in a constant stream. The formerly remote farms and villages became fodder for development. Heavy trucks rumbled through formerly quiet village streets. Vacation homes then permanent homes sprang up all along the Bay. The bridges transformed what had truly been a backwater area into prime vacation spots for the many.

I was interested in this transformation, and the analogy with metaphor struck me. Could this situation be a metaphor about metaphor?

A metaphor is commonly thought of as a bridge—a linguistic bridge linking two separate conceptual domains. Nobody speaks of a metaphor as a ferry. Yet the root terms of a meta-phor refer to a carrying over. A metaphor could be a ferry as well as a bridge.

What would metaphor-as-ferry be? It would be slower than metaphor-as-bridge. It would require more constant attention, as the ferry needs to be manned at all times. It would carry its freight intermittently. And probably it would leave both shores pretty much the same after its journey, as opposed to the bridge, which would transform them.

It occurred to me that the metaphors found in poetry are the ferries. Poetic metaphors are unique, idiosyncratic, sometimes taking a lot of work to elucidate. A poetic metaphor is a ferry between two shores, carrying a small but precious cargo of delicate meanings.

The bridges, which carry a steady stream of cargo and forge strong ties between shores, are the prose metaphors. Our prose metaphors form structures for our everyday thought and discourse. We use them without self-consciousness, just as we drive over a bridge without noticing.

Do our metaphors start out as ferries—poetic metaphors laboriously interpreted? Then, across some of these links, do bridges get built—do the metaphors become prosaic, undergirding the prose and carrying steady streams of conceptual traffic? Such, anyway, is my guess at the metaphorical history of metaphor.

* * *

Our vacation then took us to the southern New Jersey seashore, where we sat on the beach and tried not to get too sunburned. The sound of the surf was calming as it steadily crashed into the shore. The straight stretches of beach were bare and clean and lovely. One cloudy day I took a walk and started picking up seashells.

The most common shells were clamshells, with their distinctive flat oval shapes, whitish-multicolored insides, and parallel curved lines on the outsides. In our family, long ago, they had served as ashtrays.

What struck me on this day, however, was the similarity in color between the inside of the seashells and the colors of the cloudy sky. Both had lines of soft whites, grays, and occasional tinges of blue and pink. Even the translucent quality of the pink-shaded areas was similar between the sky and the shell.

I held a shell up to the sky—the colors matched. The cloudy sky blended with the cloudy inside of the seashell.

What does this match mean? I felt the presence of a mystery. I wondered if I was looking at a visual metaphor. Is color a clue to deeper meanings of process in the universe?

Often when we talk about mysteries, we know the answers, or at least have some clues about what the answers will be like. But this, to me, was a real mystery, because it was not clear what the clues were, or what the answer might look like.

Are the processes of moisture and cloud-formation in the sky somehow analogous to the processes of life in the ocean for the lowly clam? Do these analogous processes leave their traces in the seashells lying randomly around the shore, underneath the cloudy sky, waiting for someone to come along and read their proper meanings?

If I wanted to get a poetic metaphor out of it, as I am sure many have, I could write about the sky as a seashell, enclosing our lives as the shell protects life inside it. The sky-seashell closes at night and opens in the day. Or, I would write about the seashells as pieces of the sky, washed up from the ocean depths.

But I was thinking in terms of prose metaphors on this day—scientific bridges that could serve as structures for heavy traffic. Is color a clue to process? Or are we merely dealing with the paintbrush of the Creator, artistically applied?

The lines on the reverse side of the shell seem to mirror the lines of the ocean waves as they progress up the shore, and the lines the ocean waves leave on the sand seem to be of a similar family to the lines on the shells. Or here again, am I being misled by aesthetics? Do I see the fingerprint of similar underlying processes? Or just beauty put there for our delight?

One thing I did notice about the seashells. When I found one with meat still clinging to it, left behind after some gull's breakfast, I tended to leave it alone. I prefer the dry abstractions of structure, rather than the messy remains of organic activity.

* * *

There is a new branch of mathematics, known as fractals, which studies self-similar structures. These are often illustrated by examples from nature: for example, how the shapes of rocks on a mountain often resemble the much larger shapes of the mountain itself.

Do the seashells illustrate such fractal processes? Do some fractal processes ultimately generate metaphors, embodied in the thousands of seashells lying randomly on the beach? For once I could enjoy a real mystery. All I could follow was my intuition, which tells me that these visual embodied metaphors of sky and wave are clues to larger processes. Just how they work will have to await the opening of some larger conceptual shell, to reveal, hopefully, a beautiful mathematical pearl.

References

Ackaway, J. C. (1991). *The devious decade, a new approach to finding a job in the 90's.* Chicago: Adams Press.

Allen, R. (Ed.). (1987). *Channels of discourse.* Chapel Hill: University of North Carolina Press.

Anderson, B. (1983). *Imagined communities.* New York: Verso.

Anderson, D. (1983). Television literacy and the critical viewer. In J. Bryant & D. Anderson, (Eds.), *Children's understanding of television* (pp. 297-327). New York: Academic Press.

Arbib, M. (1985). *In search of the person.* Amherst: University of Massachusetts Press.

AT&T. (1993). *Connections* (video). Basking Ridge, NJ: Corporate Television.

Ayres, W. (1988, July 22). McDonald's to court: "Mc" is ours. *The New York Times,* Section I, p. 8.

Baldwin, T., McVoy, D., & Steinfeld, C. (1996). *Convergence.* Thousand Oaks, CA: Sage.

Barfield, O. (1985). *History in English words.* West Stockbridge, MA: Lindisfarne Press.

Barnes, S. (1996). Cyberspace: Creating paradoxes for the ecology of self. In L. Strate, R. Jacobson, & S. Gibson, (Eds.), *Communication and cyberspace* (pp. 193-216). Cresskill, NJ: Hampton Press.

Barrett, W. (1979). *The illusion of technique.* Garden City, NY: Anchor Books.

Baudrillard, J. (1983). *Simulations.* New York: Semiotext(e).

Baudrillard, J. (1989). *America.* New York: Verso.

Benhamou, E. (1993, March 14). Let's get going on a data highway. *The New York Times,* Section 3, p. 11.

Black, J. (1962). *Models and metaphors.* Ithaca, NY: Cornell University Press.

Blankenship J. (1976). The search for the 1972 democratic nomination: A metaphorical perspective. In J. Blankenship & H. Stelzner (Eds.), *Rhetoric and communication* (pp. 236-260). Urbana: University of Illinois Press.

Blumenfeld, W. (1989). *Pretty ugly.* New York: Perigee Books.

Bolter, J. (1984). *Turing's man.* Chapel Hill: University of North Carolina Press.

Booth, W. (1978). Metaphor as rhetoric. In S. Sacks (Ed.), *On metaphor* (pp. 11-28). Chicago: University of Chicago Press.

Bosmajian, H. (1984, Autumn). The metaphor marketplace of ideas. *Midwest Quarterly, 26,* 446-462.

Botein, M. (1993, March 14). Low tech at a high price. *The New York Times,* Section 3, p. 11.

Boulding, K. (1956). *The image.* Ann Arbor: University of Michigan Press.

Braiman, L. (1992, September 14). The U.S. keeps spending more.... *Business Week,* p. 73.

Brooke, J., Protzman, F., & Wines, M. (1990, December 23). Iraq's nuclear quest. *The New York Times,* Section 1, pp. 1, 4.

Butler, J. (1994). *Television.* Belmont, CA: Wadsworth.

Carey, J. (1989). *Communication as culture.* Boston: Unwin Hyman.

Chesebro, J., & Bertelsen, D. (1996). *Analyzing media.* New York: Guilford Press.

Chira, S. (1992, May 31). Splashy school venture creates lots of ripples. *The New York Times,* Section 4, p. 3.

Corteen, R., & Williams, T. M. (1986). Television and reading skills. In T.M. Williams (Ed.), *The impact of television* (pp. 39-86). Orlando, FL: Academic Press.

Culler, J. (1982). *On deconstruction.* Ithaca, NY: Cornell University Press.

Darrach, B. (1970, November 20). Meet shaky, the first electronic person. *Life,* pp. 58B-68.

Davis, D., & Baran, S. (1981). *Mass communication and everyday life.* Belmont, CA: Wadsworth.

DeFleur, M., & Ball-Rokeach, S. (1989). *Theories of mass communication* (5th ed.). New York: Longman.

Deming, W. (1992, May 10). *Deming of America* (videotape). Cincinnati, OH: Petty Consulting Productions, Inc., PBS.

Derber, C. (1979). *The pursuit of attention.* New York: Oxford University Press.

Derrida, J. (1996, October 4). *My independence of Algeria.* Address given at Algeria: In and Out of France Conference, Cornell University, Ithaca, NY.

Dery, M. (1990, December 23) The merry pranksters and the art of the hoax. *The New York Times,* Section 2, pp. 1, 36.

Deutsch, C. (1990, December 23). 007 it's not, but intelligence is in. *The New York Times,* Section 3, p. 24.

Deutsch, C. (1991, October 6). The fast track's diminshed lure. *The New York Times,* Section 3, p. 25.

Dick, P. (1968). *Do androids dream of electric sheep?* London: Rapp & Whiting.

Dick, P. (1969). *The preserving machine.* New York: Ace.

Dreyfus, H., & Dreyfus, S. (1986). *Mind over machine.* New York: Free Press.

Eastman, S. T., & Newton, G. (1995). Delineating grazing. *Journal of Communication, 45*(1), 77-93.

Edge, D. (1974). Technological metaphor and social control. *New Literary History, 6,* 135-147.

Editor and Publisher International Yearbook. (1989). New York: Editor and Publisher.

Eisenstein, E. (1979). *The printing press as an agent of change* (2 vols.) New York: Cambridge University Press.

Elfin, M. (1992, September 28). The college of tomorrow. *U.S. News & World Report,* pp. 110-112.

Ellis, J. (1989). *Against deconstruction.* Princeton, NJ: Princeton University Press.

Embler, W. (1966). *Metaphor and meaning.* DeLand, FL: Everett Edwards.

Fernandez, J. (1977). The performance of ritual metaphors. In J. Sapir & J. Crocker (Eds.), *The social uses of metaphor* (pp. 100-131). Philadelphia: University of Pennsylvania Press.

Fiske, J. (1987). *Television culture.* New York: Routledge.

Foss, M. (1949). *Symbol and metaphor.* Princeton, NJ: Princeton University Press.

Geertz, C. (1983). *Local knowledge.* New York: Basic Books.

Gerbner, G., Gross, L., Signorielli, N., Morgan, M., & Jackson-Beeck, M. (1979). The demonstration of power. *Journal of Communication, 29*(3), 177-196.

Gibson, W. (1984). *Neuromancer.* New York: Ace.

Gibson, W. (1986). *Count zero.* New York: Arbor House.

Gibson, W. (1988). *Mona Lisa overdrive.* Toronto: Bantam.

Goody, J. (1977). *The domestication of the savage mind.* New York: Cambridge University Press.

Gozzi, R., Jr. (1990). *New words and a changing American culture.* Columbia: University of South Carolina Press.

Gozzi, R., Jr., & Haynes, L. (1992). Electric media and electric epistemology: Empathy at a distance. *Critical Studies in Mass Communication, 9*(3), 1-12.

Graber, D. A. (1988). *Processing the news* (2nd ed.). New York: Longman.

Gumpert, G., & Cathcart, R. (1986), *Inter/media.* New York: Oxford University Press.

Gumpert, G., & Drucker, S. (1996). From locomotion to telecommunication. In L. Strate, R. Jacobson, & S. Gibson (Eds.), *Communication and cyberspace* (pp. 25-38). Cresskill, NJ: Hampton Press.

Halliday, M. A. K. (1987). Language and the order of nature. In N. Fabb, D. Attridge, A. Durant, & C. MacCabe (Eds.), *The linguistics of writing* (pp. 135-154). New York, Methuen.

Havelock, E. (1963). *Preface to plato.* Cambridge, MA: Harvard University Press.

Hawkes, T. (1972). *Metaphor.* London: Methuen.

Hawkes, T. (1977). *Structuralism and semiotics.* Berkeley: University of California Press.

Hayakawa, S. I. (1954). What is meant by Aristotelian structure of language? In S. Hayakawa (Ed.), *Language, meaning, and maturity* (pp. 217-224). New York: Harper.

Hilts, P. (1988, November 4). Saboteur's "virus" infects computer network. *Peoria Journal Star,* p. 1.

Innis, H. (1950). *Empire and communications.* Oxford: Oxford University Press.

Innis, H. (1951). *The bias of communication.* Toronto: University of Toronto Press.

Ivie, R. (1987). Metaphor and the rhetorical invention of cold war "idealists." *Communication Monographs, 54,* 165-182.

Jacoby, R. (1992, June 1). Those campus CEOs. *The New York Times,* p. A-15.

Jakobson, R. (1971). *Studies on child language and aphasia.* The Hague: Mouton.

Jaynes, J. (1976). *The origins of consciousness in the breakdown of the bicameral mind.* Boston: Houghton Mifflin.

Johnson, M. (1987). *The body in the mind.* Chicago: University of Chicago Press.

Jung, C. G. (1960). *Collected works* (Vol. 8). New York: Pantheon Books.

Kelly, K. (1994). *Out of control.* Reading, MA: Addison-Wesley.

Kerouac, J. (1976). *On the road.* New York: Penguin. (Original work published 1957)

Kilborn, P. (1990, December 23) Workers using computers find a supervisor inside. *The New York Times,* Section 1, p. 1.

Korzybski, A. (1948). *Science and sanity* (3rd ed.). Lakeville, CT: Institute for General Semantics.

Krol, E. (1992). *The whole internet user's guide and catalogue.* Sebastopol, CA: O'Reilly & Associates.

Kubey, R., & Czikszentmihalyi, M. (1990). *Television and the quality of life.* Hillsdale, NJ: Lawrence Erlbaum.

Kurtzman, J. (1988, November 13). Curing a computer virus. *The New York Times,* p. F1.

Lakoff, G. (1993). The contemporary theory of metaphor. In A. Ortony (Ed.), *Metaphor and thought* (2nd ed., pp. 202-251). New York: Cambridge University Press.

Lakoff, G. (1996). *Moral politics.* Chicago: University of Chicago Press.

Lakoff, G., & Johnson, M. (1980). *Metaphors we live by.* Chicago: University of Chicago Press.

Landow, G. (1992). *Hypertext.* Baltimore, MD: Johns Hopkins University Press.

Langer, S. (1951). *Philosophy in a new key* (2nd. ed.). New York: Mentor Books.

Lanham, R. (1993). *The electronic word.* Chicago: University of Chicago Press.

Larson, C. (1982). Media metaphors. *Central States Speech Journal, 33*(4) 533-546.

Larson, C. (1996). Dramatism and virtual reality. In L. Strate, R. Jacobson, & S. Gibson (Eds.), *Communication and cyberspace* (pp. 95-104). Cresskill NJ: Hampton Press.

Lecercle, J.J. (1990). *The violence of language.* New York: Routledge.

Lehman, D. (1991). *Signs of the times.* New York: Poseidon Press.

Levi-Strauss, C. (1966). *The savage mind.* Chicago: University of Chicago Press.

Lewis, J. (1991). *The ideological octopus.* New York: Routledge.

Lewis, L. (March 17, 1993). Deconstructing Derrida (letter). *Chronicle of Higher Education,* p. B3.

Lewis, P. (1990, December 23). On electronic bulletin boards, what rights are at stake? *The New York Times,* Section 3, p. 8.

Lifton, R. (1993). *The protean self.* New York: Basic Books.

Lippert, P. (1996). Cinematic representations of cyberspace. In L. Strate, R. Jacobson, & S. Gibson (Eds.), *Communication and cyberspace* (pp. 261-270). Cresskill NJ: Hampton Press.

Logan, R. (1986). *The alphabet effect.* New York: St. Martin's Press.

MacCormac, E. (1985). *A cognitive theory of metaphor.* Cambridge, MA: MIT Press.

Machines compute, but people think. (1988, October 20). *The Labor Paper,* p. 1.

MacPhail, M. (1994). *The rhetoric of racism.* Lanham, MD: University Press of America.

Marc, D. (1995). *The bonfire of the humanities.* Syracuse, NY: Syracuse University Press.

Markoff, J. (1988a, November 6). How a need for challenge seduced a computer expert. *The New York Times,* p. 1.

Markoff, J. (1988b, November 8). Loving those whiz kids. *The New York Times,* p. 1.

Markoff, J. (1988c, November 11). U.S. is moving to restrict access to facts about computer virus. *The New York Times,* p. 1.

Markoff, J. (1990, December 23). Another way to get to the global village. *The New York Times,* Section 4, p. 6.

Martin, J. (1996). Computational approaches to figurative language. *Metaphor & Symbolic Activity, 11*(1), 85-100.

McCloskey, D. (1990). *If you're so smart.* Chicago: University of Chicago Press.

McLuhan, H. M. (1951). *The mechanical bride.* New York: Vanguard.

McLuhan, H. M. (1962). *The Gutenberg galaxy.* Toronto: University of Toronto Press.

McLuhan, H. M. (1964). *Understanding media.* New York: McGraw-Hill.

McLuhan, H. M., & Fiore, Q. (1969). *War and peace in the global village.* New York: Touchstone Books.

McLuhan, H. M., & McLuhan, E. (1988). *Laws of media.* Toronto: University of Totonto Press.

McMillen, L. (1993, February 17). Deconstructionist fights editor of book on heidegger. *Chronicle of Higher Education,* p. A8.

McReading. (December, 1988). *Harper's Magazine,* p. 32.

Merriam-Webster. (1983). *Webster's ninth new collegiate dictionary.* Springfield, MA: Author.

Merriam-Webster. (1986). *12,000 words.* Springfield, MA: Author.

Messaris, P. (1993). Visual "literacy". *Communication Theory, 3*(4), 277-294.

Messaris, P. (1994). *Visual literacy.* Boulder, CO: Westview Press.

Meyrowitz, J. (1985). *No sense of place.* New York: Oxford University Press.

Meyrowitz, J. (1993). Images of media. *Journal of Communication, 43*(3), 63-74.

Minsky, M. (1966, September). Artificial intelligence. *Scientific American,* 246-260.

Moffatt, M. (1989). *Coming of age in New Jersey.* New Brunswick, NJ: Rutgers University Press.

Morse, M. (1992). *Transformed by the light.* New York: Villard Books.

Mumby, D., & Spitzack, C. (1983). Ideology and television news. *Central States Speech Journal, 34,* 162-171.

Mumford, L. (1963). *Technics and civilization.* New York: Harcourt, Brace, Jovanovich.

Nietzsche, F. (1992). Truth and falsity in an extra-moral sense. *ETC., 49*(1), 58-72. (Original work published 1873)

Norris, C. (1991). *Deconstruction, theory, and practice* (rev. ed.). London: Routledge.

Norris, F. (1989, March 5). Time Inc. and Warner to merge, creating largest media company, *The New York Times,* p. 1.

Noth, W. (1995). *Handbook of semiotics.* Bloomington: University of Indiana Press.

Ong, W. (1971). *Rhetoric, romance, and technology.* Ithaca. NY: Cornell University Press.

Ong, W. (1977). *Interfaces of the word.* Ithaca, NY: Cornell University Press.

Ong, W. (1982). *Orality and literacy.* London: Routledge.

Osborn, M. (1967). Archetypal metaphor in rhetoric. *Quarterly Journal of Speech, 53*(2), 115-126.

Patterson, T. (1980). *The mass media election.* New York: Praeger.

Peirce, C. S. (1932). *Collected papers* (Vol. 2). Cambridge, MA: Harvard University Press.

Pepper, S. (1942). *World hypotheses.* Berkeley: University of California Press.

Perkinson, H. (1995). *How things got better.* Westport, CT: Bergin & Garvey.

Petit, C. (1988, November 4). Vicious "worm" spreads havoc through computers in U.S. *San Francisco Chronicle,* p. 1.

Petit, C. (1988, November 5). How "worm" was defeated. *San Francisco Chronicle,* p. 1.

Piaget, J. (1970). *Structuralism.* New York: Basic Books.

Plat, J-L. (1995). "Like." *ETC., 52*(1), 66-69.

Platt, C. (1995). Interactive entertainment. *Wired, 3*(9), 144-149.

Polanyi, M. (1958). *Personal knowledge.* Chicago: University of Chicago Press.

Poster, M. (1990). *The mode of information.* Chicago: University of Chicago Press

Postman, N. (1976). *Crazy talk, stupid talk.* New York: Delacorte.

Postman, N. (1979). *Teaching as a conserving activity.* New York: Dell.

Postman, N. (1982). *The disappearance of childhood.* New York: Vintage Books.

Postman, N. (1985). *Amusing ourselves to death.* New York: Viking.

Postman, N. (1993). *Technopoly.* New York: Vintage.

Pratt, M. L. (1987). Linguistic utopias. In N. Fabb, D. Attridge, A. Durant, & C. MacCabe (Eds.), *The linguistics of writing* (pp. 48-66). New York: Methuen.

Ramacharaka, Y. (1905). *Advanced course in yogi philosophy.* Chicago: Yoga Publication Society.

Reddy, M. (1979). The conduit metaphor. In A. Ortony (Ed.), *Metaphor and thought* (pp. 284-324). Cambridge: Cambridge University Press.

Rheingold, H. (1993). *The virtual community.* New York: HarperPerennial.

Richards, I. A. (1936). *The philosophy of rhetoric.* New York: Oxford University Press.

Rosenau, P. M. (1992). *Postmodernism and the social sciences.* Princeton, NJ: Princeton University Press.

Roszak, T. (1986). *The cult of information.* New York: Pantheon.

Salomon, G. (1984). Television is "easy," print is "tough." *Journal of Educational Psychology, 76*(4), 647-658.

Saussure, F. de. (1969). *Course in general linguistics.* (W. Baskin, Trans.). New York: McGraw-Hill. (Original work published 1916)

Schon, D. (1979). Generative metaphor. In A. Ortony (Ed.), *Metaphor and thought* (pp. 254-283). Cambridge: Cambridge University Press.

Schutz, A. (1964). *Collected papers* (Vol. 2). The Hague: Martinus Nijhoff.

Schwartz, T. (1973). *The responsive chord.* Garden City, NY: Anchor Press.

Searle, J. (1982, April 29). The myth of the computer. *New York Review of Books,* pp. 3-6.

Shannon C., & Weaver, W. (1949). *The mathematical theory of communication.* Urbana: University of Illinois Press.

Sheridan, T., & Zeltzer, D. (1993, October). Virtual reality check. *Technology Review,* 27-35.

Shibles, W. (1971). *Metaphor.* Whitewater, WI: The Language Press.

Stelzner, H. (1965). Analysis by metaphor. *Quarterly Journal of Speech.* 51(1), 52-61.

Sterling, B. (1988). *Mirrorshades.* New York: Ace.

Sterling, B. (1992). *The hacker crackdown.* New York: Bantam Books.

Stevenson, R. (1988, November 1). World leader in consumer goods. *The New York Times*, p. 33.

Strate, L. (1996). Cybertime. In L. Strate, R. Jacobson, & S. Gibson (Eds.), *Communication and cyberspace* (pp. 351-378). Cresskill, NJ: Hampton Press.

Superhighway hits roadblock in poll. (1994, May 9). *Ithaca Journal*, p. 10A.

Tenner, E. (1991, March-April). Revenge theory. *Harvard Magazine*, pp. 27-30.

Toynbee, A. (1972). A study of history (new edition). New York: Weathervane Books.

Turbayne, C. (1970). *The myth of metaphor* (rev. ed.). Columbia: University of South Carolina Press. (Original work published 1962)

Turner, M. (1991). *Reading minds.* Princeton, NJ: Princeton University Press.

Turner, M., & Fauconnier, G. (1995). Conceptual integration and formal expression. *Metaphor & Symbolic Activity, 10*(3), 183-204.

Wallace, J., & Mangan, M. (1996). *Sex, laws, and cyberspace.* New York: Henry Holt.

Wallraff, B. (1988). The literate computer. *Atlantic, 261*, 64-71.

West, D., & Travis, L. (1991). The computational metaphor and artificial intelligence. *AI magazine, 12*(1), 64 79.

Wheelwright, P. (1962). *Metaphor and reality.* Bloomington: University of Indiana Press.

Whorf, B. (1956). *Language, thought, and reality.* Cambridge, MA: MIT Press.

Wittgenstein, L. (1953). *Philosophical investigations.* Oxford: Basil Blackwell.

Zorn, B. (1988, November 27). In computers, as in nature, variety is desirable. *The New York Times*, Section 4, p. 14.

Author Index

Subject Index

291